FOCUS ON SOUTHEAST ASIA

Other titles in the
focus *series*
of regional introductions

focus *on the Middle East*

focus *on South America*

focus *on Africa South of the Sahara*

focus *on Eastern Europe and the U.S.S.R.*

focus *on East Asia*

focus *on South Asia*

focus on
SOUTHEAST ASIA

edited by ALICE TAYLOR

Published in cooperation with
The American Geographical Society

Praeger Publishers
New York • Washington

BOOKS THAT MATTER

Published in the United States of America in 1972
by Praeger Publishers, Inc.
111 Fourth Avenue, New York, N. Y. 10003, U.S.A.

© 1972 by Praeger Publishers, Inc.

Library of Congress Catalog Card Number: 72 – 188045

Printed in the United States of America

CONTENTS

Foreword — Alice Taylor   vii

I   AN OVERVIEW

1   The Political Dimension: Regionalism and Extra-
    regional Relations — Norton S. Ginsburg   3
2   International Cooperation for Development: The
    Mekong Project — Louis A. Cohen   13
3   The Primate Cities of Southeast Asia and Their
    Problems — Donald W. Fryer   31
4   Planning the Future of the Southeast Asian City
    — Norton S. Ginsburg   43

II   NATIONS OF SOUTHEAST ASIA

5   Burma — Robert E. Huke   63
6   Thailand — Leonard Unger   82
7   Cambodia — William A. Withington   100
8   Laos — Leonard Unger   119
9   Vietnam   131
10 Malaysia — Kenneth Thompson   152
11 Singapore — Yue-man Yeung   166

12   Indonesia — William A. Withington   185
13   The Philippines — Alden Cutshall   202
      Index   221
      The Contributors   230

MAPS

Southeast Asia   4
Southeast Asia: Relief   17
Southeast Asia: Rainfall   18
Main Mekong Projects   28
Southeast Asia: Population   33
Burma   64
Thailand   84
Cambodia   101
Laos   120
Vietnam   132
Malaysia   153
Singapore   167
Indonesia   186
The Philippine Islands   203

FOREWORD

Political and social inequalities, hunger, unemployment, illiteracy, and poor health have been the lot of much of mankind throughout history. Today they are critical problems for millions of people living and working in the less developed nations of Asia, Africa, and South America—the so-called third world—where new ideas, attitudes, and technology have only recently begun to challenge ancient traditions and patterns of living. Seeking solutions, these people are beginning to question political, economic, and social organizations that fail to alleviate poverty and injustice. They are becoming increasingly aware of the consequences of inequitable distribution of land, great disparities in income, rapid and chaotic urbanization, rapidly increasing population, and ecological imbalances. They see the urban rich minority retaining most of the political and economic power while the majority continues to eke out a living barely above the subsistence level. They know that in the highly industrialized affluent nations of the West the average income exceeds theirs greatly—in some cases as much as 10 to 1.

How can such problems be tackled in a nation where a privileged group pursues policies aimed at its own enrichment (the tax system, for instance) while the lowest income and employment group is unorganized and has little means to make itself heard? If there are no broadly based democratic forces that can bring pressure to change the political and economic system, how can it be changed?

Unemployment in the third world has now reached the proportions of the Depression of the 1930's in the West. How can it be reduced when most of the people are undernourished and illiterate, when production and productivity are so low that there is little opportunity to accumulate capital investment for agricultural and industrial development? Moreover, a large portion of the foreign aid received, which might be used as capital investment, now goes to pay foreign debts and the interest on them. Unemployment spells poverty, discouragement, alienation, and unrest.

Frustration is greatest among the members of the new middle class and the young, those most imbued with ideas of equality and material progress. They seek innovations that will give them greater influence in government and society and bring a greater measure of economic well-being. Thanks to education and modern means of communication, they are more aware of injustices than their parents and grandparents, reared in societies where hierarchies in all realms were traditional and unquestioned. The political consequences of economic and social inequalities, unemployment, and increasing population pressures are likely to become more serious in the 1970's. Local governments that ignore such problems may well find it difficult to survive. Nor can any citizen of this small planet afford to ignore them.

In its monthly publication, *focus,* The American Geographical Society has been attempting to disseminate up-to-date and accurate information on problems prevalent in the less developed nations and on the solutions being sought for them. Of particular concern has been the dissemination of such information among young adults in the United States, for they need to learn more about the peoples and cultures of the third world if they are to contribute to the solution of its problems.

Grateful thanks are due to the following people for their contribution to this book: Nancy Kreitler, Trina Mansfield, and Chih Chwen Pinther drew the maps; Kathleen Cole, Nancy Gidwitz, and Sally Kennedy assisted in the checking and editing of the articles; and Nancy Gidwitz and Molly Laird read proof.

New York
November, 1971
                                                              ALICE TAYLOR

I AN OVERVIEW

1 THE POLITICAL DIMENSION

Regionalism and Extra-regional Relations

Norton S. Ginsburg

The Idea of the Region • Extra-regional Relations • The Problem of China

Until World War II, Southeast Asia was often linked with India, and the name "Farther India" was sometimes employed by Europeans. The Chinese and the Japanese perceived it as the southern extension of the Far East— that is, East Asia. But with the war in the Pacific came the recognition that this corner of Asia was in fact a subcontinent, half the size of the United States, with a population comparable in size to that of Africa south of the Sahara and of a heterogeneity unmatched perhaps anywhere else in the world outside Europe. It is also a subcontinent with historical antecedents and contemporary significance not exceeded by any other developing region.

In 1940 Southeast Asia was dominated by foreigners. Only one nation, Thailand (then called Siam), was not a formal dependency of an imperialist power, whether European or American; and even it was strongly influenced in economic terms by European advisers and interests. In the next several years Southeast Asia came under the domination of the Japanese in their drive to create a Greater East Asian Co-Prosperity Sphere. The Americans were forced out of the Philippines; the Dutch out of their East Indies; the British out of Malaya and Burma; the French out of Indochina. Shortly after the close of the war, Southeast Asia had become

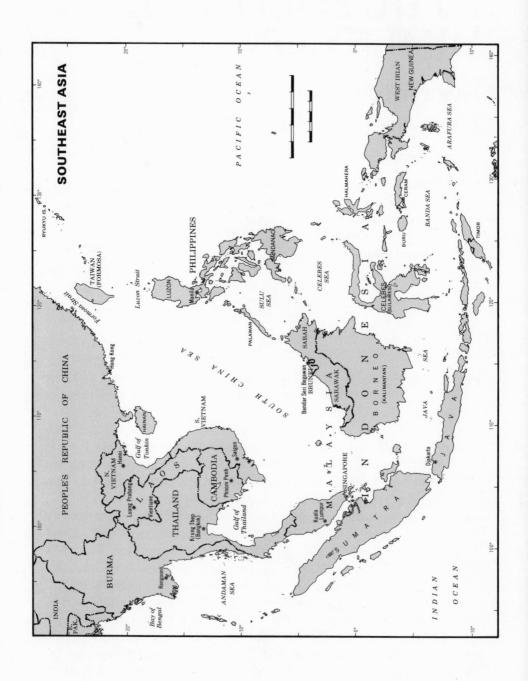

SOUTHEAST ASIA

in effect a congeries of parochial nationalisms and newborn nation-states, independent of one another but linked by a common hostility toward colonialism and domination by foreigners, including the Japanese.

By the close of 1957, the political map of Southeast Asia had been transformed. All major areas had attained independence. Only British Borneo (sometimes called Kalimantan) and West Irian (Irian Barat) remained under the control of non-Asians, and these in due course also were absorbed by the Southeast Asian nations. By 1963 the region included nine nations—Burma, Thailand, Laos, Cambodia, North Vietnam, South Vietnam, the Philippines, Malaysia (including Singapore), and Indonesia. In 1965, Singapore left the Federation of Malaysia, thus bringing the number to ten. Only the oil-rich sultanate of Brunei remained, by choice, attached to the United Kingdom. All the rest of this vast region, with its quarter of a billion people, had become independent.

Even then, the nations of Southeast Asia resembled their progenitors of 1940 in that they, in Jan Broek's terms, stood back to back, looking outward toward a world in which the former colonial powers still appeared to be dominant. This was not so much the case with Burma or with Indonesia, which had deliberately severed its political connections with the Netherlands in 1957; but it surely was true of most of the rest of the region, including the states of Indochina. Interrelations among the various new or older states chiefly occurred through the hinge points of entrepôts such as Singapore and Pinang. Even in these instances, the principle of autarky required that trade flow through the ports of the nations in which it originated or for which it was destined; and Indonesia looked to Singapore as a succubus draining income from the fragile and mismanaged Indonesian economy. A more highly fragmented part of the globe could scarcely be imagined.

The Idea of the Region

In fact, however, there had long been an interest in intra-regional cooperation. For a while the possibility of a Pan-Buddhist confederation was considered: It would have associated Burma, Thailand, Cambodia, and Laos, and possibly Ceylon and Vietnam. Other proposals included Pan-Malay or Pan-Indonesian confederations, which would have included all of Indonesia, Malaya, and the Philippines, and parts of Malay-populated peninsular Thailand. In 1963, under Sukarno, Indonesia took the initiative in encouraging the creation of a confederation to be known as Maphilindo (Malaysia, the Philippines, Indonesia), but the concept soon broke upon the rivalries between Malaysia and Indonesia. About the same time (1962), there came into being the so-called Association for Southeast Asia (ASA), composed of the Philippines, the Federation of Malaysia, and Thailand, but its activities were few and its effective history comparatively short, in part because of Filipino claims to Malaysian Sabah. In 1967 a successor organization was created, following the overthrow of Sukarno in Indonesia and the separation of Singapore from Malaysia, the so-called Association of Southeast Asian Nations (ASEAN), which includes all of Southeast Asia except Burma and the Indochinese states.

Although ASEAN has as yet done little toward regional cooperation, it is symptomatic of the deeply held feelings of many of the leaders in Southeast Asian nations that they are a part of a regional entity that demands further and clearer definition and recognition. Some see in ASEAN the beginnings of a Southeast Asian common market; others, the germs of a degree of regional political cooperation and even confederation, which had never existed either before or during the colonial period.

It should be made clear, on the other hand, that the Southeast Asia Treaty Organization (SEATO) provides no substantial basis for cooperation, let alone integration, within the region. Only Thailand and the Philippines are party to the Treaty of Manila of 1954, which gave rise to SEATO, and only Thailand is particularly active in the organization, although Filipino officers hold high positions in it. In fact, the only other Asian nation in SEATO is Pakistan, which appears to be uninterested in Southeast Asia, at least at the moment. The more active members of the organization, other than Thailand, are from outside the region—the United States, Australia, Great Britain, and New Zealand.

Southeast Asian regionalism is illustrated further by the requests made by several nations to the Asian Development Bank, founded in 1965, to undertake comprehensive regional studies of transportation problems and prospects and of the probable direction of the economy in the 1970's. These requests assume special importance when it is understood that the bank is not a Southeast Asian regional organization but is concerned with what the United Nations terms "Asia and the Far East"—that is, the great area extending from Afghanistan to Japan. Moreover, the request for the transportation study was couched in terms of determining ways in which transportation could be used to further the integration of the region of Southeast Asia and the development of its economies. All this is evidence of interest in the *idea* of Southeast Asia as a regional entity.

The thrust toward Southeast Asian integration has, of course, been viewed differently in different nations. Burma is to all intents and purposes out of it, but then the Burmese have withdrawn not only from cooperative regional affairs but substantially from relations with other nations except where circumstances do not permit them to do so. For example, Burma is not a member of the Asian Development Bank. Laos and Cambodia (and, indeed, the entire Indochinese Peninsula) have been so involved in civil strife, albeit with strong international connections, that regional matters have received comparatively little attention. Yet, in September of 1970, an official delegate from South Vietnam attended an international conference on problems of Southeast Asian cities, and the South Vietnamese at least have maintained some overt concern with regional development problems.

Even though the official position of most of the nations in Southeast Asia has favored expanded regional cooperation and development insofar as it is possible, in fact there are strong interest groups in each country that place a lower priority on intra-regional cooperation. These groups argue that the development of each individual nation is of such over-whelming importance that concern with regional identity and intra-regional cooperation is a luxury. Certainly, nation-building is a prime concern here as it is in other parts of the so-called Third World. Yet, some qualification is required. Unlike Black Africa, for example, several of the Southeast Asian nations have long histories of independent existence and strong cultural as well as political identities. Burma, Thailand, Vietnam, Cambodia—indeed, most of mainland Southeast Asia—fit into this category. In these countries the idea of the state has long been established, although it has been weakened by a massive multi-ethnicism, reflected in the constitution of the Burmese modern state as a federation, in theory if not in fact. Even the Philippines, although never a state even in premodern times, has a history of 400 years of centralized administration under the Spanish and another fifty years under the Americans, which provides a basis for national integration despite strong ethnolinguistic differences. Indonesia also was never a single country inclusive of all its present territories, but a long history of Indonesian nationhood, centered either in central Java or in southern Sumatra, substitutes for that lack. Laos is largely the product of French colonial policy, but for a relatively short period one of its ruling dynasties controlled about half of what is now included within its territory, as well as parts of northeastern Thailand.

Malaysia, on the other hand, has no tradition of nationhood, and it is confronted, perhaps more than any other country in Southeast Asia (other than Laos), with the need to create and reinforce what Richard Hartshorne has called the "idea of the state." Since it came into being in

August, 1957, Malaysia has appeared to be one of the more successful of the Southeast Asian units in its search for a new or renewed identity, but the stresses of a multi-ethnic society operating in so new a state have been eroding the bases of support for effective centralized government. In 1971 it is possible to say without reservation that the future of Malaysia depends largely upon the resolution of its racial problems.

Singapore deserves special attention in this context, for at least three reasons: its recent political history; its economic role in Southeast Asian trade and shipping; and the fact that it is the only city-state in the world.

After attaining partial independence from Britain in 1960 and then separating from the Federation of Malaysia in 1965, Singapore found itself confronted with seemingly insurmountable problems—a populace rapidly increasing in numbers and with very high rates of unemployment; a strong internal communist threat to its government; a vendetta waged against it by the Indonesian Government; and an economic base poorly equipped to provide the infrastructure for a modern state, especially for a modern welfare state. The miracle of Southeast Asia has been the ability of Singapore to deal with most of these problems constructively and effectively.

One of the reasons this could happen is the traditional role of Singapore as a hub of the archipelagic Southeast Asian universe. True, the Philippines were traditionally little involved in the Singapore trade, either directly or through Chinese agents; Burma's orientation was toward British India and that of the Indochinese area toward France and Hong Kong. But, even in prewar times, much of Indonesia's trade, despite the best efforts of the Dutch, was organized by Singapore interests. In fact, so intimate were the connections between Singapore and parts of Indonesia that, when the Japanese took over Southeast Asia after 1941, they attached central and northern Sumatra administratively to Singapore. The power of Singapore inhered less in its strategic location at the southern tip of the Malay Peninsula, where the Indian and Pacific Oceans join, than in the entrepreneurship of its Chinese merchants and the stability of its government and currency. Through these two powerful forces, the influence of the city-state affected a much wider hinterland than the facts of its commodity trade would indicate.

To a considerable degree, the influence of Singapore has again been extended over much of Southeast Asia. The entrepôt trade with Indonesia has revived; the Singapore dollar remains a model of stability; capital moves in and out of the city at a scale matched only by Hong Kong; and the port is the world's third or fourth largest in total tonnage served. Moreover, Singapore has become the staging center for petroleum explorations in the South China Sea, one of the more promising such projects in Asia; and it has attracted massive capital investment in industry. Thus it shows signs of becoming another Hong Kong, but one deep in Southeast Asia and without the constraints imposed by a colonial administration and a location on the edge of China.

Extra-regional Relations

As noted above, only two nations in Southeast Asia are members of the Southeast Asia Treaty Organization and thus are more or less formally identified with a policy of "containment" of communism on a continental scale. In fact, however, most of the governments are anticommunist. Although several recognize the People's Republic of China, for example, only the government of North Vietnam and the communist revolutionary governments in South Vietnam, Laos, and Cambodia maintain friendly relations with Peking. The relations of Burma and Indonesia with that government are highly strained, after periods in both cases of relative warmth and friendliness.

Extra-regional economic ties are another story. With regard to the former imperialist powers, most of the nations in Southeast Asia still maintain intimate commercial relations with their erstwhile "mother" countries. This does not mean that commodity trade itself necessarily is primarily with these countries; in fact, this is seldom the case. It does mean, however, that most commercial transactions are with or through intermediaries associated with these countries—commercial houses, banks, shipping companies. The chief exception to this generalization is Indonesia, which severed ties with the Netherlands in such drastic fashion that commercial relations declined to near zero for some years following 1957. But, since 1964, Dutch commercial activities, including trade, have been expanding rapidly in Indonesia, although they are still far below prewar levels. Burma also has placed severe constraints upon its commercial relations with the United Kingdom, through the nationalization of industries and banks. And, in the case of the former French-Indochinese states, commercial relations with France have been much curtailed.

The United States has come to occupy a position of increasing importance in commercial relations, not only as a major ultimate market for the exports of most of the nations concerned, but also as a provider of credit and aid to those that accept it. Some, like Burma, do not. In the

Philippines, of course, the United States is the dominant trading partner as well as the largest creditor.

Even more significant is the resurgence of Japan to the position of first, second, or third trading partner with almost every nation in the region, although the former imperialist country usually retains a greater hold on more general commercial transactions. So dominant is Japan in the external commercial life of most such countries that fears of Japanese commercial, and even political, domination haunt the administrative halls of Southeast Asian governments. There is concern not only about becoming part of a new Japanese Greater East Asian Co-Prosperity Sphere but also about the possible resurgence of Japanese political and military expansionism. In March of 1971, for example, when President Ferdinand Marcos of the Philippines expressed his apprehension that the United States might withdraw from Southeast Asia and thereby leave the region vulnerable to external aggression, it was not China to which he referred as the prospective danger but Japan. The expansion of Japanese trade and other commercial interests, such as mining and manufacturing, into Southeast Asia reflects in part the miraculous restoration and expansion of the Japanese economy in the postwar period, but it also reflects Japan's long-standing interest in the areas to the south of it, always of greater appeal than the prospect of expansion on the nearer Asian mainland. Moreover, Japan's payment of reparations to many nations in the region, which took the form chiefly of payment in kind, had the effect of creating a substantial market for many kinds of Japanese goods. At current rates of Japanese investment in Southeast Asia and expansion of trade, most of the region will probably become a commercial subsidiary of Japan in economic terms, perhaps with Singapore a quasi-autonomous competitor within the region; the economic influence of most of the external powers other than China is likely to be much diminished.

The Problem of China

The relation of China to Southeast Asia remains an enigma, but it looms large in the thinking of many leaders in Southeast Asia, depending, generally, on their nation's distance from China. *Ceteris paribus,* the farther away, the less the concern. Another variable relates to the numbers and influence of ethnic Chinese in a given country. Where they are numerous and influential, the problem of China seems to loom larger, but even this proposition is difficult to apply without qualification.

In general, the nations that share boundaries with China are more keenly aware of and sensitive to the fulminations of their gigantic neighbor, although few recognize its government officially. Burma, which does, thought its relations with China were settled by the boundary convention of 1960, but within the past three years or so it has been the target of Chinese invective; more serious is the extensive Chinese support of rebels against the Ne Win government. Thailand, which does not recognize the Peking government but is said to maintain ephemeral, clandestine relations with it, does not share a boundary with China, but its northern frontiers run through areas inhabited by ethnic groups also found in China as well as in other countries adjacent to Thailand. The Indochinese states, rent by war, are, of course, intimately linked with their northern neighbor either as friend or potential enemy; but even among the communist governments involved, such as that in Hanoi, there is reason to suppose that the Chinese are viewed with suspicion, if not with alarm, despite a basic ideological consensus.

In short, the mainland states of Southeast Asia are keenly aware of the Chinese presence. Moreover, all of them at one time or another were in effect "client states" of the Chinese Empire and paid tribute to the Chinese court. An especially intimate relationship, although by no means always a cordial one, exists between the Vietnamese and the Chinese, since Vietnamese culture is a Sinitic variant. the consequence of Chinese domination of northern and central Vietnam between the second century B.C. and the tenth century A.D., when the Vietnamese successfully revolted against the then weakened Chinese state.

The other nations of Southeast Asia are less sensitive to the nuances of Chinese foreign policy, although their own large Chinese minorities have created an omnipresent "Chinese problem," which is less a matter of direct international relations than of domestic policy. The most important internal political problem in Malaysia, for example, is the racial one; there the Chinese minority accounts for about 35 per cent of the total population. In Indonesia, persecution of the substantial Chinese minority by the Indonesians and repression of a major communist uprising in 1965 have resulted in almost complete deterioration of relations between the two countries, despite recognition by the Indonesian regime of the Peking government. In the Philippines, hostility toward a much smaller Chinese minority still is a major factor in Filipino internal politics, but it is interesting to note again the statement of President Marcos that Japan rather than China is the potential enemy.

From the Chinese point of view, mainland Southeast Asia constitutes a traditional sphere of Chinese influence, the reconstitution of which appears to be a primary objective of Chinese foreign policy. Yet there is little evidence to suggest that the Chinese have any intention of actually occupying the mainland Southeast Asian nations, even if they could do so in military terms, which appears most doubtful. Most of the *terrae irredentae* of the Chinese state lies not to the south in Southeast Asia but in the north and west, in the Soviet Union and the Mongolian People's Republic. On the other hand, the Chinese place heavy emphasis on ridding mainland Southeast Asia of all foreign, particularly non-Asian, troops and advisers. It seems clear that the Thai, for example, are well aware of the Chinese position and would be prepared to make significant shifts in their foreign policies were American military forces to be removed from the region. Moreover, the Thai have led in attempts to create closer relations with other countries in Southeast Asia through their participation in ASA and ASEAN, despite their prior participation in SEATO and in the Vietnam war (from which they have profited substantially). Their ambivalence is indicative of the dilemmas facing all Southeast Asian governments, related to the continued American presence in parts of Southeast Asia.

Singapore, the world's "third Chinese state," has urged that the Americans remain, on the grounds that their presence is what enables most of Southeast Asia to maintain a position of relative neutrality toward the colossus to the north. It also helps to restrict the amount of Chinese aid given to revolutionary movements within these nations. On the other hand, Singapore, too, has taken the initiative in urging intra-regional cooperation among the Southeast Asian states as an alternative to excessive dependency upon the United States; and amid efforts toward these objectives, Singapore has granted permission for elements of the Russian fleet in the Indian Ocean to use its port facilities.

Southeast Asia thus plays the role of a buffer region, parts of which are of special interest to the Chinese for cultural-historical reasons, parts of which are far less significant. The American presence in the region is assumed to be ephemeral in the long run; so is the incipient Russian presence. Japan is regarded by many to be a greater potential influence on the region as a whole than any of these other nations.

2 INTERNATIONAL COOPERATION FOR DEVELOPMENT

The Mekong Project

Louis A. Cohen *

The Need for Development and International Cooperation • The Mekong Committee • The Indicative Basin Plan • Environmental Problems • Prospects for the Future

The nations of the Lower Mekong River Basin form a politico-geographic region of great complexity. The topography is varied, providing avenues and barriers to communications and transportation. The climate is affected by the monsoon, with unevenly distributed rainfall, tropical jungles, mountains, river deltas, and lowland swamps. The people vary in ethnic composition, religious affiliation, and linguistic usage. Agriculture still dominates the economies; the road to industrialization has proved to be paved with difficulties inseparable from the broader problems of modernization.

Of the six nations in the Lower Mekong Basin, two—Burma and North Vietnam—have not yet participated in the Mekong Development Project. Of the four participating riparian states, two—Laos and Thailand—are kingdoms, and two are republics—South Vietnam and Cambodia (Khmer Republic). Nationalism on occasion has proved to be an effective force in helping to bind together the dominant peoples in each nation and has

* The views and historical interpretations presented here are the author's and not necessarily those of any organization with which he is affiliated.

been utilized by the leaders in pursuit of their own aspirations. It varies in intensity from time to time and from country to country, but it can be aroused against a neighboring state or a minority within a given state.

Still, the four participating riparian nations share many interests and problems evolving from their shared cultural heritage, historic experience, geographic proximity, and the challenge of moving from the stage of colonial dependency into the development of viable modern nation-states. They all have the tensions, both internal and external, that accompany the emergence from neofeudalism into the restrained anarchy of the mid-twentieth-century international system. They also, of course, share one great and potentially significant physical feture: Through or along their borders runs the Mekong River.

What is impressive about the Mekong as a natural resource is not its great length (2,600 miles), its vast drainage basin (318,800 square miles), or the huge volume of its flow, but the negligible extent to which it and its tributaries have been developed to benefit the people of the basin. It is truly, in the words of Dr. C. Hart Schaaf, former Executive Agent of the Mekong Committee, "a sleeping giant . . . a source of tremendous potentialities for power production, irrigation, navigation, and flood control, a source virtually unutilized." In his 1958 report to the United Nations, Lieutenant General Raymond A. Wheeler, former Chief of the U.S. Army Engineers, stated, "This river could easily rank with Southeast Asia's greatest natural resources. Wise conservation and utilization of its waters will contribute more towards improving human welfare in this area than any single undertaking." Eugene R. Black, former President of the World Bank and later Special Adviser to President Lyndon Johnson on Asian Economic and Social Development, noted in 1968 that "Harnessing the Mekong River to improve the living conditions of millions of people in . . . Cambodia, Laos, Thailand, and Vietnam [is] one of the most challenging and potentially rewarding development plans ever proposed. Its full promise can be realized only by cooperation among all four countries."

The river rises in the snow-covered mountains of the great Tibetan Plateau in the People's Republic of China, and it is wild in its upper reaches. It is a good deal more placid in the Lower Basin, but still majestic and powerful. Its drainage basin includes an area larger than France or Texas. An average of over 650 billion cubic yards of water flows into the sea each year. Among Asian rivers, only the Yangtze (Chang) and Ganges (Ganga) exceed it in minimum flow. At Kratie, in Cambodia, at the head of the delta slightly more than 310 miles from the mouth, the Mekong's minimum flow of 1,764 cubic yards per second is nearly twice that at the

The Nam Ngum dam and power station in Laos, now nearing completion, is one of many internationally sponsored projects designed to develop the immense irrigation and hydroelectric potential of the Mekong Basin once peace has been restored to Southeast Asia.

mouth of the Columbia River. Its maximum flow at Kratie averages about 52,000 cubic yards per second, or about thirty times the minimum. This wide range, which is seasonal, is due to the monsoon rains from mid-May into October each year.

For 150 miles south of the China border, the Mekong forms the border between Laos and Burma. Beyond the point at which Burma, Laos, and Thailand meet, it continues to form most of the border between Laos and Thailand; it then traverses central Cambodia and at Phnom Penh divides into the Mekong and Bassac arms; then it empties into the South China Sea through a broad delta south of Saigon in southern South Vietnam. As Table 2.1 indicates, the Lower Basin below Burma covers an area of nearly 250,000 square miles, or about 75 per cent of the whole basin.

TABLE 2.1

THE LOWER MEKONG BASIN

Geographical Area	Area in Square Miles	Total Population (000)	Rural Population (000)	Wet Rice Production (000 tons)	Estimated Population in Year 2000 (000)
Cambodia	70,898	6,701	5,935	2,504	14,934
Laos	90,428	2,893	2,590	680 [a]	6,556
Thailand	198,455	34,738	29,713	10,722	78,482
South Vietnam	66,897	17,866	14,471	4,366	33,565
Total	426,678	62,198	52,709	18,322	133,537
Cambodian Basin Provinces	53,242	6,239	5,509	2,354	13,866
Laos Basin Provinces	85,135	2,701	2,407	680	6,131
Northeast and North Thai Basin	72,984	12,803	12,330	4,003	28,740
Vietnam Delta and Highlands in Basin	26,810	6,829	6,211	3,134	13,637
Total	249,172	28,572	26,457	10,171	62,374

[a] There are no data for outside the basin.
SOURCE: *Annual Statistical Bulletin* (Mekong Committee), 1969.

The total area of the four riparian states is some 637,000 square miles, almost twice the size of France. They have an abundance of natural resources. A combination of climate, soils, topography, and human endeavor has long enabled the region to produce a sizable rice surplus. Rubber and

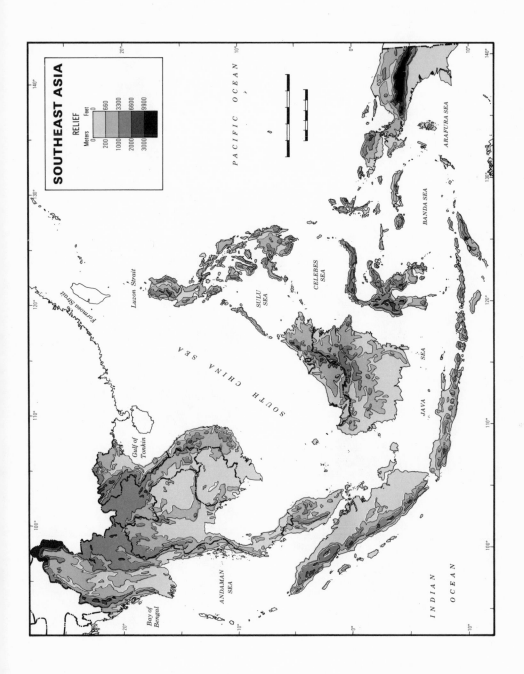

SOUTHEAST ASIA

RELIEF

Meters   Feet
0   0
200   660
1000   3300
2000   6600
3000   9900

PACIFIC OCEAN

ARAFURA SEA

BANDA SEA

CELEBES SEA

SULU SEA

SOUTH CHINA SEA

JAVA SEA

Luzon Strait

Formosa Strait

Gulf of Tonkin

ANDAMAN SEA

Bay of Bengal

INDIAN OCEAN

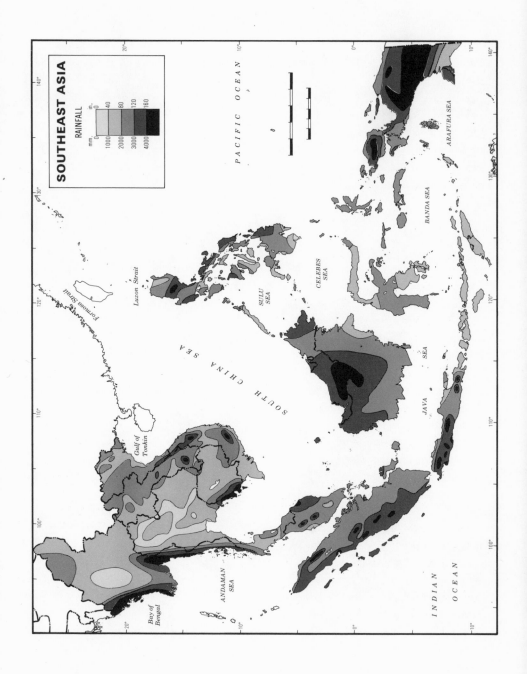

SOUTHEAST ASIA

RAINFALL

mm.	in.
0	0
1000	40
2000	80
3000	120
4000	160

PACIFIC OCEAN

Luzon Strait

Formosa Strait

SULU SEA

CELEBES SEA

BANDA SEA

ARAFURA SEA

SOUTH CHINA SEA

Gulf of Tonkin

JAVA SEA

ANDAMAN SEA

Bay of Bengal

INDIAN OCEAN

30°

20°

120°

110°

100°

20°

10°

10°

0°

140°

130°

120°

110°

100°

140°

20°

10°

0°

forest resources are significant on the world market. Mineral wealth and fisheries are also important economic assets.

The four nations have a population of more than 62 million, of whom nearly half live within the basin, despite the fact that the two major cities—Krung Thep (Bangkok) and Saigon—lie just outside the physical drainage area of the Mekong. While the over-all population density of 109 per square mile is not high by world standards, the growth rate, over 3 per cent per year, poses problems for development planning.

Agriculture dominates the basin economies, but migration from rural to urban areas is of considerable significance and is accelerating. The rapid growth of urban centers is not yet matched by the growth of industry and employment opportunities.

The Need for Development and International Cooperation

Many observers, both within and outside the Mekong region, see the harnessing of the river as the key to solving major problems of the riparian nations stemming from poverty and political instability. The present per capita income in the Lower Mekong Basin is under $150 per year. Although the people in these nations are somewhat better off than those in most other parts of Asia, standards of living are low.

If there is no significant reduction in population growth rates, there will be nearly 135 million people in the riparian nations by 2000, and the increase in food production has so far not kept pace with population growth. A Ford Foundation study in 1961 and a 1966 report by the Carnegie Endowment for International Peace found a need for an increase in milled rice production from 8 million tons to 17 million tons by 1990. This will require not only the introduction of new seeds and fertilizer practices but a great increase in the controlled use of water and dry-season irrigation.

In addition to the required expansion of agricultural output (about 4 per cent per year), these reports indicate that industrial output should increase by 7 per cent per year. Much of this increase could be achieved by expanding the processing of agricultural and forest products, which is contingent to some degree on the provision of cheap electric power—obtainable by development of the same projects needed to provide irrigation water and flood control.

Storage of flood flows at projects on the mainstream and on some of the tributaries would help to overcome the flooding problems that have plagued riparian populations from earliest times. At the same time it would aid irrigation and power generation and would permit the improvement of navigation below Phnom Penh and its extension farther upstream.

Although there is no conclusive evidence, experience suggests that broadly conceived water-management projects will foster interest in other measures needed to accomplish economic and social evolution. Water-management projects alone, however, cannot ensure the desired changes. They must be accompanied by other measures—road improvement, industrial promotion, agricultural reorganization, more education and training, extension of agricultural credit and marketing facilities, and, in effect, modernization of the rural political structure. These measures assume special significance in the Lower Mekong region because both economic infrastructure (such as transportation and communications) and agricultural methods are inadequate to cope with the revolution in agricultural and industrial inputs and outputs required to realize the potential of the vast Mekong scheme.

Drastic changes would need to be made in farm practices to take advantage of the river regulation that could be provided by the system of control structures envisioned or in various stages of implementation on the Mekong and its tributaries. Similarly, major changes would have to be made in political and social institutions and in sociocultural habits to permit a change-over from a partly commercialized agrarian society to one in which industry has a significant role.

Perhaps the Mekong program, with its promise of economic development, may provide the political and emotional stimulus to bring about these ancillary measures. The administrative and political leaders of the riparian states have, from the beginning, sensed the political and social, as well as the economic, significance of undertakings with the magnitude and scope of the projects included in the Indicative Mekong Plan, which has now been put in final form for publication in late 1971. Tensions and struggle for control of the planning mechanism, characteristic of political processes everywhere, have not been lacking in the growth of the idea of Mekong Basin development. However, the Mekong is an international river, and its ultimate development for the benefit of the riparian states requires their cooperation.

Prior to World War II, few political figures thought of Southeast Asia in regional terms. Indeed, the very term "Southeast Asia" came into common usage in English only as a result of the creation of an Allied military command for the region under Lord Louis Mountbatten in 1943. The predominant point of political focus before the war was national liberation from colonial control. World War II strongly stimulated Southeast Asian regional feeling, though, through common experience with the Japanese invaders and with the Allies and emergence of independent national entities. In general, however, the political regional organizations either have failed or are only slowly developing significance as factors in the national and international life of Southeast Asian nations. It is in the less tense areas of economic and sociocultural cooperation that there has been clear progress.

The United Nations regional entity, ECAFE, with headquarters in Krung Thep, has active participation from every regional country except North Vietnam, and its conferences and projects are considered essential by each of the regional states. All of them, except North Vietnam and Burma, have joined the Asian Development Bank (with headquarters in Manila, in the Philippines). The Southeast Asian Ministers of Education Organization has met regularly for five years and has drawn considerable regional and international support for its series of regional centers of academic excellence. These include: English language training in Singapore; agricultural graduate training at Los Banos, in the Philippines; science and mathematics teacher training in Pinang, Malaysia; graduate engineering training in Krung Thep; tropical biology research in Bogor, Indonesia; tropical medicine in Krung Thep; and educational innovation and technology in Saigon. Similarly, the Organization of Southeast Asian Ministers of Transport and Communication has successfully developed a continuing program of regional cooperation and mutual help in their field of expertise.

Perhaps it is because organizations devoted to economic development and social and cultural evolution appear to be depoliticized that they have been more successful than those devoted to political and military integration or to trade and monetary schemes. By far the most successful of all these regional economic-development organizations has been the Committee for Coordination of Investigations of the Lower Mekong Basin (the Mekong Committee), which, though suffering all the tensions and strains of the national and international political problems afflicting its four members— Cambodia, Laos, Thailand, and South Vietnam—has never allowed them to disrupt its organization, planning, and programs.

The Mekong Committee

The first international effort to cooperate in the use of the Mekong River occurred in 1926, when France and Thailand agreed that neither would impede navigation on the river. In 1949, Cambodia, France, Laos, and the

Republic of Vietnam signed a Convention of Maritime and Inland Navigation, which provided for a consultative commission. Although the commission was set up in 1950, it never was active. A similar convention was signed by the three former French colonies in 1954, whereby the parties agreed to coordinate action on navigation and police rules, river improvement, and industrial and agricultural projects that might affect navigation, as well as to share costs, duties, taxes, and payments relating to river commerce and navigation and to observe the 1926 Franco-Thai agreement.

When ECAFE was established by the United Nations in 1947, the real stimulus for international cooperation was initiated. ECAFE sponsored a series of conferences on water problems and water-resources planning and basin development, as well as providing guidelines for basin planning that have since been utilized. In May, 1952, the first ECAFE report on the Mekong discussed a power project at Luang Prabang and an irrigation project at Pa Mong, between Laos and Thailand, but stressed the need for more intensive studies before the feasibility of potential projects could be determined. After the 1954 Geneva Agreement ended hostilities in Indochina, the United States, Japan, and France expressed a desire to help develop and investigate the potential of the Mekong. The United States provided a study by the Bureau of Reclamation and the Corps of Engineers which, in 1956, became a basic document for planning the river's development.

A 1957 ECAFE study identified five potential mainstream project sites for power and irrigation development, provided a conceptual framework for a basin-wide planning effort, and recommended establishment of an international clearinghouse for the exchange of information, which might become a permanent instrument charged with the responsibility for planning and coordinating the development of the basin.

In response, the four riparian states convened a meeting in Krung Thep to consider further action. In September, 1957, a Preparatory Commission adopted the Statute of the Committee for Coordination of Investigations of the Lower Mekong Basin. North Vietnam was not invited to participate, ostensibly because it was not a member of ECAFE, but primarily because two of the four conveners of the meeting (Thailand and South Vietnam) did not recognize North Vietnam. Burma was formally invited to participate but at the time was deeply involved in internal rebellion and a developing split in the ruling political party; therefore, while apparently keeping open the possibility of future participation, it declined to express interest in development of the Mekong resources available to Burma.

Late in 1957 the United Nations and the World Bank provided a mission headed by Lieutenant General Wheeler, which produced a comprehensive plan of basin data-gathering with the then staggering cost estimate of $9.2 million (U.S.). Outside donors soon filled the funding gap, and the Mekong Development Program was under way. In 1961, a Ford Foundation team headed by Dr. Gilbert F. White, of the University of Chicago, provided the framework to determine the effects the development of the river might have on the economic and social structure of the basin population and a list of ancillary programs that should be undertaken to ensure that the benefits of river development would be maximized.

By the end of 1970 the Mekong Committee had operational resources of more than $202 million contributed or pledged by the four member nations, twenty-six donor nations from outside the basin, twelve United Nations agencies, and several private firms and foundations. Of this total, over $59 million was for preinvestment investigations and planning, and the remaining $143 million was for construction investments. The four member states had contributed more than the equivalent of $89 million. The United States funding was in excess of $36 million, and Germany and Japan together roughly matched the U.S. contribution.

Three substantial multipurpose dams on tributary streams are completed (two in Thailand and one in Laos), eight are under construction or financed (five in Thailand, two in Laos, one in Cambodia), and sixteen are fully studied and awaiting funding (five in Thailand, one in Cambodia, ten in Vietnam). In addition, four mainstream projects have been examined for economic and technical feasibility: Pa Mong, between Laos and Thailand; Sambor, in Cambodia; Tonle Sap, in Cambodia; and delta flood control and irrigation in South Vietnam. The Mekong Committee's Indicative Basin Plan will pull together twelve years of data-gathering and sophisticated systems analysis of electric power and flood flows and will identify the priority of investments for the immediate future. At this point, the riparians and their friends from outside the basin will be faced with decisions concerning up to $5.3 billion in investment for construcion of huge projects that could alter the economic and political course of the Mekong Basin.

The Indicative Basin Plan

The Indicative Basin Plan is a sectoral plan for the orderly development of the water and related resources of the Mekong Basin to provide the infrastructure and the services—for example, flood control, salinity control, irrigation and drainage for increased agricultural production, electric power for industrial and other uses, and related social and institutional development—which are necessary for the over-all economic growth and social evolution of the riparian countries and the adjacent region.

The plan undertakes to analyze development of the water resources of the basin as a comprehensive system; each component project is appraised in terms of its contribution to the welfare of the people in the basin as a whole. It enables the four riparian states to anticipate how management of water flow at one place would be likely to affect conditions elsewhere in the basin. Some of the judgments are tentative pending completion of additional studies, but a rough sketch of both physical and social effects is now available. The plan establishes a framework for selecting projects for implementation during the initial years covered by the plan. It provides a program of interrelated studies to determine more precisely both the needs and the means of meeting these needs. It offers an analysis of the basin's assets and potential that should help the riparian governments' planners to formulate their economic and social development programs.

The comprehensive development of the Lower Mekong Basin is a long-range undertaking extending far into the future—the Indicative Basin Plan examines a thirty-year period. The needs of the basin as indicated by present conditions and those of the immediate future are quite apparent. Conditions that may prevail in the more distant future are less distinct, but the plan has addressed the fundamental needs of the basin and the

TABLE 2.2

INCREASE IN IRRIGATED LAND AREA (DOUBLE CROP) REQUIRED TO MEET
ANTICIPATED DEMANDS FOR AGRICULTURAL PRODUCE (IN 1,000 ACRES) [a]

Year Ending	Cambodia	Laos	Northeast and North Thailand	South Vietnam	Total
1965 (base year)	0	0	0	0	0
1970	37.0	12.0	106.0	39.5	194.5
1975	86.5	26.0	229.0	84.0	425.5
1980	193.0	49.0	462.0	201.5	905.5
1985	326.0	70.0	699.0	321.0	1,416.0
1990	514.0	95.0	1,139.0	510.0	2,258.0
1995	798.0	127.0	1,482.5	797.0	3,204.5
2000	1,255.5	209.0	2,167.0	1,176.0	4,807.5

[a] Agricultural produce includes wet rice (paddy), maize, peanut, soya bean, mung bean, sesame, fruit, vegetables, potatoes, and sugar cane.
SOURCE: Draft Indicative Basin Plan.

region, considering those for agricultural and industrial development of paramount importance, along with improvement of social welfare. Table 2.2, for example, indicates required increases in the irrigated land area to meet demands for agricultural produce.

The Indicative Plan comprises (1) a group of independent small to medium-sized single and multipurpose projects, situated on the tributaries of the main river, to meet local needs; and (2) an integrated system of mainstream and major tributary projects capable of meeting basin and regional development needs. It is envisaged that the first group will be studied, constructed, and operated before any of the large mainstream projects in the integrated system can be realized.

The short-range plan (1971–80), therefore, includes a group of tributary projects designed specifically to satisfy developing needs during the next decade. A tributary-development plan to continue beyond 1980 is to be proposed at a later stage, when more accurate data are available on needs

TABLE 2.3

Projects Considered in the Long-Range Plan

Project	Irrigation (acres)	Flood Control	Installed Power (megawatts)	Capital Costs ($ millions)
1. High Pak Beng	nil	9,500 m³/sec	1,850	535
2. Low Pak Beng	nil	nil	350	114
3. High Luang Prabang	nil	nil	1,500	418
4. Low Luang Prabang	nil	nil	350	121
5. Sayaboury	nil	nil	240	89
6. Pa Mong	4,027,000	11,000 m³/sec	4,800	1,066
7. Bung Kan	nil	nil	220	179
8. Upper Thakhek	nil	nil	400	256
9. Thakhek	nil	nil	250	291
10. Khemmarat	nil	nil	420	159
11. Ban Koum	nil	nil	900	320
12. Pakse	nil	nil	350	181
13. Khone Falls	494,200	nil	750	263
14. Stung Treng	1,729,700	25,000 m³/sec	3,400	1,023
15. Sambor	84,020	nil	875	321
16. Tonle Sap	5,742,700	80,000 acres	nil	nil
17. Delta Development	6,520,900	12,246,300 acres	nil	2,247
18. Nam Theun No. 2	nil	nil	1,500	198
19. Ten minor South Vietnam hydro-electric projects	nil	nil	1,759	530

Source: Draft Indicative Basin Plan.

and all aspects of potential. A suggested sequence of tributary-project development for each country has been prepared to meet the short-range needs for irrigation and power. The total estimated cost of this ten-year program of hydroelectric power, flood control, and pioneer agricultural projects is $784.55 million.

The second part of the plan, to be brought into operation between 1981 and 2000, consists of fifteen identifiable mainstream multipurpose projects, one water-control project on the Tonle Sap, a major tributary hydroelectric project, a related group of ten minor hydroelectric power projects outside the drainage basin in South Vietnam, and the vast Delta Development Project in Cambodia and South Vietnam. From this group of projects, many of which are mutually exclusive or alternatives for one another, the most favorable can be selected to comprise an integrated system for flood control, power generation, salinity control, and irrigated agriculture. The

TABLE 2.4

Principal Targets for Agricultural Development in the Lower Mekong Basin, 1971–2000 (Annual Production in Tons)

Year	Food Crops [a] in Wet Rice Equivalent	Cotton Fiber	Livestock [b] (Dressed Weight)	Fish (Live Weight)
1970	12,714	35.6	43.1	4.5
1975	14,908	45.9	98.1	10.0
1980	17,642	59.1	163.2	36.0
1985	21,048	76.2	241.6	70.0
1990	25,243	98.1	330.0	96.0
1995	30,424	126.5	440.1	128.0
2000	37,054	162.9	571.5	152.0
	Capital Investment ($ million U.S.)			
1971–75	37.3	1.3	6.1	2.0
1976–80	46.3	1.6	7.1	5.4
1981–85	57.9	1.9	8.6	4.5
1986–90	71.3	2.3	9.7	9.0
1991–95	88.1	2.8	12.0	5.0
1996–2000	112.7	3.5	14.4	6.0
Total	413.8	13.4 [c]	57.9	31.9

[a] Includes all major crops. Conversion to wet rice equivalent made on basis of calorie content.
[b] Refers to livestock development in project areas only and includes poultry.
[c] Investment in this case includes ginning facilities.
Source: Draft Indicative Basin Plan.

principal features of these major projects are summarized in Table 2.3; however, it must be kept in mind that the reliability of the present data varies substantially (for example, Pa Mong has a completed feasibility study, while Stung Treng has only a preliminary desk study of old maps and initial core drill logs).

The thorough analysis contained in the plan report indicates that Pa Mong, Stung Treng, and Delta Development are the key projects for any integrated plan and identifies several combinations and sequences that can be built around them.

Also included in the plan are a comprehensive program of agricultural development (see Table 2.4), related industrial and mineral development, navigation and inland water transport, other transportation, and domestic water supply, and social policy, foreign-investment policy, and community-development programs. The total cost estimate for the complementary program to support the long-range plan (direct investment) is $2.6 billion. The plan also includes discussions of financial implementation and organizational aspects and necessary international agreements.

Environmental Problems

Aware of the potential impact on ecology of its vast program of water-resources development, the Mekong Committee has planned studies to minimize negative environmental effects on water, soil, animal life, and vegetation and the entire ecology and human environment of the basin. It has concluded that any decision to go ahead with a construction project requires an estimate of the probable environmental impact, how serious it may be, and whether further studies or changes in project design are necessary.

In moving toward understanding and controlling the effects of basin development on the environment, the committee has already undertaken a survey of the problems of aquatic weeds; a basin-wide study of water-borne diseases, with special emphasis on snails as a vector; extensive studies of fish migrations and habits; and examination of sedimentation patterns and the role of silt deposits in the delta. It has monitored the effects of year-round irrigation on return flows and water quality of tributary projects.

Clearly, the initial studies of watershed management, ground-water conditions, and human influence on hydrological phenomena are far ahead of work done in other river basins when they were at this stage of development. But the magnitude of the potential dangers from inadvertent disturbance of the ecology and from the sheer numbers of people to be affected

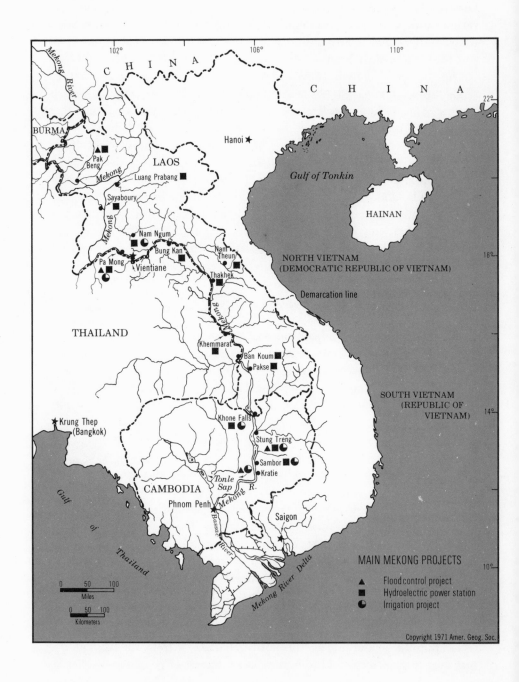

MAIN MEKONG PROJECTS

▲ Flood control project
■ Hydroelectric power station
◐ Irrigation project

Copyright 1971 Amer. Geog. Soc.

by the proposed projects led the November, 1970, Seminar on the Plan, held by the Mekong Committee in Krung Thep, to recommend that (1) future findings on project feasibility should contain explicit discussion of what is known and—more important—what is not known about the project's probable environmental consequences; and (2) the committee, as part of its future planning, should organize more general investigations of the ecological systems in the basin: the effects of the whole range of changes in land use, farming technology, water flow, water quality, and waste management.

Prospects for the Future

To date, the Mekong Committee and its supporters have brought together and analyzed a vast amount of data and have begun the monumental task of developing one of the world's great rivers. With the completion of the Indicative Basin Plan, a plateau has been reached in this effort. Security conditions in much of the basin prevent or inhibit extensive field studies and construction. The sites of easiest access and lowest cost to develop on the tributaries have already been used. Problems of cooperation and coordination have been overcome in order to raise a vast sum of money for studies and construction of essentially national tributary efforts. Now the greater task of securing international agreement on water allocation, operation, and management must be faced to develop the mainstream for the benefit of all the people in the basin, without distinction as to nationality or politics.

For the first time the great reservoir of technical expertise and funds, the World Bank, and the Asian Development Bank have become donors and project implementers. This bodes well for accelerated activities, particularly in the area of pioneer irrigated agricultural projects and further feasibility investigations of river-control projects. Many of the studies and activities recommended by the Basin Plan and many of those suggested by the development banks can be carried out at the present time or in the near future. These include not only studies, investigations, and pilot projects but also, where judged feasible, water-control structures, particularly on the tributaries and in the delta, and further refinement of the systems analysis of the entire Lower Mekong Basin system. There are other major studies and structures that cannot now be undertaken because of technical, financial, or security considerations. It is hoped that conditions may soon permit major reconnaissance studies of projects identified by the plan as of high priority, but about which little accurate information is available. Such studies will permit a more definitive formulation of alternative sequences for feasibility analysis and the design and construction of projects with the highest priorities.

The Indicative Basin Plan and its implementation scheme must be refined and revised as new information becomes available. The Mekong Committee's planning and development schemes must be carried out in full coordination with the economic and social development of the riparian nations, whose policies and decisions will be the major determinants of the future of the Lower Mekong Basin and its peoples.

3 THE PRIMATE CITIES OF SOUTHEAST ASIA AND THEIR PROBLEMS

Donald W. Fryer

The Origin and Growth of the Great Cities • The Morphology and Functions of the Great Cities • Major Problems

With an estimated 80 per cent of its population living in rural conditions in 1970,* Southeast Asia is one of the least urbanized regions of the world. Only in the neighboring Indian region and in intertropical Africa does the proportion of rural dwellers reach comparable levels. The Indian region has cities larger than any in Southeast Asia, and these are growing very rapidly; but, on the whole, its urban population is fairly evenly distributed in large, medium, and small cities. Southeast Asia's urban population, on the other hand, is concentrated in cities of very large size by the standards of the region. With the important exception of Indonesia, few nations have cities of intermediate size (100,000–500,000), so that the remainder of the urban population in each country is divided among a number of small cities and towns with a population of less than 100,000, and often much less. Such a situation is indicative of urban primacy, and it can be

* Kingsley Davis, *World Urbanization 1950–1970*, vol. 1. Berkeley and Los Angeles: University of California Press, 1969. Table C, p. 126.

TABLE 3.1

URBANIZATION IN SOUTHEAST ASIA, 1970

	Population (in millions)	Urban Population (per cent)	Population of Largest City (millions)	Four-city Index of Primary Davis [a]	Ginsburg [b]
Burma	27.6	15.8	1.8	2.1	68.3
Rangoon					
Cambodia	7.0	12.8	1.0	—	—
Phnom Penh					
Indonesia	124.0	17.9	5.1	1.2	56.5
Djakarta					
Laos	3.0	13.4	0.2	—	—
Vientiane					
West Malaysia	9.4	45.8	0.7	0.9	48.2
Kuala Lumpur					
Singapore	2.1	—	—	—	—
Philippines	38.3	23.2	4.3	4.6	82.0
Manila					
Thailand	35.9	13.0	3.4	12.4	94.1
Krung Thep–Thon Buri					
North Vietnam	22.1	23.9	1.4	1.7	59.4
Hanoi					
South Vietnam	18.4	27.1 [c]	2.0	2.8	74.0
Saigon					

[a] The population of the largest city divided by the combined populations of the next three largest.

[b] The population of the largest city as a percentage of the four largest.

[c] The Agency for International Development places this figure much higher.

SOURCES: Based mainly on Kingsley Davis, *op. cit.*, and Ginsburg, *Atlas of Economic Development*, with additional material from national sources.

measured in various ways (see Table 3.1). A high degree of urban primacy is also found in many countries of Latin America and Africa and, it has been claimed, is typical of countries at a low level of economic development. But some countries at a high level of economic development, such as Denmark, also demonstrate extreme primacy; eighteenth-century London and Paris were primate cities *par excellence*. In Southeast Asia the primate cities are very large: In 1970 Djakarta had more than 5 million inhabitants, Manila more than 4 million, Krung Thep (Bangkok) 3 million, and Singapore and Saigon 2 million each. Intertropical Africa has no cities as large as these.

What is perhaps the most remarkable characteristic of the primate cities

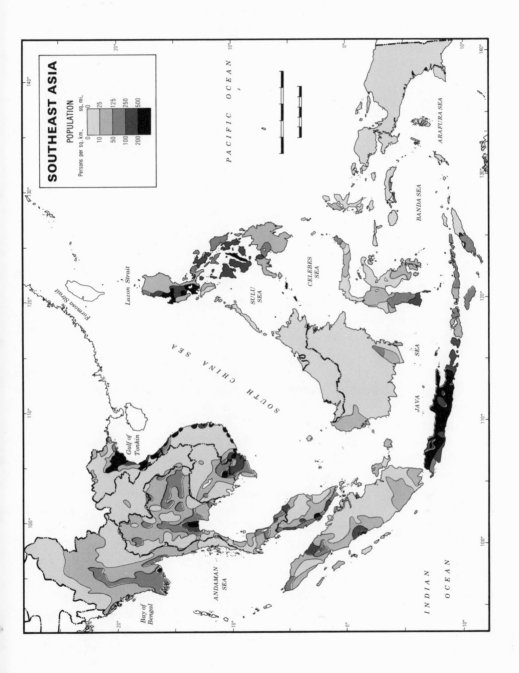

SOUTHEAST ASIA

POPULATION

Persons per sq. km.   sq. mi.

0	0
10	25
50	125
100	250
200	500

PACIFIC OCEAN

ARAFURA SEA

BANDA SEA

CELEBES SEA

SULU SEA

Luzon Strait

Formosa Strait

SOUTH CHINA SEA

JAVA SEA

Gulf of Tonkin

ANDAMAN SEA

Bay of Bengal

INDIAN OCEAN

of Southeast Asia, and unquestionably the cause of their most intractable problems, is the rapidity with which their populations have grown; within the lifetime of many of its residents, the population of Djakarta has increased tenfold. In the early 1930's, Batavia, as the city was then called, had a population only a little over 500,000, and was smaller than its old commercial rival, Singapore, which then had about 600,000. Djakarta is now the region's first city on a population basis, and it is first in the enormity of its problems, which are perhaps better judged in comparison with those of Calcutta, "the world's worst city," than with those of opulent Singapore or Krung Thep. But the growth of the other major cities has been almost as spectacular; in the mid-1930's Manila numbered only some 600,000, Krung Thep less than 800,000, and Saigon-Cholon merely 250,000. By such standards, the growth of cities during the early nineteenth century in the Western world seems almost pedestrian.

Moreover, the population of the great cities will continue to grow rapidly in the near future, and by the end of the 1980's the region will probably have at least one city with a population of 8 to 10 million, and two with 5 million or more. It is now widely believed that only a thermonuclear Armageddon can prevent world population from doubling some time before the end of the century; but what is perhaps the most important aspect of the population explosion—the urban revolution—is much less well understood. Between 1950 and 1970 the population of Southeast Asia increased from 170 to 285 million, but the population living in urban conditions (the varying national definitions of "urban" create some problems here) increased from around 23 to 57 million. The cities of the largest size (those with a population exceeding one million), however, increased from 4.3 million to 20.1 million over this period. By 1970 not only was a larger share of the total population living in urban conditions, but a larger share of the urban population was living in big cities.

Such rapid social change is unprecedented in history. For many inhabitants of the Third World, the city offers the only prospect of escape from a life of unending and grinding poverty. The great cities of Southeast Asia are the region's chief ports and administrative centers. They contain the largest range of manufacturing industries, constitute the repositories of the national cultural tradition, are the principal locations for domestic and foreign private investment, and absorb a large proportion of budgeted national expenditure. To the landless and to those whose family holdings offer only minimum subsistence and no relief from the crushing burden of debt, the great city offers by far the best prospects of employment and shelter, of adequate medical, educational, and social facilities for their dependents.

Thus the great cities attract an enormous flow of in-migrants, and, because they have a youthful population structure, they also have high rates of natural increase. Their enlarged populations encourage still larger investment in both public and private sectors, so that they grow through a cumulative causation mechanism, sometimes epitomized in the expression "nothing succeeds like success." Apart from broken-down Rangoon and austere Hanoi, whose respective miseries and shabby faces are the direct result of national development policies, the primate cities of Southeast Asia thus present an opulent and industrious appearance to the Western visitor. Poverty and squalor, it is true, can be found in superabundance by any who care to look for it, and the search will scarcely be protracted. But in burgeoning Singapore, Krung Thep, or Malaysia's Kuala Lumpur (not yet a primate city but the nucleus of one in the 1970's), it is sometimes difficult to realize that the teeming millions of rural Southeast Asia are very close at hand. Even decrepit and chaotic Djakarta has taken on a new look since the fall of the prodigal Sukarno regime; if not yet a city of hope, it is no longer in such desperate straits as in the early 1960's.

The Origin and Growth of the Great Cities

With the exceptions of Krung Thep and Hanoi, all the great cities were founded by Europeans; the Western appearance of the commercial and administrative areas and the large numbers of nonindigenous residents testify to the fact that the cities have always served international, mainly Western, ends. With the creation of new nation-states, attempts have been under way to make the great city a worthy repository for the local great tradition and to serve primarily national ends. But attempts to replace the bastions of colonial rule with new national capitals have come to naught, and relocation of the administrative center in most countries in the region now appears out of the question. In effect, the great city is now more significant than it was in the colonial period, and success in national development plans and the modernization process strengthens the ties between the great cities and the world.

The indigenous city was small and ephemeral; the Philippines is unique in having no urban tradition at all before the coming of the Europeans. But in other parts of the archipelagic Malay world trading settlements were numerous. Local rulers or sultans levied a toll on produce such as pepper, tin, or gold moving downstream to the *kualas,* or estuaries, and, as custodians of the communal lands along the valleys, they exacted their share of the rice harvest. Trade was the life blood of the coastal cities, and, as accounts of the great emporium of Malacca indicate, it could bring a high degree of organization. In mainland Southeast Asia, with its broad river valleys, and in the more open and accessible coastal plains of Java, the development of water-control systems made it possible to establish large agricultural states capable of supporting one large urban center. Such centers served, in effect, a combination of administrative, military, religious, and commercial functions of a high order, a combination usually achieved through the deification of the ruler, whose seat provided the main incentive to industrial arts and trade. The accession of a new ruler or dynasty, however, usually brought the relocation of the capital, and the ephemeral nature of the indigenous state, in large part a reflection of the difficulties of the terrain and the diversity of peoples, produced a multiplicity of short-lived urban centers, whose location owed much to the whim of the ruler and his religious advisers.

Krung Thep, founded in 1782 by the first of the Chakri monarchs (the present dynasty), originated in this way. It remained little more than a floating village around the royal palace for decades, and it was mainly the incorporation of Siam (now Thailand) into the world economy under European pressure that saved Krung Thep from the fate of the previous dynastic capitals, Thon Buri (now part of the greater Krung Thep area) and Si Ayutthaya. In its economic functions and large nonindigenous population—some 60 per cent of the city's people were of Chinese or mixed Chinese-Thai origin at the outbreak of World War II—Krung Thep was identical with the capitals of colonial territories. Similarly, Hanoi, the only other indigenous city to have a population exceeding 1 million in 1970, was the capital of the Annamite Empire when independence was achieved from China in the tenth century. But it was displaced by Hue with the dynastic quarrels of the sixteenth and seventeenth centuries, and its restoration as the capital of the Annamite (Vietnamese) lands and its development as a major industrial and commercial center were a result of French rule.

The sites of the European-founded cities originally had little significance for the indigenous people. The two oldest, Manila (1571) and Batavia (1619)—now called Djakarta—products of the mercantilist era, both occupied the sites of mere villages; they were selected to provide fortified settlements and trading posts alongside good sheltered harbors. Singapore

(1819) was founded as a trade emporium on a site quite unoccupied at the time. The cities founded in the nineteenth century, such as Rangoon (1852), Saigon (1859), and Hanoi (occupied in 1873), all absorbed older dynastic urban centers, although only Hanoi really merited the name of city. Saigon consisted of little more than a few flimsy huts around the imperial fortress in the newly colonized Vietnamese lands of Cochin China. Some three miles westward, however, on the Kinh Ben Nghe (Arroyo Chinois), a branch of the Saigon River, was a Chinese settlement, Cholon (great market), founded by refugees in the late eighteenth century. Cholon was destined to become the principal industrial center of French Indochina, and, although it was made a single administrative unit in 1931, the Région de Saigon-Cholon right up until World War II consisted of a twin-city symbiosis unique in Southeast Asia.

As products of an era of intense colonial expansion, the cities of the nineteenth century acquired high administrative functions almost from the beginning. Although never the official capital of the British Raj in the Malayan Peninsula, Singapore nevertheless came to share responsibility with Kuala Lumpur, partly through the establishment of common departments for the directly administered British territories (Straits Settlements) and for the indirectly ruled Malay States (Federated Malay States—FMS), and partly because the offices of Governor of the Straits Settlements and High Commissioner for the FMS were held by the same person. National policy now viewed Western capital as a major engine for the development of colonial territories. Land was made available on very easy terms for large-scale European agricultural enterprise; roads, railways, and improved communications were undertaken by the state to assist the opening up of estates and mines. New harbors were constructed in the great cities to replace the old silted harbors and roadsteads, which could no longer serve larger steam vessels; the organization of a labor supply, drawn from immigrant populations or from congested parts of the territory, was undertaken by the state to staff the new mines and plantations. All these activities were reflected in the growth of the great cities, which also became the headquarters of Western extractive and agricultural enterprises and provided them with financial and commercial links with the world economy. At the ports large new processing plants were erected to handle the output of the new export-oriented industries, and the state almost invariably selected the great cities as the sites for the repair shops and yards servicing the transport infrastructure. Thus the nineteenth-century cities grew rapidly, and even the older cities of Manila and Djakarta burst their confines.

The Morphology and Functions of the Great Cities

The great cities were planned urban developments, and traces of the original layouts can still be seen in the old cores. Close to the harbor, on eminences safe from flooding, was the administrative and European quarter; grouped around were the quarters of other alien groups, Chinese, Indians, or Arabs, each under the control of a headman or *kapitan*. Beyond the city were the *kampongs* or *barrios* of the indigenous population, which, as the city spread, were gradually engulfed and eventually converted to other uses. But almost from the beginning, in-migration from the rural areas and the development of indigenous unplanned settlements thwarted the planner's intentions. Most of the old European quarters have long been abandoned in favor of more spacious and salubrious suburbs, but the Chinese quarter has frequently persisted; in the pullulating "Chinatowns" densities of 2,000 or more persons to the acre are to be encountered, with the inhabitants jammed into two-storied shop-houses. As was the practice in the indigenous city, and indeed in that of medieval Europe, workers in similar trades and occupations were grouped together. Initially, of course, no provision was made for industry; this gradually appeared *in situ*, so that many blocks of the old cores are blighted with small workshops and manufacturing establishments.

In the earliest European-founded cities the influence of the colonial ruler was strong. The old walled city of Manila reproduced the patterns of seventeenth-century European fortified settlements, its walls providing protection from Moro (Muslim) raiders from the south. Djakarta was provided with narrow streets and tall houses, together with a system of canals and water gates as in cities of contemporaneous Holland. The initial layout inevitably was largely determined by topography. Old Singapore had a dumbbell shape athwart the Singapore River, while Rangoon was developed in a series of south-to-north zones parallel with the Rangoon River, in which were respectively arranged the port and industrial activities, the administrative-commercial district, and the better residential districts and European quarter on higher land toward the Shwe Dagon Pagoda. As if to match the elegance of the contemporary reconstruction of Paris, Saigon was tastefully laid out with wide tree-lined boulevards. In being primarily a port and an administrative center, Saigon stood somewhat apart from the other great cities, a fact reflected in its rather small population; service and manufacturing industries were largely banished to Cholon.

Courtesy Yue-man Yeung

Near the site where Raffles landed in Singapore, lighters and renovated godowns still stand, servicing and storing cargoes from ships moored in the Roads (one of the main anchorage areas), much as they did a century ago. Public housing has been forcing the pace of change. The juxtaposition of the old and the new is a familiar sight in the cities of Southeast Asia.

The growth of new residential districts and the appearance of subsidiary administrative and commercial quarters in the inner urban fringes was, of course, greatly encouraged by improvements in transport. Djakarta was unique in its eventual acquisition of an electrified suburban railway system, but elsewhere tramway systems helped the spread of cities. But, except in the Malayan Peninsula, the impact of the motor vehicle was long delayed, in part through the dislocation of World War I and the Great Depression, a traumatic experience throughout the region. The violent, almost explosive growth of the great cities is largely a postwar development.

The primate cities of Southeast Asia are sometimes said to be more compact than the Western city of equivalent population, but such statements are apt to be misleading, for they overlook the enormous *kampong* and squatter fringes. Djakarta Raya has an area of almost 1,550 square miles and Greater Manila is larger still. The whole of Singapore Island, 225 square miles in extent, is effectively urbanized with the exception of the extreme northwest and the water-supply catchments in the center. In the densely populated city centers, however, traffic congestion is no less acute than in Western counterparts: Manila, Djakarta, and Krung Thep have about half the national stock of motor vehicles, and Singapore, the richest city in the region, has almost two thirds as many vehicles as all of West Malaysia. The city-state is in fact well up to the standards of the poorer parts of Europe in this respect. Saigon is notorious for its swarms of motorcycles and scooters, and although the number of cyclists is not large compared with the Netherlands or Denmark, it is large by the standards of most Western cities. Djakarta additionally has over 50,000 *betjaks* (pedal trishaws), and, although Krung Thep has banished its equivalent *samlors*, their motorized successors appear almost as numerous. There are few aids to traffic control, and road discipline is poor. New roads become clogged almost immediately by lines of shops, restaurants, and hawkers, and the journey from Kebajaran Bahru, Djakarta's satellite city to the southwest, to the center of the financial district, a distance of five miles, can take two hours. Defective circulation, however, is among the least of the cities' problems.

Major Problems

The great cities demonstrate in even more acute form all the problems that beset the great cities of the West, and they are compounded by a chronic and severe shortage of employment. The creation of new jobs encourages still further in-migration from the rural areas, and there is no prospect of relief from this treadmill until the demographic transition to a new balance of low birth-and-death rates has been achieved and the modernization process is far advanced.

The shortage of housing is immeasurably more acute than in any Western city. Its most obvious manifestation is the extensive squatter camps which rapidly spring up on any patch of unoccupied land, especially near the city center or in the port area, where jobs are most likely to be found. The squatter encampments represent a major challenge to government authority, utilize land often urgently needed for other purposes, including social facilities, distort the pattern of land values by vastly inflating the price of squatter-free land, and constitute a serious fire danger and hazard to health. Squatters are well organized, with important political connections, and ejecting them is difficult and expensive. Nevertheless, the squatter camp cannot be judged by the standards of the Western city, and, under certain conditions, if given security of tenure, squatters have shown themselves to be capable of transforming their settlements into acceptable and even attractive districts.

Apart from squatters, who occupy land illegally, there are vast areas of slums whose tenants, though legal occupants, endure conditions little if at all better than those of the squatter camps. Of the estimated 600,000 "housing units" that have to accommodate Djakarta's more than five million inhabitants, some 80 per cent are judged to be in such poor state of repair as to be unfit for habitation; only 10 per cent are served by the capricious city water system and only some 12 per cent by the equally uncertain electric supply. The provision of adequate utilities, especially a sewage system, is a necessity that has little prospect of fulfillment in most of the cities in the foreseeable future. Existing services were constructed long ago and for populations only a fraction of the present size; in many cities replacement and maintenance are long overdue. The problem of providing adequate schooling and other social facilities is compounded by the extremely youthful and rapidly increasing population. Even the ports, the original *raison d'être* for the cities, are failing to keep abreast of technical progress in oceanic transportation. Singapore, one of the five premier ports in the world, is unique in the provision of facilities for the new techniques of containerization and is determined to maintain its position as the region's first port. Singapore also appears to have the will and the resources to grapple with problems of rapid urbanization; its public housing program, which has provided accommodation for no less than one third of the republic's population, is the best in Asia, Japan included.

THE PRIMATE CITIES AND THEIR PROBLEMS 41

In the efficiency of its services, the almost universal provision of water and electricity (no part of the island is more than a quarter-mile from a standpipe), the competence of its administration, and its clean and well-ordered appearance, Singapore differs markedly from most other cities in Southeast Asia.

Singapore owes much, of course, to the industry and intelligence of its largely Chinese population. But its success indicates also that the principal problems of Southeast Asian cities are political, just as they are in the West. Problems will yield to appropriate organization and resources, but the national governments have often denied both to the great cities of Southeast Asia. Governments throughout history have regarded their big cities with suspicion, for cities by their nature are pragmatic places, in which social changes are most likely to arise, menacing the security and privilege of the ruling elite. Thus the government of the great cities is parceled out among a multiplicity of departments of state or special agencies. Only Manila has an elected mayor and city council; but the city of Manila proper covers only a small part of the effective urban area, and responsibility is thus divided among many urban authorities, whose principal concern is to keep the appalling problems of Manila from spilling over into their areas.

Because of divided responsibility, it is impossible to plan adequately for the future of the cities; moreover, division does not encourage an equitable allocation of revenue between the national exchequer and the city—revenue generated in very large part by the city itself. Although Djakarta remains poverty-stricken, with an effective budget only about one tenth that of Singapore, the establishment of a unitary city administration under General Sa Dikin in place of the military and paramilitary groups that treated the city as their own private fiefs during the Sukarno regime was an important step forward. The general has a Twenty-Year Plan, which could transform the city into a viable and prosperous metropolis; fanciful it may be, but it is scarcely less realistic than the planning provisions of some other great cities, both in the East and the West.

Meanwhile, unencumbered by expensive and protracted irrigation and community-development schemes, Singapore spends all its budget on improving its own physical and human resources and enhancing its industrial and commercial efficiency. Its experience strongly reinforces the claim that the city is the fundamental agent in the modernization process.

4 PLANNING THE FUTURE OF THE SOUTHEAST ASIAN CITY*

Norton S. Ginsburg

The Southeast Asian City • Forces and Trends • Implications for Planning

All definitions of "modernization" refer in some measure to change and to concepts of efficiency, increased human and spatial interaction, and extraordinarily complex human relationships. These concepts also are associated with cities and with the process by which cities come into being and societies become increasingly urbanized. Yet, cities have existed from very early times. The city is at once both very old and very new, both evolutionary and revolutionary. The cities that arose in the Fertile Crescent of Southwest Asia some 6,000 years ago were associated with modernization in that period, just as the cities of medieval Europe were associated with modernization then, and the cities of the contempory world with modernization today. Modernization is a phenomenon found in every era; so is the growth of cities. One can reasonably propose, in fact, that every major development in history leading to increased efficiency in the production of goods and services, to increased spatial interaction, and to the more effective mobilization of resources has been associated with the growth of cities and of the prominence of their role in society.

* Based on material published in D. J. Dwyer, ed., *The City as a Centre of Change in Asia*. Hong Kong: Hong Kong University Press, 1971.

It is a truism that all cities have come into being to perform certain functions that cannot be carried out except through them. From the dawn of history, cities have performed at least two such basic functions—administrative and commercial. Both functions are associated with the concentration of certain activities in central places. Both imply the dominance of the city over contiguous hinterlands. From the first, then, the city could not properly be considered apart from the rural areas to which it was most closely, even symbiotically, related. One of the grievous failings of much analytical work on the evolution and functions of cities has resulted from the separation of the city from its hinterlands, as if their problems were not interrelated.

The accumulation of capital in the form of grain and other types of storage was one of the major functions of the earlier cities. Lewis Mumford has suggested that the history of civilization could be written in terms of the kinds of containers that given cultures created for themselves—containers for storage of grain, water, or wine; for the channeling of irrigation water or the control of floods; for the cartage and movements of goods and people; for the containment and shelter of kings and prelates, soldiers and servants, tradesmen and artisans. The city was almost from the first a central place for the storage of wealth. It consequently also was a central place for the distribution of that wealth, and in this capacity it assumed the commercial function of distributing goods drawn from certain parts of its hinterlands to other parts that needed or wanted them. It also exchanged part of this wealth with other cities that had different kinds of wealth, and in the process its people became familiar with the products and ways of life of other places. The city became a storehouse of geographical and historical knowledge. It often also became a center in which new ideas circulated and where conditions for change therefore were particularly favorable. The earliest cities were centers of modernization in the sense of social innovation.

The early city was also a producer of goods, and it engaged in manufacturing. The market for its goods consisted primarily of residents of the city itself, particularly the aristocracy and merchant elites, the holders of power, and their retainers. Thus, even very early, as now, the city was a primary consumer of its own goods and services. The concentration of artisans in cities led to some economies of scale, but for the most part the market was too small for these to become significant except in certain trades—the weaving of fine cloths, the manufacture of arms, and construction. In short, although cities of this type were manufactural, they were for the most part not industrial, in that production was for a market of limited size, technological innovations were slow to develop, units of production were minute, specialization of manufactural occupation was more by craft than by tool or process, and animate energy underlay almost all production. The difference between this type of city, which Professor Sjoberg has called the preindustrial, and more recent types of Western cities lies primarily in the consequences of the shift from *manufactural* to *industrial* activities, in the substitution of inanimate for animate energy, and in the consequent flexibility of the distribution of activities within the city. However, we should understand that *all* cities in history have been multifunctional, that *most* have been as much manufactural as commercial and administrative, and that *all* have had relations with hinterlands of varying sizes and degrees of contiguity.

The Industrial Revolution meant not only changes in the manner in which goods could be manufactured; it also meant, through a concomitant transportation revolution, the freeing of cities from dependency upon their immediate hinterlands. This greatly increased the capabilities of cities for specializing in certain kinds of activity, whether commercial or manufactural, and it also modified relations between town and country. However, it would be a mistake not to recall that the Industrial Revolution in Western Europe also was associated with marked changes, even revolutionary changes, in agricultural organization. In fact, then, the modernization associated with the Industrial Revolution was urban-focused, but by no means restricted to cities alone. Rural areas also became free to specialize in products for which they possessed either natural or locational advantages.

One trouble with the term "preindustrial city" is that it suggests that there is another type, an "industrial city." In fact, there are very few contemporary cities so heavily committed to industrial activity that a great majority of their labor force is engaged in it. Most cities today are multifunctional, just as they always were. Moreover, the trend is for Western cities to become even more multifunctional than they have been. Technological innovations, particularly in transportation, have made this possible. At national scales, centrality has become an ever more powerful force.

The contemporary Western city that has evolved since the Industrial Revolution—or perhaps out of it—has a characteristic morphology, related to its functions. A spatial model of such a city would show a central business district of limited size and low population density, with wholesaling functions at its periphery and perhaps some light manufacturing, the latter associated with higher-density, low-income residential areas. Toward the periphery of the urbanized area, one would find higher-income residential land uses extending well into the countryside. Manufacturing, even that commonly called "heavy," might be found well within the built-up area, at sites adjacent to tidewater or with other transportation advantages. Other manufacturing areas might be located nearer the margins of the urbanized areas, on less favored sites and in sectors that do not conflict with the high-income, low-density residential areas. Multiple nuclei may also develop, usually subdominant to the central business district, as a consequence of the history of the area. Expanding cities often swallow up smaller towns, and these also may provide the focus for smaller business centers within the city.

The principles that are at work creating this highly simplified and constantly changing model relate to *centrality*, to *situational advantages*, to the *specialization of functions and of land uses* associated with those functions, and to *inertia*. Each of these helps to account for the distance-density decay in land values, which are many times higher at the center than at the periphery; for the location of particular types of activities such as industrial; for the separation of places of work from places of residence; and for the existence of otherwise inexplicable landscape elements.

To these principles, however, one must add the importance of *values*. Although the Western city may seem to be more rather than less "rational," in fact many aspects of it can be explained only by reference to, if you please, sentiment; for example, the notion long held in America that an American landed yeomanry is an ideal to be pursued, even though attainment might mean only a detached house with a postage-stamp-sized lawn front and rear. That notion underlies the very rapid suburbanization of American cities during the past thirty years—not that it is the only cause—since it was the basis for the legislation making credit available primarily for single-family detached dwellings rather than for other forms of urban residential containers. On the other hand, not only Americans are sentimental; so are all other peoples. At least, all have cultures, and what those cultures specify as desirable has much to do with what sorts of cities evolve.

The Southeast Asian City

One of the difficulties in discussing the Southeast Asian city, let alone planning for it, is defining what we mean by it. It might almost be said that a real Southeast Asian city is hard to find; particularly when one considers the larger ones, remarkably few represent an indigenous tradition of urbanism. Much of the urban development that has taken place in Southeast Asia in the past two centuries has been the result of foreign enterprise or domination. The coasts of Southeast Asia are dotted with "colonial" cities—Rangoon, Singapore, Djakarta, Surabaja, Manila. Almost all of these are relatively modern in that their most rapid growth took place within the past century or so, and even more spectacularly within the past few decades. All were, moreover, the products of Europe's expansion into Southeast Asia, in the form of either direct conquest or indirect political or commercial control. To a considerable degree, then, these very large cities developed, not to serve immediately contiguous hinterlands, but more to act as linkage points between the European imperialist powers on the one hand and the territories they controlled or were interested in on the other. Until recently they may be described as representing alien enclaves rather than indigenous urbanism. Clearly, one of the basic problems underlying the host of more immediate problems associated with these great cities is finding guidelines for their cultural transformation into predominantly indigenous phenomena and for their more effective integration with national, rather than colonial, hinterlands. This problem is exacerbated by the fact that a number of them are now capitals of independent states.

The Southeast Asian cities also differ from their Western counterparts in their relation to population distributions. In the United States, for example, most people are in the regions where the cities are, and this is, of course, because most people live in these cities. In Southeast Asia, for the most part, people also are concentrated in areas where the cities are, but *not* because they live in those cities. In Southeast Asia, there is a truly remarkable areal coincidence, with some exceptions, between the distribution of the larger cities and the distribution of agricultural and therefore over-all population. Exceptions like Singapore only serve to underscore the point, which has considerable significance for developing a national planning strategy.

Southeast Asian cities also differ from their Western counterparts in their rank-size and functional relations to other cities within given countries. This refers not only to the widespread phenomenon of primacy, which is more characteristic of the smaller countries, but, more important, to the existence within countries of so-called dual economies, with a modernized sector with which the largest cities are associated, and a more traditional rural, agricultural sector, with which the smaller cities are associated. In other words, one commonly finds in Southeast Asian nations a dual stratification of cities rather than a regular, highly integrated hierarchy. The modernized sector, which sometimes consists of only one primate city or of several large ones, has better connections with other primate and large cities and with the outside world than with the smaller cities in the bifurcated domestic hierarchy. This situation has given rise to the proposal that the urban hierarchy must become "balanced" if development is to occur. There is merit in this position, but it is controversial enough to deserve further attention later on.

Morphologically and organizationally, the Southeast Asian city differs from the Western model in a number of important respects, besides its predominantly Asian population. The spatial distribution of that population is less by socio-economic classes than by ethnic, racial, and occupational distinctions. Land uses most frequently are mixed, and place of work and place of residence tend to be associated. Suburbanization is relatively slight, and with some exceptions, conspicuously Manila among the largest cities, such suburbanization as has taken place is associated with lower-income rather than higher-income groups. Even where suburbs in a strict sense are nonexistent, given frequent overbounding of municipalities, settlement on the outskirts of the expanding cities may be associated with squatters. The central business districts are underdeveloped and diffuse. Centralization as a principle is clearly not nearly so heavily at work as it is in the West. Industry has the qualities of artisan types of manufacturing or is located in larger space-demanding modern plants well on the outskirts of the built-up area.

Moreover, in some cities one can identify an old walled city, a newer residential-cum-commercial city, a military cantonment, a railway cantonment, industrial estates with housing, themselves almost small towns with recent higher-income housing estates on the peripheries—all of these representing different stages or events in the historical evolution of the urban landscape. Many Indonesian cities display these qualities, and Manila is the very model of such diversity. Linkages among these various types of units may have been poor in colonial times; most often they still are. An important problem in most Southeast Asian cities relates to the integration of these various enclaves into a better articulated, more efficient spatial system.

Even more important, it is reasonable to propose that these cities are less effective modernizing media than those of the West. I do not mean to suggest that they are *not* modernizing media, because I think they are. I merely wish to distinguish them from Western equivalents in effectiveness as modernizing agents. Why might this be so? In large part it relates to the multi-ethnic character of most of them, although the differences among them are very great in this respect. In part it has to do with the inherent fragmentation that is less a product of the history of territorial-administrative structures, as in Manila, than it is of the polynodal character and "spatial stickiness" of most of them. To a large degree it has to do with the lesser significance of modern manufacturing in the occupational structure of most Southeast Asian cities, other than Singapore. Industrial employment commonly is much lower than might be expected even in cities that are formally based upon industry. Moreover, much of even this industrial activity may be more traditional than modern, and relations with suppliers and customers more often than not are personal.

Forces and Trends

If these are some of the characteristics and problems of the Southeast Asian city, let us move to some of the forces at work upon it. Some of these are associated with cities everywhere; others with those only in the developing countries; others only with Southeast Asian developing countries.

It is clear that the populations of Southeast Asian cities are growing rapidly, for two obvious reasons: high rates of natural increase and substantial immigration. The importance of the first often is underestimated. In most countries it is fully as important as immigration, and it is associated with declining mortality rates in most large Asian cities, improbable though this may appear in the cases of a few. The urban populations of such cities are generously reproducing themselves, and there are few signs that rates of increase are declining. Whether they will or not is hard to say. The Japanese model, often alluded to, may not be applicable if only because it was associated with a very rapidly developing economy.

As for immigration, it is a fact that although water will not ordinarily flow uphill, people will—that is, up the gradients representing income levels in given countries. Since larger cities have higher incomes than smaller ones, it is almost certain that people will continue to stream upslope to places where the opportunities both seem to be and in fact most often are greater. Of course, special cases of rural insecurity, as has been the case in South Vietnam, represent "push" forces of great significance; but, even there, where the urban population of the country is now about 45 per cent as compared to less than 15 per cent about twenty-five years ago, should one reasonably expect a massive ebb of population back to rural areas from the cities when peace comes at last? I doubt it. There

In many less-developed nations, large numbers of poor rural people are migrating to the cities in search of jobs and a higher standard of living. Nearly one quarter of the inhabitants of Manila live in makeshift houses such as these, made of tin, cardboard, and old lumber. Governments, often aided by private groups, including the United Nations International Children's Emergency Fund, are trying to provide more adequate housing and various social services in such areas.

is, in fact, no documented case in modern times of large numbers of urban migrants returning to rural areas, other than those who deliberately seek temporary employment, like the *samlor* drivers of Krung Thep (Bangkok). Policy-makers must face it: Rural migrants to cities are there to stay, and many more of them will be following. Although some will double-stage their migration, most will come to the big cities first. For reasons not entirely clear, Samuel Stouffer's "law of intervening opportunity" has apparently ceased to operate in most rural-urban migrations. Perhaps improved transportation technology has something to do with this. If so, the implications may be considerable with regard to a number of related problems of development and planning strategies.

At the same time, all Southeast Asian nations are committed to a policy of modernization, whatever interpretation they may place upon that term, and in almost every case this means industrialization as a key element in the modernizing process. Since industrialization means urbanization, this suggests increasing investment in cities, which in turn will add further stimulus to urban growth. But what kind of urban growth? Surely not one in which manufactural employment suddenly looms large. Modern industry, in which most governments are interested, is a relatively light employer of labor, especially unskilled and semiskilled. Here lies one of the major problems of economic development in Southeast Asian nations, the evolution of a pattern of industrial activity that provides productive employment for rapidly expanding labor forces.

At the same time, a commitment to raising productivity and increasing wealth must mean not only industrialization in cities but also the modernizing of agriculture. For generations, scientific knowledge about agriculture in the lower latitudes was minimal, constrained by the lack of interest among most Western nations and scientists in the agricultural problems of the tropics except as they related to specific industrial crops for export, such as rubber. Now science and technology are beginning to make their contributions to agricultural development in tropical areas. The results will be twofold: first, an enormous increase in agricultural production in both absolute and per capita terms in all Southeast Asian nations; and second, effective rationalization of agricultural activity, which will bring unprecedented rural labor surpluses. The cities will be inundated by migrants from rural areas. Nothing will keep them down on the farm— not better roads, not higher literacy, not improved sanitation, not farmers' cooperatives, not even higher incomes or other consequences of governmental welfare policies! All of these will stimulate, rather than retard, migration.

Not only will there be unprecedented numbers of people descending upon the cities of Southeast Asia, but they will be people with higher expectations than those who have gone before them. More will be literate; more will have had some glimpse of the benefits possessed by other societies. Most will believe the propaganda of their own leaders. In fact, they probably will be better off on the whole, and their increased demands will be in keeping with the realities of their situation. This is, of course, highly speculative, but the times would indeed be out of joint if over the next several decades living levels were to decline rather than rise, albeit slowly, in most Southeast Asian nations. Thus, the burdens upon the municipalities will be greater than ever before to provide those services and amenities that ever larger, more demanding populations will require. The implications for more effective municipal administration and for consideration of technological innovation are immense.

Thus far, only very general trends have been considered, as they will affect all sizable cities in Southeast Asia, but there also are forces at work at the metropolitan level that cannot help but influence the spatial and organizational structure of the individual city. At present most Southeast Asian cities are more compact than their Western equivalents, and population is more evenly distributed throughout them; or, to put it in other terms, the distance-density gradient of population is very low as compared, for example, with a Chicago. However, this characteristic is changing, not only because of the growth of urban populations, but also because of an increasing reliance on the automobile, rather than mass transit facilities, to move people and goods within the urban area. Moreover, modern industries can find few sites well within the built-up area, and they therefore seek sites on the outskirts, where land is cheaper and access relatively easy. These plant locations are already generating residential-commercial developments around them, some carefully planned, most not; the total effect is to enlarge the areas for which urban services are required and to reduce over-all population densities somewhat. Unlike the situation in, say, the United States, industries, rather than higher quality residential land uses, will lead the way to suburbanization.

In this connection, it is well to note that the Southeast Asian cities' connections with other places, both intra- and extranational, also are affected by changes in transportation technology. Most American and European cities developed either prior to or during the railway era, and railway stations and yards continue to be the foci for a host of clustered service and industrial activities. Although many Southeast Asian cities are well supplied with rail connections, their most rapid growth is taking place at a time when the relative importance of the railways is declining and the importance of air transport for the movement of people, and trucks and buses for the movement of people and goods, is looming ever larger. Growth corridors between city and airport are common features of the Southeast Asian landscape already; their further development is inevitable. And bus terminals, more flexible of location than the railway terminals, are providing further impetus to the trends toward dispersion.

Indeed, it is possible that the future Southeast Asian city will continue to be much less highly focused, although more compact, than its Western counterpart. The various parts of the whole can be better integrated than ever before by transportation devices well within the means of even the poorer nations. In fact, the tendencies toward dispersion may become so great that the advantages of concentration of people and resources may be lost or diminished. One can see indications of this prospect in the case of Manila, the Los Angeles of Asia, a great metropolis in search of a center.

Implications for Planning

These trends and forces indicate increasing rather than declining problem intensities for most Southeast Asian cities, compounded by vast ignorance as to their functions as spatial and social systems. Yet, cities in Southeast Asia, as elsewhere, are ordered, comprehensible entities. Their characteristics and functions are as amenable to systematic inquiry as any artifact or institution. If a single clear need can be identified, it is for systematic, comprehensive, and continuing research on the city and urbanization in Southeast Asian nations. What may be needed is a center, an urban observatory, an interdisciplinary institute of inquiry into the basic forces that make Southeast Asian cities what they are.

Equally important is the need to inquire into the possibilities new technologies present for dealing with various urban problems as they appear to be developing. I refer not merely to the investigation of means for producing mass housing or parts of housing or for substituting cheaper materials for dearer in the construction of sewers, drains, and other hardware; nor even to the improvement of transportation at economic levels suited to the needs as well as the resources of the developing nations. I do refer to the use of modern communication devices, such as television, for raising literacy levels and providing vocational training; for assisting the institutions of social assimilation in doing their work; and for developing new industrial patterns based upon the small firm. Most important, I refer also to technological innovation as a basis for rethinking the entire process of urbanization.

For example, earlier we discussed the dualism that characterizes the urban hierarchy in most Asian nations and the incomplete or skewed distribution of places within that hierarchy. One line of thought holds that this characteristic is a serious structural fault in the space economy of any country, and that its rectification through the development of a large number of middle-sized regional centers or growth-points is essential to economic integration and therefore development. In that way one could achieve "regional balance" in development, bridge the gap between the dual sectors of the economy, and increase the so-called trickle-down effects from larger to smaller places. Persuasive though this argument might at first appear, it could be based on a confusion of ends and means. The stunted hierarchies in most Southeast Asian nations probably do derive in part from dualism in their economies, but expanding and balancing the hierarchies need not lead to the correction of structural difficulties within the economy. The seemingly balanced hierarchies that exist in most developed countries grew up in association with certain transportation and marketing technologies. Changes in those technologies already are producing changes in the hierarchies whereby increasing numbers of people and functions are concentrating in the larger metropolitan areas and the smaller towns are relatively declining. In the Southeast Asian setting, as elsewhere, it is possible that the middle-sized city may already have become an anachronism. This is because the integration of rural and urban very likely is feasible directly between the very small rural center, on the one hand, and the great metropolis, on the other. These surely can be connected through efficient highway transport, without intermediation through the smaller cities, in ways not conceivable even fifty years ago in the West. The Southeast Asian nations, like all developing nations, have one very great advantage over nations that were developing in the past— access to an enormously greater range of technological devices for overcoming the frictions of distance and the dissonance in marketing and manufacturing systems.

Of course, it will be argued that middle-sized towns are essential to slow down the movement from rural to urban areas, but the evidence for this, as noted above, is contradictory at best. The probabilities of direct movement from farm to metropolis appear greater now than ever before, if only because it is easier to bridge the physical distances from one to the other.

At the same time, strategies for urban development cannot neglect the rural sector. Modernization through urbanization and industrialization, if history is any guide, assumes a parallel modernization of agriculture. This does not mean, however, that more people will or should remain in rural areas. On the contrary, it means more rapid movement from country to city. This suggests that, in addition to investment in agricultural infrastructure, the most productive investment in the rural areas and small towns would be in education to prepare potential migrants for life in the cities, education that would take them out of the unskilled, illiterate category and place them in the literate and at least partly skilled category.

The problem then assumes a new dimension: how to take advantage of the vast resources of manpower that the growing cities provide? This was in effect the main question posed at the first Pacific Conference on Urban Growth in Honolulu in 1967; it remains the most important question for the future.

There is, however, yet another issue of policy that relates to regional development within developing nations. For the most part, governments tend to view all parts of their territory as having equal value, and in their planning for development they adhere to the principle of regional equity rather than that of regional comparative advantage. In federal political systems such as that of India, Australia, and the United States, different though they may be, there are, understandably, strong pressures to allocate government support in equal measure to all parts of the spatial system. Indeed, in the United States, federal government investment on a per capita basis has been much greater in the sparsely populated western states, with limited over-all resources, than elsewhere. However, there is another way of looking at the space polity of any country, and that is the way the Chinese, for example, are believed to have looked at theirs. They assigned higher value to some areas than to others, in general because they were more accessible and more productive, and because investment in them meant greater returns for larger numbers of people and therefore for the state itself.

A similar point of view might be explored for at least some of the Southeast Asian nations. In such an exercise, any reasonable measurement of benefits and costs probably would suggest the concentration of investment in the major metropolitan areas and in the agricultural regions which are readily integratable with them. Both industry and agriculture in these urban-centered regions would receive their share of investment, as would urban services. The possibilities of doing this in most Southeast Asian countries are greatly enhanced by the areal association of large cities with hinterlands having dense agricultural populations.

A basic assumption in these arguments is that planning for the future of the Southeast Asian city is planning for change; it is planning, not only for cities as they now are, but for cities as they seem to be becoming; it is planning, not only at the scale of the city and its parts, but also at regional and national scales, where the functions and the benefits and costs of urbanization assume quite different proportions; it is planning, not only for the physical city, but, more important, for the kinds of people who will be residing in it; it is planning for modernization, for development, and for urban forms that need not replicate those of the West and that indeed may vary significantly from nation to nation within the region. Even as they are, cities *are* the centers for change in Southeast Asia. The challenge and the opportunity lies in creating a setting for the kind of change that will bring the most benefits to the largest number of people.

Suggested Readings for Part I

COEDÈS, GEORGES. *The Making of South East Asia.* Translated by H. M. Wright. Berkeley and Los Angeles: University of California Press, 1966. A superbly translated study of the region by one of the foremost historians of Southeast Asia.

Committee for the Coordination of Investigations of the Lower Mekong Basin Annual Report. United Nations, Economic Commission for Asia and the Far East; Bangkok, annually.

Development of Water Resources in the Lower Mekong Basin, Flood Control Series no. 12. United Nations, Economic Commission for Asia and the Far East; Bangkok, 1957.

DWYER, D. J. "The Problem of In-Migration and Squatter Settlements in Asian Cities: Two Case Studies, Manila and Victoria-Kowloon." *Asian Studies,* II (1962), pp. 145–69. Reprinted in *Ekistics,* XXI (1966), pp. 196–200. A graphic account of some squatter settlements and the problems they have created, together with the differential administrative responses elicited by uncontrolled urban settlements.

————, ed. *The City as the Centre of Change in Asia.* Hong Kong: The University of Hong Kong Press, 1971. A collection of interdisciplinary papers presented at an international conference held in Hong Kong in 1969, which explore various problems of Asian cities and their prospects.

FISHER, C. A. *South-East Asia: A Social, Economic and Political Geography.* New York: Dutton, 1964. The standard regional geography of Southeast Asia, strongly emphasizing historical development and political relationships.

FRYER, D. W. *Emerging Southeast Asia: A Study in Growth and Stagnation.* New York: McGraw-Hill, 1970. An up-to-date analysis of political, social, and economic changes. Chapter 3 discusses the origins and development of the great cities and their role in national economic life.

GOLAY, FRANK H., *et al. Underdevelopment and Economic Nationalism in Southeast Asia.* Ithaca, N.Y.: Cornell University Press, 1969. Examines the impact of economic nationalism on economic policy and development in the postwar period.

McGEE, T. G. *The Southeast Asian City: A Social Geography of the Primate Cities of Southeast Asia.* New York: Praeger, 1967. An excellent study of the great cities and the process of urbanization, with special emphasis on social and demographic patterns and a fine bibliography.

MORGAN, THEODORE, and NYLE SPOELSTRA, eds. *Economic Interdependence in Southeast Asia.* Madison, Wisc.: University of Wisconsin Press, 1969. Discusses the prospects for economic cooperation among the nations of Southeast Asia. Sponsored by the University of Wisconsin Research Project on Economic Interdependence in Southeast Asia.

MURPHY, RHOADS. "New Capitals of Asia." *Economic Development and Cultural Change,* V (1957), pp. 216–43. Describes sociopolitical and economic factors associated with city growth in newly independent countries in monsoon Asia.

MYRDAL, GUNNAR. *Asian Drama: An Inquiry into the Poverty of Nations.* New York: Pantheon, 1968. A three-volume study analyzing the problems of underdevelopment, development, and planning for development in South Asia.

Resources for the Future. *Agricultural Development in the Mekong Basin: Goals, Priorities and Strategies.* Washington, D.C., 1971. Explores agricultural development in the Mekong Basin with special attention to human factors and social and cultural strategies for modernizing an agrarian society.

SEWELL, W. R. D., and GILBERT WHITE. *The Lower Mekong: An Experiment in International River Control.* New York: Carnegie Endowment for International Peace, 1966.

SHAND, R. T., ed. *Agricultural Development in Asia.* Berkeley and Los Angeles: University of California Press, 1969. An analytical and descriptive account of the main trends in agricultural development and assessment of prospects for future agricultural and general economic development.

SHAPLEN, ROBERT. *Time out of Hand: Revolution and Reaction in Southeast Asia.* New York: Harper and Row, 1969. Reports on events and problems by a correspondent for *The New Yorker.*

Southeast Asia Development Advisory Group. *Agricultural Revolution in Southeast Asia.* New York: The Asia Society, 1970. Deals with the impact of grain production and trade and the consequences for development.

STEINBERG, DAVID J., *et al. In Search of Southeast Asia: A Modern History.* New York: Praeger, 1971. Six historians explore anew the process by which Southeast Asians have been adapting their cultures to a changing world.

VAN NIEL, ROBERT, ed. *Economic Factors in Southeast Asian Social Change.* Hawaii: University of Hawaii, Asian Studies Program, 1968. Analyzes aspects of rural and urban evolution in the Philippines, Indonesia, and Malaysia.

WHITE, G. F., *et al. Economic and Social Aspects of Lower Mekong De-*

velopment. Bangkok, 1962. This report to the Committee for Coordination of Investigations of the Lower Mekong Basin investigates the types of economic and social studies and organizations needed for development of the region and the potentialities of various projects.

See also: Asian Survey, Economist Intelligence Units, Far Eastern Economic Review, Journal of Tropical Geography, Pacific Affairs.

II NATIONS OF SOUTHEAST ASIA

5 BURMA

Robert E. Huke

Ethnic Diversity and Population Distribution • The Landscape and Climate • Agricultural Regions • Fish and Forests • Mining and Manufacturing • Persistent Problems • focus *on Political Factors in Burma's Rice Economy*

Of the nations that have achieved independence since World War II, Burma has suffered more than most from economic, political, and social instability. Like most of the new and developing nations, it has been struggling with poverty, illiteracy, unemployment, and the conflict of interests between traditional and modernized groups. It has also had to contend with conflicts between the Burmans, who have largely controlled the government, and various ethnic minorities, who have had little say in it. Some improvement has been made in education, public health, and public works, but food shortages persist, and the government has failed to bring about the desired economic development and to reconcile peacefully internal political and social rivalries. Few periods since independence from Great Britain was joyfully celebrated on January 4, 1948, have not been marred by militant protests by communist insurgents, ethnic rebels, or other groups opposed to the government's centrally planned economy or to its other methods of seeking solutions to the nation's problems.

The Japanese occupation of Burma during World War II left this potentially rich land battle-scarred and deeply divided in political ideologies. Years of clashes between government forces and various rebellious factions led to a military takeover, followed in 1962 by a bloodless coup and the setting up of a dictatorship under General Ne Win. In 1967–68, widespread demonstrations against the Chinese minority led to the declara-

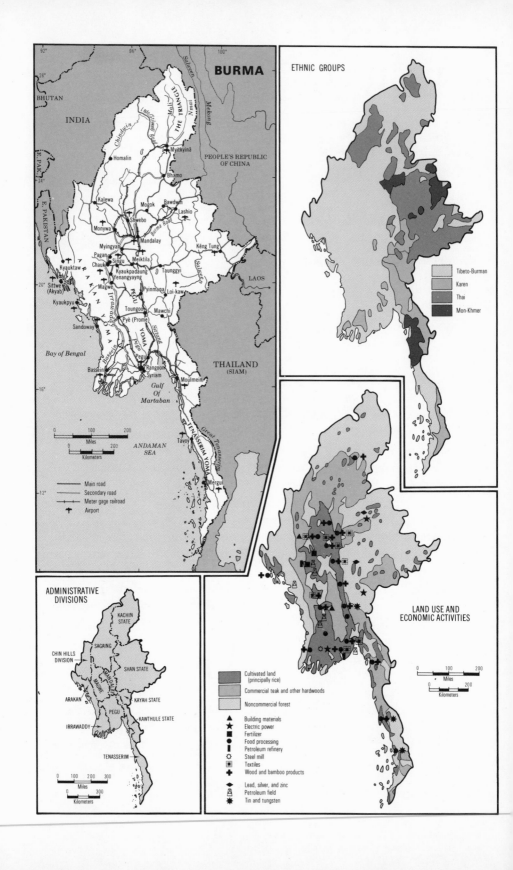

tion of martial law. Meanwhile, banks, trade, and industries were wholly or partly nationalized, and, in an attempt to calm separatist movements, several semi-autonomous ethnic states were established, namely Shan, Kachin, Kayah, and Kawthule; and Chin Hills acquired a special territorial administration.

In the early years of indepedence, Burma sought the aid of various United Nations and other foreign experts in drawing up plans for economic development. Once the decision was made to sever all ties with foreigners and go it alone, the lack of trained and experienced personnel and of capital for investments became all too evident; as a result, numerous ambitious development plans and projects have been shelved or initiated only half-heartedly.

A basic cause of the continued turbulence is the fact that Burma, like many other societies in the developing world, is torn between a desire to preserve its ancient social and essentially Buddhist traditions and a desire to enjoy the material benefits of a modern, industrialized economy.

Ethnic Diversity and Population Distribution

Although about 60 per cent of the 27.6 million inhabitants of Burma are Burmans, ethnically related to the Tibetans, a long history of migrations, which continue even today, has created a patchwork of ethnic groups, each with its own traditions and languages.

During the sixty-three-year-period when Burma was administered as part of British India, large numbers of Tamils, Telegus, and Chettyars migrated from India to less crowded Burma, where labor was scarce and land more easily available. In 1960 persons of Indian origin comprised some 7 to 8 per cent of the nation's population and were concentrated in the Irrawaddy Delta region, where they worked as agricultural laborers, and in the urban areas, where they made up a sizable portion of both the coolie and the retail-trade groups. Nationalization of industry and trade in the early 1960's, combined with bitter rioting between factions, caused a major exodus of Indians and, to a lesser extent, of the Chinese, who had also played a major role in retail trade throughout the country.

The largest minority group is the Karens, who comprise about 11 per cent of the national total. They have settled mostly in the southern Shan Upland, in Kawthule, and in the Irrawaddy Delta. The Shan, closely related to the Thai of neighboring Thailand, make up some 8 ½ per cent of the population; they are concentrated in their own state but have also spread into the Irrawaddy and Chindwin valleys. The Kachins, in their own northern state and the northern parts of the Shan state, number some 700,000, or just under 3 per cent of the national total.

In addition to these groups, the census recognizes some 120 "races" and a total of 126 languages within the country. Burmese, a monosyllabic Tibeto-Chinese language, is the official language, although English is sometimes used in government, business, and the universities.

In contrast to India and Pakistan to the west and China to the northeast, Burma is relatively uncrowded. Its 1970 population of 27.6 million, if equally distributed over its Texas-size area of 261,789 square miles, would give an average density of slightly over 100 persons per square mile, roughly equal to that of North Carolina. Actually, the population is strikingly concentrated in the deltas of the Irrawaddy and Sittang rivers, in the central dry belt, and along the northern Tenasserim Coast. But even in these areas the density seldom exceeds 250 persons per square mile and the nutritional density averages less than 500. The least populated areas are the extensive mountain and hill peripheries of the Irrawaddy lowland, home of most of the 10.8 million non-Burman peoples.

In Burma, as in many other Southeast Asian nations, one city dominates urban life. Rangoon, the capital, has a population of 1.8 million, five times that of Mandalay and nearly eleven times that of Moulmein, the second and third cities. International transportation and trade routes focus on it, and more than 85 per cent of the nation's foreign trade moves through its port. As the political and financial hub of the country, it has attracted a considerable volume and variety of industrial development. Here is the center of the chief industries: rice milling and textiles. Here also are the biggest sawmills and furniture plants, a major oil refinery, and the nation's only steel mill.

Despite modest industrial growth in Rangoon and elsewhere in recent years, Burma cannot yet supply its needs for textiles and other products of light industry, and only the barest beginnings have been made in heavy industry. Most of the needed machinery and transport equipment, textiles, dairy products, chemicals, and iron and steel have come from abroad.

The Landscape and Climate

Burma is shaped like a huge kite with its top touching eastern Tibet and its tail extending down the Tenasserim Coast. From the Himalayan system a series of rugged mountain ranges runs southward, separating Burma from

India, and then southeastward parallel with the Arakan Coast. Passage across these mountains is possible only by precipitous trails through a few transverse gaps.

The northeastern and eastern borders are also marked by rugged ranges, high to the north and lower behind the Tenasserim Coast. Almost the whole of the Shan state is a deeply dissected plateau averaging 3,000 feet in elevation, the western edge of which is a fault scarp that in places rises 2,000 feet in a single step. The famous Burma Road connects Burma with China's Yunnan Province across the northern part of the Shan Upland.

Between these formidable mountain systems is a central lowland, formed by the valleys of the Irrawaddy, Chindwin, and Sittang rivers, which is cut down the middle by the wooded rolling hills of the Pegu Yoma. The northern part of the lowland is known as the dry belt. The southern part, known as the delta region, where the Irrawaddy and much smaller Sittang distributaries approach one another to form an alluvial plain some 12,000 square miles in area, is Burma's rice bowl. Narrow coastal plains provide additional agricultural land on the Arakan and Tenasserim coasts.

For centuries, Burma's major arteries of economic and cultural development have been its rivers, one of which, the Irrawaddy, was immortalized in Kipling's lyric evocation "Can't you 'ear their paddles chunkin' from Rangoon to Mandalay?"

The Irrawaddy is born of snow fields in the rugged, tangled, 19,000-foot mountains where China, India, and Burma meet. Its twin sources, the Nmai and Mali rivers, flow southward and join at the base of the triangle, an area so wild and unexplored that during World War II it was never occupied by the Japanese. Bhamo, the year-round head of navigation, is 900 miles from the sea and 872 miles from Rangoon, with which it is connected by regular freight and passenger service.

Nearly 150 miles from the Andaman Sea the river breaks up into a series of distributary channels that wind their way across the flat delta to reach the sea along a 150-mile mangrove-lined tidal front. Rangoon lies to the east of the main delta but is connected with the Irrawaddy by the 22-mile Twante Canal.

Sixty miles southwest of Mandalay the Irrawaddy is joined by its main tributary, the Chindwin, which during the rainy season is navigable for 380 miles to Homalin, near the Indian border. The Chindwin is doubly important in Burma's future because of the more than 2.5 million acres of virtually unsettled and apparently cultivable land along its upper course.

The longest of Burma's great rivers is the Salween, which rises in the mountain knot of eastern Tibet and flows 1,750 miles to reach the sea at Moulmein. Spectacular gorges and rapids mark its route and prevent significant long-haul transportation. But the last fifty-five miles are used extensively, and country boats navigate some portions of the middle reaches. The Salween, like several other rivers in Burma, has considerable potential hydroelectric power, which is slowly being developed.

The Sittang is a misfit stream occupying a former channel of the Irrawaddy and emptying into the Gulf of Martaban sixty miles northeast of Rangoon. It is navigable for only short distances, and its mouth is famed for dangerous tidal bores.

Burma's location on the northeastern shores of the Bay of Bengal exposes it to the full effects of the Indian monsoon. Starting in late May and continuing until mid-October, southwest winds cross the bay and intersect the Arakan Coast at right angles. As the moisture-laden air reaches the mountains, it rises and cools, inducing heavy rainfall. At Sittwe (Akyab), for instance, 197 inches may fall during the monsoon season. From mid-October through mid-May the winds are from the north-northeast and Sittwe's rainfall totals only about six inches.

This same seasonal pattern is typical of most other parts of the country, although rainfall totals are lower. The Irrawaddy Delta averages some 125 inches a year. In the dry belt, around Magwe, the total drops as low as 21 inches. Monsoon winds reaching this area have traveled 200 miles north along the Irrawaddy Valley and have already lost much of their moisture, or they have crossed the Arakan Yoma, producing heavy rain on the windward slopes and a rain shadow in their lee. Farther north, rainfall again increases, averaging some eighty inches at Myitkyina.

Agricultural Regions

Stimulated by the introduction of political stability in the Irrawaddy Delta region under British rule, by the first steam shipping, by the opening of the Suez Canal, and by increased demands for rice on the world market, Burma was transformed within a period of seventy-five years from a country with little agricultural surplus and almost no foreign trade to the world's leading exporter of rice. By 1940, it was annually selling abroad 3 million tons of rice, 95 per cent of which came from the delta region.

Conditions for growing rice are highly favorable in this region. Not only is there a reliable rainfall averaging eighty inches a year, most of it in the peak growing season, but the swampy lands are easily converted into diked

Courtesy United Nations

Religion plays a key role in many Southeast Asian societies and has inspired the creation of countless magnificent works of art. This is a view of the inner court-yard of the main Buddhist pagoda in Rangoon. Shoes must be removed before entering.

fields where the flow of water can be regulated to suit cultivation needs throughout the growing season. Not surprisingly, therefore, rice predominates almost to the exclusion of all other crops in the delta. This concentration on one crop has its disadvantages, however. During the six weeks or so of the transplanting season starting about June 20, and again during harvest season from November through January, there is a severe shortage of labor. At other times widespread underemployment is the rule. (For additional information on factors that contributed to the rise and fall of Burma's rice economy, see pp. 74-81.)

In 1956 the government began efforts to introduce jute cultivation so as to eliminate the importation of bags for rice, but by 1970 only about 70,000 acres had been converted to jute. Rice production continues to dominate the landscape, just as rice milling dominates the industrial scene in the hundreds of trading centers perched on river banks throughout the region.

In the delta, less than 1 per cent of the farm land is double-cropped, despite favorable temperatures for year-round production. Double-cropping of rice and a dry crop has proved to be effective on experimental farms, but the practice has not spread. Even for rice, fertilizers are seldom used, seed selection is poor, pest damage is high, and cultivation methods are not efficient. As a result, yields average only 1,300 pounds of wet rice per acre, compared with 4,300 pounds in the United States and nearly 7,000 in Japan. Burma's latest program for economic and social development emphasizes raising rice yields through greater use of fertilizers, more intensive farming practices, and irrigation projects that would permit double-cropping in the delta. At the same time, it aims at greater diversification of crops to cut down on imports.

The dry belt includes the central Irrawaddy and lower Chindwin valleys and the northern extension of the Sittang Valley. It has one fourth of the nation's people and one third of its cultivated land. With an average rainfall of less than forty inches, almost all of it between May and October, water deficiency is a problem. Tanks, wells, canals, and streams provide irrigation water for about one third of the agricultural land, and these fields are devoted largely to rice. Nevertheless, the dry belt does not normally grow enough of it for local needs.

In contrast to the delta, the dry belt produces a great variety of crops. Food crops include maize (corn), millet, sesame (an herb whose seeds yield an oil), peanuts, chili, pulses (edible seeds of plants such as peas and beans), and a variety of vegetables. These, together with cotton and tobacco, occupy twice the acreage of rice. Although dry-farming techniques are used, crops frequently fail because of fluctuations in rainfall. At one time such failures caused famines, but in recent decades rice surpluses from the Irrawaddy Delta have been available. Sesamum and peanuts from the dry belt supply a large part of Burma's requirements of cooking oil, while the cotton, even though of a rather short-staple length, finds a ready market in the nation's textile mills. Millet, in addition to serving as the dietary staple for the less well-to-do people in the region, also is important as a fodder crop for Burma's several million cattle and buffalo. These are mainly work animals; faithful Buddhists do not eat meat. Those who adhere less strictly to Buddhist tenets do, however, and many farmers keep cattle, pigs, and chickens to supplement their rice and fish diet.

Broad terraces paralleling both the Irrawaddy and the Chindwin, which are now dry-farmed, appear to be well suited to irrigation. And there is plenty of water in these rivers. At such time as the government has funds available for the construction of dams, storage reservoirs, and additional canals, at least 2 million acres of now low-yielding farm land could be converted into high-yielding irrigated land capable of growing two crops a year.

In all the mountainous areas of Burma, shifting (slash-and-burn) cultivation, known as *taungya*, is practiced. *Taungya* involves cutting and burning the forest cover, then planting and harvesting the crops. Often as many as forty-five different crops are planted in a single field, including several varieties of rice, maize, beans, tobacco, cotton, sesamum, potatoes, and numerous vegetables. Usually, a given field loses its fertility after one or two years; it is then abandoned in favor of a new field and is not planted again until it has naturally regained its fertility, a decade or more later.

This technique of land use often results in a moderately well-balanced diet for the people who practice it, but it is destructive of timber reserves and may cause soil erosion. Furthermore, as the population increases (and it is growing at the rate of 2.2 per cent per year), fields are used more frequently, yields gradually decline, and erosion becomes serious.

Fish and Forests

After rice, fish is perhaps the most common foodstuff in Burma. Commercial fishing on a small scale takes place in the major rivers and off both the Arakan and Tenasserim coasts. Much of the total catch, amounting to about 85 million pounds a year, is provided by part-time fishermen. Traps are common in standing water and in streams, large and small. Farmers cast nets in almost any body of water while their children fish with hook and line.

One of Burma's greatest resources is its immense forests. Up to 1940 it was the world's leading producer of teak wood. Disruptions caused by the war, insurgent activities, and nationalization have cut the annual exportable surplus from about 500,000 cubic tons to half that. Much of the heavy forest work is done by elephants, about 900 of which continue to haul and pile the logs.

Good forestry practices have been in use for a number of years, but regulations are frequently disregarded. Reserves are large enough to provide for a sustained cutting of about 400,000 cubic tons a year. The best teak forests are on hill and mountain slopes where rainfall is between forty and eighty inches a year, especially on the lee slopes of the Arakan Yoma, on both flanks of the Pegu Yoma, and in the Shan Uplands.

Mining and Manufacturing

More than fifty minerals are known to exist in Burma. In 1940, minerals provided almost 40 per cent of the export earnings. The most important developed mineral resources are petroleum, tin, tungsten, and lead-silver. The most romantic are jade, rubies, sapphires, and gold. Jade has been mined since time immemorial in a rough mountain area about sixty miles west of Myitkyina. Moderate quantities of ruby, sapphire, garnet, and aquamarine have come from near Mogok. Gold is mined in several places along the banks of the Chindwin and the Irrawaddy.

Although petroleum occurs in a number of places, the only fields of any size are at Chauk (the major area), Yenangyaung, and Myingyan, immediately east of the Irrawaddy in the dry belt. During World War II, wells, pipelines, and refining capacity were destroyed, and rehabilitation has been hampered by insurgent activity and by the lack of capital and managerial skills. A number of new wells have been opened, however, and refineries are operating at Syriam, near Rangoon, and at Chauk. By 1970 domestic production had reached 810,000 tons, or more than double the figure in the late 1950's. This is not sufficient for the country's needs; output could be much greater provided adequate capital and technical skills became available.

Ores of tin and tungsten occur together in a belt running from the west-central part of the Shan state south through the Kayah state, Kawthule, and on into the Tenasserim coastal district. The largest production has come from hydraulic mining of alluvial and eluvial deposits at Tavoy, while the most consistent output has come from underground mining of quartz veins at the Mawchi Mines. Annual production totals for the two metals together had once averaged 8,000–9,000 tons, but by 1969–70 this total had fallen to 1,100 tons.

Lead and silver are produced at the Bawdin Mines, thirty miles northwest of Lashio, one of the largest high-grade silver-lead-zinc ore bodies in the world. Here, too, problems associated with nationalization, lack of capital, and political turmoil have seriously curtailed output. In 1969–70 production totals were 12,000 tons of lead and 1 million ounces of silver, only one sixth the 1938–39 levels.

Burma has never produced coal in appreciable volume, nor do its reserves appear to be large, though occurrences are common. The best possibilities apparently are near Kalewa on the Chindwin River, where several ten-foot seams having a total thickness of fifty feet are located.

Substantial supplies of iron have been discovered in the Shan Uplands, and lateritic ores are common, but neither can be exploited economically with current technology.

As in many developing nations, industrialization is a prime goal of development plans, especially because of the chronic unemployment or underemployment of the farming population. Before World War II, food processing, textiles, machine shops, handicrafts, and industries making consumer goods were mainly in the hands of local Burmese. Most mining and modern manufacturing—petroleum refining, shipbuilding, railways, electrical industries—were established and operated by foreigners, principally British and Indian entrepreneurs. With nationalization in 1963, almost all foreign owners, managers, and technicians left Burma. Since then, industrial production appears to have dropped considerably, mainly because of inexperienced government management and because reduced rice exports have not provided sufficient funds to buy imported factory equipment. Barter-aid agreements with several foreign nations have, however, resulted in the establishment of new metal-smelting, chemical, plywood, tractor, paper, and vehicle-assembly plants. Further development of industries depends partly on larger supplies of power. Petroleum production can undoubtedly be increased, and several hydroelectric stations now in operation can be greatly expanded. Also, there is a tremendous amount of potential hydroelectric power in Burma's untapped rivers.

Persistent Problems

Measured by the usual Western standards, this young nation is very poor indeed: The average income per person, for instance, is about $75 a year.

Some idea of the enormous problems facing the inexperienced military administrators is provided by the following information drawn from the revolutionary government's budget for 1969–70. In 1969 there were 3,469 agricultural tractors owned by the government, but 2,663 were unusable because of lack of spare parts and maintenance. The tractors that were serviceable worked in the fields an average of 280 *hours* during the *year* and plowed an average of 189 acres each. Because of a serious lack of trucks, each put in 160 hours of additional work in road transport. Payment received for field work during the year averaged Kyats 1,996 while the costs of operation averaged Kyats 11,311.

Measures that will have to be taken to make Burma a more viable nation include, first of all, the creation of a political structure that can provide greater internal stability and the integration of the alienated non-Burman minorities into national society. A second goal is improvement in the quality of education and the training of more capable managers and technicians to develop modern manufacturing industries and expand the presently inadequate transport system. Recovery of prewar export levels of rice, teak, petroleum, and metals would make it possible to buy abroad the equipment needed to develop more factories making consumer goods. To do this, limitations on imports will have to be relaxed, and there is some evidence of a trend in this direction. Given the lack of immediate concern over population pressure, and given the untapped resources of the land, mines, and rivers, the Burmese are better off than many Southeast Asians. Much depends on the policies evolved to make better use of their resources, both physical and human, during the 1970's.

focus *on Political Factors in Burma's Rice Economy*

Burma's dramatic transformation from a subsistence economy with negligible international trade in rice to a system of commercial agriculture based overwhelmingly on rice has seldom been equaled. Unhappily, the meteoric rise in production and exports during the decades prior to World War II has been almost matched by a catastrophic decline in recent years. This metamorphosis is directly related to changing political regimes, first under the Burmese kings, then colonial rule, and finally emerging nationhood.

Rice and the Burmese Kings

In 1569 Caesar Frederick visited Lower Burma and its then capital and principal trade center, Pegu, in search of new products for the European markets and new markets for European products. He reported: "The merchandizes that go out of Pegu are Gold, Silver, Rubies, Sapphires, Spinelles, great store of Beniamin [bensoin], long Pepper, Lead, Lacca

[lac], Rice, Wine, some sugar. . . ." * Frederick nowhere mentions the volume of the rice export or its destination. However, from its place as number ten on the list, we are probably safe in assuming that the volume was at that time quite small.

During the last half of the sixteenth century, various Portuguese traders visited Pegu, and at the turn of that century a small trading post was established at Syriam, across the Pegu River from the present site of Rangoon. This post did not last long, however; it was overrun and destroyed by the Burmans in 1613, during one of the frequent Mon wars. The captured Portuguese were impressed in the Burmese army, and their trade attempts ceased.

In 1635, King Thalun transferred his capital from Pegu to Ava in the central Burma dry belt. Ava was 400 miles up the Irrawaddy from Syriam, and the trip took as long as two months. The delta lands and the kingdom's only significant ports were now at the very margin of Burma's military control and, more than ever before, were subject to raiding and pillage by the Mons. Settlement of the delta was limited to a few thousand hardy souls who practiced a semimigratory form of subsistence agriculture. Thalun and subsequent rulers saw the dry belt as the focus of Burmese life, devoted little effort to the development of Lower Burma, and actively discouraged foreign contact and trade.

Thus cut off from the outside world, the Burmese kings came to believe that their capital was the "center of the universe." This period of isolation lasted for almost 200 years. "At the beginning of the nineteenth century, although rice was the most abundant product of Burma, exports were entirely prohibited by the King and the Court of Ava as it was feared that if Lower Burma once began exporting rice for profitable consideration it would be difficult to prevail upon cultivators to retain a sufficient quantity to supply the needs of Upper Burma." †

The Colonial Period

In 1824 a series of incidents on the Burma–East Bengal border led to the First Burmese War, which resulted in British control of the Arakan and Tenasserim coastal areas. Twenty-eight years later, in 1852, the Second Burmese War brought about Great Britain's direct control of the vast delta lands of the Irrawaddy and Sittang rivers.

* D. G. E. Hall, *Burma*. London: Hutchinson House, 1950, p. 52.
† *Burma Rice*. Burma Pamphlets No. 4, Calcutta: Longmans, Green and Co., Ltd., 1944, p. 2.

The beginning of the colonial era under Britain roughly coincided with the great expansion of British overseas trade and with the development of steam navigation. Shortly after annexation, two events of great importance to Burma's future occurred: first, the American Civil War, which cut off Europe's supply of rice from the Carolinas, and, second, the opening of the Suez Canal in 1869, which provided a cheaper route to Europe for Burma's rice and to Burma for British manufactured goods. Each of these events, in turn, caused a sharp rise in the price offered to Burma for its rice and a much increased demand by volume.

Under Burmese rule the economy had been of the feudal type, and very little money was used. The British immediately introduced the then-popular *laissez-faire* economy, with its freedom of action, its individualistic attitude, and its abandonment of barter in favor of money. The end of the rule of kings and the introduction of the British system also led to a revolution in the prevailing system of land tenure. British laws enabled, and in fact encouraged, individual ownership of the land a man farmed. This was in marked contrast to the former system, under which all land was owned by the king, thus precluding permanent tenure on the part of any cultivator. The concept of private property encouraged a permanency of settlement never before typical of the delta region. British rule was also accompanied by the introduction of strong military and police forces, which provided a degree of personal and property security not previously enjoyed here.

Vast areas of empty yet potentially productive land in Lower Burma were suddenly attractive for settlement. A major migration from three directions, representing three contrasting cultural groups, began almost immediately. From the north came the Burmans of the dry belt; from the east, out of the hills on the border between Burma and Siam (now Thailand), came the Karens; from the west across the Bay of Bengal came the Madrasi and others from south India. All were encouraged by the government policy of granting freehold rights to any person willing to occupy, farm, and pay taxes on a plot of land for twelve consecutive years. Especially in the early decades of this migration, farms tended to be quite large, on the order of twenty acres, while population density was low.

Under Burmese rule, agriculture had been on a family basis, and of a subsistence type. With the British in power, it immediately shifted to what Furnivall calls "industrial agriculture," * because of its similarity to the factory system. In this "industrial agriculture" seasonal labor was needed

* John S. Furnivall, *The Political Economy of Burma,* revised by J. Russell Andrus. Rangoon: Burma Book Club, 1938.

to transplant, reap, and mill the crop. This labor was recruited from outside the region and consisted chiefly of Indians from Madras and Bengal who came to Burma without their families. Some of these laborers settled in Burma, but many returned home after the season was finished. This was commercial agriculture, producing chiefly for the export market and concentrating almost exclusively on rice. The emphasis on rice was so great that many farm families depended on market purchases to supply their needs, not only for household goods, but even for food other than rice.

At the beginning of British administration of the delta region, the area devoted to rice was less than 500,000 acres, most of it farmed under a system of shifting cultivation. From 1853 on, more permanent systems of farming became the rule, and the total area planted in rice expanded dramatically. Between 1860 and 1870 the acreage in Lower Burma alone increased by about 400,000 acres. During the following three decades it went up by more than 3 million acres. By 1930 the total rice area in Burma had risen to 12.4 million acres, nearly 10 million of which were in Lower Burma.

In an attempt to increase and improve the production of rice, the country's main food and main source of income, Burma has established state farm schools. Here rice is being winnowed and rewinnowed by hand to obtain the purest possible strain for replanting. *Courtesy United Nations*

At the beginning of World War II, Burma was producing more rice per capita than any other country and had become the world's fourth largest producer, exceeded only by China, India, and Japan, in that order. It was by far the largest exporter of rice in the world, having about 38 per cent of the exportable surplus, more than twice as much as French Indochina (now Cambodia, Laos, and North and South Vietnam), its nearest rival.

In the last season before the Japanese occupation, the gross area sown to all crops in Burma was 18.8 million acres; of this 12.5 million were sown to rice. Thus, rice occupied two thirds of the total cropped area. Clearly, rice dominated both the landscape and the economy. This was mono-cultivation with a vengeance.

Emerging Nationhood

When the Japanese took over Burma, in early 1942, one of the first results was an almost total cessation of shipping, cutting off the nation from its European, Indian, African, and American markets. Almost equally damaging was the loss of domestic transport. Constant Allied bombings of the ports, railroads, and roads put many of them out of operation. Simultaneously, the occupation forces confiscated and slaughtered a major portion of the work-animals, thus seriously hindering both plowing and hauling. Disruptions to the transport network were so serious that normal trading patterns all but ceased to exist. Rice surpluses accumulated on the farms and at milling centers while serious food shortages occurred in Rangoon and Mandalay.

The Burmese had expected that once the Japanese were in control of the country there would be a bountiful supply of such Japanese industrial goods as textiles, cement, ironware, and miscellaneous consumer goods. However, the Japanese had neither the shipping to bring these goods to Burma nor the exportable surplus that Burma wanted. Consequently, the once prosperous Burma bazaar trade dropped to almost nothing.

The total loss of foreign markets, the great difficulties of internal transportation, the decimation of the work-animal population, and the recruiting of military and paramilitary forces from among the farm population led to a drastic decrease in rice production: The 1944–45 harvest was 500,000 tons *less* than the amount of rice normally consumed locally, while markets in the delta were glutted with a backlog of the grain, and the dry belt was close to famine.

Rice output increased rapidly after the British reoccupation and probably would have reached or even surpassed the 1940–41 figure by 1949–50 had it not been for a series of unfortunate incidents that overtook Burma after it became independent in 1948. During the following year, several political factions within the country went underground and turned to armed insurrection. By the summer of 1949 about half of Burma's rice area was in the hands of the White Flag Communists, the Red Flag Communists, the Army Mutineers, the People's Volunteer Organization, the Democratic Front, or the Karen National Defense Organization.

In the 1950's the internal political situation improved gradually, and in the last half of the 1960's total rice production and the area sown to rice returned to 1940 levels. Unfortunately, exports did not. Burma's population had grown from 16 to 27.6 million, or nearly 65 per cent, during this period, and per capita consumption of rice had increased simultaneously. By 1970 a production of 8 million tons left a potential exportable surplus of roughly 800,000 tons, less than one third of the actual exports of 1940. Not only were surpluses much reduced, but by 1970 the domestic economy was only just beginning to revive. Chinese, Indian, and British millers had been forced to leave the country. Rice trade had been completely nationalized and was being directed by relatively inexperienced military personnel. Internal transportation was overloaded, milling facilities were in serious need of modernization, and prices for rice at the farm level were low. The prices were fixed by the central government, which by law controlled the purchase, milling, export, and retail sale of the grain. The price for standard-quality rice delivered at the mill averaged about $32 per ton compared with roughly $70 in the Philippines. The low farm price has permitted the Peoples Shops in Burma to provide retail rice at one of the world's lowest rates ($2.25 per 100 pounds), but it has also discouraged the farmers from attempting to increase production.

Nationalization of land formerly owned by large landholders reduced tenancy and the crushing burden of debts that had been the common lot of Burma's farmers, but it resulted in uneconomic fragmentation of holdings among the new owners.

Yet another problem, perhaps the worst of all, has been insecurity in the agricultural regions. Rebels and *dacoits* (armed robbers) have operated over large rural areas, extracting taxes and hindering the free movement of rice from farm to mill. This has further lowered farmers' incentives to produce and, while relatively little land has been abandoned, production techniques over large areas have remained haphazard.

Yields per unit area are low, averaging a bit less than 1,300 pounds per acre. The use of chemical fertilizers on rice is insignificant, averaging less than 1/40 that of the Philippines and 1/600 that of Taiwan. The low rate of fertilizer use is a direct reflection of government pricing policy. The Burmese farmer receives the lowest return per unit weight of rice of any farmer in Asia, yet his cost for nitrogen fertilizers is high. The nitrogen-rice price ratio is roughly 10 to 1, twice that of any other Asian country.

The paucity of fertilizer application on Burmese ricelands may begin to show significant change in the early 1970's. Two chemical-fertilizer plants of modest scale are scheduled for completion. These plants, located on the banks of the Irrawaddy in central Burma, are designed to utilize natural gas, locally available in adequate volume, and to be of sufficient capacity to satisfy domestic needs.

For many years Burma's agricultural experiment stations have been carrying on research in seed improvement. Also in 1967, 200 tons of IR8 * were imported for experimental purposes. From this seed a new strain, known in Burma as *Yagyaw* (100 basket), was developed for local use. In 1969 this improved seed was planted on almost 500,000 acres. Approximately half this area was on irrigated lands in the dry belt divisions of Sagaing, Mandalay, and Magwe. The remainder was concentrated in the Irrawaddy Delta with only token plantings in the Arakan, Tenasserim, and other peripheral areas. Yields in the areas of major *Yagyaw* plantings averaged 2,900 pounds per acre, well over double the national average for all rice. Clearly, improved seed together with new technology holds great promise of vastly improved yields in the years ahead.

Outside the dry belt, irrigation plays little part in Burma's rice production. Less than 5 per cent of the rice receives supplemental water, a figure well below that of any other rice-exporting nation. While rainfall is more reliable than in other Southeast Asian rice-producing regions, periodic flood and drought conditions do occur, as in 1966, when at least 15 per cent of the total sown area was destroyed, and in 1968, when torrential rains breached numerous small dams and caused serious damage to the crop along the Arakan Coast. Since 1962 several irrigation systems of modest scale have been opened. These all make use of tributary streams showing great fluctuations in the volume of water available from year to year. To date no important system makes use of the vast resources of the major rivers.

Despite an uninspired history of rice production since independence, Burma's potential remains great. The man-land ratio is the most favorable in Asia even though recent increases in the rate of population growth are

* The first high-yielding variety released by the International Rice Research Institute, Los Baños, Laguna, Philippines, often referred to as "miracle rice" (see pp. 215–19).

now being felt. Burma's monsoon rainfall not only provides adequate water over vast areas but its reliability from year to year, despite occasional problems, is greater than in any other Southeast Asian nation. Burma also has at least 4 million acres of undeveloped land, much of which is suitable for rice, and a huge volume of untapped irrigation water in the combined flow of the Irrawaddy and Chindwin rivers.

Burma has the potential for another dramatic increase in rice production and a resumption of its position as the world's leading exporter. The first order of business must be the re-establishment of political tranquility. Only then can planning strategy for renewed growth prove effective.

Suggested Readings

American University. *Area Handbook for Burma.* Washington, D.C.: U.S. Government Printing Office, 1968. A comprehensive analysis of social, political, and economic aspects of the area and its national security.

DONNISON, F. S. V. *Burma.* New York: Praeger, 1970. A general work stressing the post-1962 period; takes a somewhat gloomy view of Burma's future.

FURNIVALL, J. S. *Colonial Policy and Practice: A Comparative Study of Burma and Netherlands India.* New York: New York University Press, 1956. A thorough discussion of social and political evolution under British administration, 1826–1940.

HTIN AUNG, U. *A History of Burma.* New York: Columbia University Press, 1967. A very good history, from the earliest kingdoms to the post-independence period.

HUKE, ROBERT E. *Rainfall in Burma.* Hanover, N.H.: Geography Publications at Dartmouth, #2, 1965. A detailed study with numerous maps, graphs, and charts dealing with precipitation patterns and variability.

MAUNG, MYA. *Burma and Pakistan: A Comparative Study of Development.* New York: Praeger, 1971. Explores the question of why certain types of economic philosophy and policy are being pursued in Burma and Pakistan and examines their success or failure.

TINKER, HUGH. *The Union of Burma: A Study of the First Years of Independence.* New York: Oxford University Press, 1967. A comprehensive analysis of economic, political, and social events of Burma's first ten years of independence and prospects for further political developments.

See also Suggested Readings for Part I, pp. 57–59.

6 THAILAND

Leonard Unger [*]

Historical Highlights · *The People* · *The Resource Base* ·
The Economy · focus *on Prospects for the Future*

More and more visitors from the West have come to know Krung Thep
(Bangkok), the capital of Thailand, as one of the major stopping points
on round-the-world air travel. And Thailand has more and more impinged
on the consciousness of the world outside Southeast Asia because of the
roles it plays in connection with the political and military dramas of
Vietnam, Laos, and Cambodia. Americans, who have played a major part
in the events in Southeast Asia since World War II, have developed especially close relations with Thailand.

The location of Thailand, which was called Siam until 1932, provides
part of the explanation for the country's growing significance in world
affairs. When the seas were the main channel for world travel and commerce, Thailand lay off the beaten track that touched Southeast Asia primarily at Singapore and also at Saigon, Djakarta (Batavia), Pinang, and
Rangoon. The more direct air routes have tended increasingly to gravitate
to Krung Thep as a stopping place in its own right and as a junction
point for the routes to Malaysia, Singapore, Indonesia, and Australia.
When Western attention was focused primarily on colonial possessions, in
the period before World War II, Thailand received little notice, and it
was French Indochina, Burma, and Malaya that one heard most about.
Today our interest in the new groupings of Southeast Asia's independent
nations centers mainly around their development and their struggle to
maintain their independence, and this puts the spotlight on Thailand as a

[*] The views presented here are the author's and not necessarily those of The American
Geographical Society.

relatively stable area between the war zones of Laos, Vietnam, Cambodia, and to some extent Burma, and the relatively calmer lands to the south in peninsular and insular Southeast Asia.

Historical Highlights

Any historical discussion of Thailand begins with the fact that the nation, unlike all its neighbors, has never lived under colonial rule and has long been independent. This takes us back to the first millennium of the Christian era, when Thai peoples, or at least warrior groups of Thais, were moving south from or through Yunnan Province (now in southwestern China) and beginning to establish small independent kingdoms in what is now Laos, northern Thailand, the Shan state of the present Union of Burma, and the upper reaches of the Brahmaputra (Dihang) Valley in Assam (India). The rest of what is Thailand today was variously under the rule of the Khmers (ancestors of the present Cambodians, who ruled a large empire out of Angkor Wat), of the Mons, and of certain kingdoms based mostly on Sumatra, notably Srivijaya, which held sway in the Malay Peninsula area. By the early thirteenth century the first important precursor of modern Thailand was established with its capital at Sukhothai and its dominion extending down the Malay Peninsula, east toward the Mekong River, and west to the mountains separating it from Burma. Since that time the Thai people have continuously occupied and ruled a homeland, whether called Siam or Thailand, which has had as its core the valley of the Chao Phraya (Chao Phya) River.

When the capital was at Sukhothai, the famous king of that day, Ramkamhaeng (1275–1317), devised the first alphabet for the Thai tongue and also developed an administrative framework for the state. This vigorous monarch also promoted economic growth and improved the nation's armed forces to enable them to defend the country and on occasion to expand its territory, at the expense of the declining Khmer Empire, among others. In about 1350 the capital was moved to Si Ayutthaya, some forty-five miles up the Chao Phraya from the Gulf of Thailand and accessible to ocean-going ships of that day. It was in the Si Ayutthaya period that Siam became known to Europeans. First the Portuguese (1516) and the French, then the Spanish, Dutch, and English, as well as the Japanese, established trading settlements there, and the first formal relations with the West were formed. After several inconclusive wars with Burma in the sixteenth and eighteenth centuries, the Burmese moved into Siam in force and totally

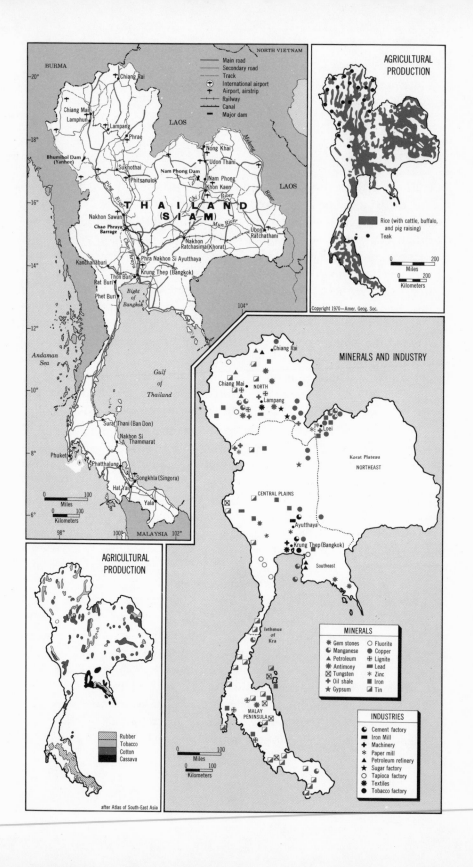

destroyed Si Ayutthaya in 1767. They were, however, pushed out of Siam soon thereafter, and by 1782 a new capital, the present Krung Thep (City of the Angels), was already being built.

The next 200 years witnessed Siam's evolution from an essentially medieval land, with some of the social and economic characteristics of feudalism and ruled by an absolute monarch, to the modern constitutional monarchy of Thailand, so named in 1932. The history of this period is inseparable from the nine monarchs of the Chakri Dynasty who guided the destinies of Thailand throughout this era and are represented today by the Ninth Rama, King Phumiphon Adunyadet. Two of his illustrious forebears, Kings Mongkut (Rama IV) and Chulalongkorn (Rama V), ruled consecutively from 1851 to 1910 and were primarily responsible for modernizing the nation at the same time that they defended it, mainly through skillful diplomacy, from the predatory colonial powers then expanding into Burma, Malaya, and Indochina. Siam's monarchs, like its subjects, were pragmatic and practical people; they knew that survival required their country's emergence from the traditional past as rapidly as possible, and they were convinced that this could be accomplished only by learning the technical ways of the West from Westerners themselves. For close to a century Thailand itself employed a corps of European and American advisers to modernize the police, the judicial system, the government's finances, the conduct of foreign affairs, and other matters. At the same time it was and is a cardinal policy to retain intact what is valuable from the traditional Thai past; the people are as proud of what has been preserved as they are of their modern institutions.

Like Turkey and China, Thailand had a history of "unequal treaties" imposed by European colonial powers to give preferred treatment to their nationals and their commerce. By about 1930 virtually all of these disabilities had been removed, but a sensitivity lingers on. Even today, in its foreign relations, Thailand is quick to take exception to any proposals or treatment that it feels might be interpreted in principle as putting it in anything less than perfect reciprocity and equality with other sovereign nations.

In earlier times national independence was defended largely through diplomacy, but in the period since World War II Thailand has sought to promote its national security primarily through mutual or collective security arrangements, notably in the context of the Southeast Asia Treaty of 1954. Still considering that it had to look above all to itself for its own internal protection, Thailand nevertheless has counted on help from outside, principally the United States, in case of external aggression such as might come from the People's Republic of China. It is in the framework of this collective security arrangement that Thailand sent forces as one of the allies in South Vietnam and has permitted the U.S. Air Force to use Thai bases to support and protect allied forces in Vietnam and to provide air protection to Laos.

The People

Thai—the name by which the people of Thailand call themselves—means "free." The name applies as a linguistic-ethnic designation also to the principal peoples living in the Mekong Valley in Laos and in the Shan state of Burma, and to certain groups still living in semitribal conditions in areas as remote as Yunnan, Kwangsi, and Kwangtung provinces of China (the Lü, Chuang, Nung, and Tung peoples), northern North Vietnam (the Nung and the Black, Red, and White Thai), and the Assam state of India. Their language, which is basically monosyllabic and tonal, is now considered by some linguistic experts as one of the two branches of the Thai-Kadai group, the other branch being spoken on southern Hainan Island and in southernmost China. In modern Krung Thep Thai, there is a strong infusion of Sanskrit and Pali words resulting from the heavy influence of Hindu culture through the Buddhist religion and through various institutions inherited through the Khmer and other Hinduized cultures. The written language devised by Ramkamhaeng borrowed a script remotely derived from India's Devanagari and more directly from Mon and Khmer scripts and applied it to the spoken language of the Thai.

While the great majority (around 85 per cent) of Thailand's people are Thai in culture, there are several important non-Thai groups. Most numerous are the Chinese, who live primarily in Krung Thep and the other cities and towns of the kingdom, where they engage mostly in trade. How many Chinese there are it is impossible to say, since assimilation is generally encouraged in Thailand and is more successful than in many other areas of Southeast Asia, but those who retain a sufficiently separate identity to be labeled "ethnic Chinese" still form a significant minority. The four or five southernmost provinces of Thailand are the home of an important Malay-speaking Muslim minority—forming in fact the majority of the population in those provinces. In the southern provinces of the northeast, bordering on Cambodia, are found a few hundred thousand ethnic Khmers.

In the west, all along the mountainous Burmese frontier, live the Karens; in the north, living in scattered groupings at higher altitudes, are the Meo, the Yao, the Khmu, the Lawa, the Lahu, the Lisu, the Akha, and others. Most of these people still live more or less in a tribal state, speak non-Thai languages, have no writing of their own, and until the advent of missionaries in recent times were animists, as many of them still are. One more group, numbering over 40,000, which is today of potential political significance, is the Vietnamese, who live mostly in the northeast along the Mekong River, and who first arrived there as refugees from the war of independence in Indochina in the early 1950's.

The Buddhist religion is another factor that ties together most of the nation's population. Except for the approximately 1.4 million Muslims (living mostly in areas adjacent to Malaysia, as already noted), a few Christians, the animists among the hill tribes, and some of the Chinese who are not Buddhists, the entire population, from His Majesty the King as head of the state religion to the ordinary villager, throughout the land respects the Buddha and his teachings. The wat, a Buddhist monastery, is the most typical feature in the landscape.

According to the 1970 census, the total population is 35.9 million. It is growing at an annual rate of some 3.3 per cent, about as fast as any in the world. This is partly attributable to a decline in the death rate (from 24 per 1,000 in 1945 to 11 in 1969) but also to an exceptionally high birth rate (45 per 1,000). The country's population is still overwhelmingly rural, with 78 per cent living for the most part in villages of several hundred people and earning their living from agriculture. The only metropolis, Krung Thep–Thon Buri, with an estimated population of 3.4 million in 1970, is both the economic and the political capital. There are now several cities with between 50,000 and 100,000 people, of which the largest are Chiang Mai (87,000) and Nakhon Ratchasima (Khorat) (79,000).

The country's most concentrated areas of settlement are in the Chao Phraya Valley. In that region there is dense and more or less continuous agricultural settlement from the Gulf of Thailand as far north as Phit-sanulok and Sukhothai, and numerous moderate-sized provincial cities are scattered through the region. Certain areas of the northeast which are more favorable to agriculture, such as the valleys of the Mun and Chi, are also rather quickly settled, as are several of the agricultural valleys of the north around Chiang Mai-Lamphun, Lampang, Chiang Rai, and Phrae. In the south, dense population is to be found primarily in the favorable agricultural areas around Nakhon Si Thammarat, Phatthalung, and Songkhla (Singora) and southward along the deltas and flood plains on the east coast of the peninsula to the Malaysian frontier.

The Resource Base

The major regions of Thailand, listed below, are distinct and easy to identify.

1. The Central Plains, the continuous flat, flood plain valley of the Chao Phraya and neighboring lesser rivers.
2. The Northeast, a low plateau mostly under 656 feet, entirely drained by the Mekong and separated from the rest of Thailand by a continuous zone of highlands and mountains. This region is sometimes called the Khorat Plateau.
3. The North, consisting of mountains up to 8,200 feet separated by flat-floored valleys with generally north-south trend.
4. The Malay Peninsula, extending south from the Kra Isthmus to the Malaysian frontier; this is a complex area of mountains and coastal lowlands. There is in addition the long and occasionally wide belt of north-south trending mountain chains lying between Thailand and Burma and extending southward to the Kra Isthmus, which is bordered to the east by terraces and rolling plains that lie alongside the Chao Phraya Valley or, farther south, the Gulf of Thailand. Another small special area lies southeast of the Central Plains and extends as far as the Cambodian frontier; it is characterized by short north-south trending mountain ranges separated by rolling plains.

Almost all of Thailand lies in the tropical wet-dry monsoon belt. Only in the south (beyond the Kra Isthmus) and in the southeast along the Gulf adjacent to Cambodia are there tropical monsoon or rain-forest climates (Am and Af, near Malaysia, according to the Thornthwaite classification), where there are not more than two to three months with less than 2.4 inches of rain. Elsewhere the climate is savanna (Aw) with a dry winter. Everywhere in Thailand where the relief and soils permit there is enough rainfall for rice agriculture in the wet season, which lasts approximately from May through October, although there are some marginal areas of the northeast and north where rainfall averages somewhat under 40 inches and drought occasionally threatens the crop. Except in elevated areas the temperature is warm to hot the year round; the average temperature varies from 86°F. in the hottest month (April or May) to 75.2°F. in the coolest (December or January).

The natural vegetation is mostly made up of the forest types typical of a wet-dry tropical climate, and the dipterocarps are the most representative genera. There is a rather open forest which is partly deciduous in the drier areas; here teak is a valuable tree. In the more humid areas, in the south and at higher elevations, the forest is tall, dense, evergreen. The rubber plantations in these latter areas are found in the south and southeast. The alluvial plains of the Chao Phraya, now almost entirely devoted to rice cultivation, were probably originally open grass plains dotted with borassus palms, with some forest perhaps along the water courses.

Soils are typical of those in a tropical humid environment, heavily leached and with frequent widespread occurrences of laterite. They are considered to be of average fertility, and many are annually enriched from the alluvium that comes with the flooding of the rice fields. In the northeast, however, there are areas where soils are excessively sandy and porous, poor water retainers, and occasionally salty.

Thailand is only moderately endowed with mineral resources. It has depended on widespread deposits of tin to provide one of its most valuable foreign-exchange earners for several decades; it is the world's third-ranking producer. No other minerals contribute significantly to the economy, although sapphires and rubies are mined and there appears to be a prospect for fluorite and tungsten, and perhaps manganese, lead, zinc, gypsum, copper, and antimony. Thailand possesses some usable iron ore but virtually no coal or bauxite of proved worth sufficient to justify large-scale exploitation; at least two lignite deposits are being mined. On the other hand, there is hope that petroleum and/or natural gas will be discovered in substantial quantities offshore under the Gulf of Thailand. Six foreign companies are now prospecting in this area, which immediately adjoins Malaysian and Indonesian offshore areas where oil has been found.

The main proved source of energy is water power, and this is potentially available in abundance at many locations, above all from the vast flow of the Mekong River which forms most of Thailand's extended boundary with Laos in the north and northeast. The most important of the mainstream Mekong dams—the Pa Mong, just west of Vientiane in Laos—is estimated to have a potential installed capacity of 4,800 megawatts. Thailand has already made considerable strides in developing its hydroelectric possibilities, most notably through the Bhumibol (Yanhee) Dam on the Ping River (140,000 kw installed capacity) and the Nam Phung Dam in the northeast (25,000 kw).

The Economy

Agriculture is the basis of Thailand's economy in every sense: 78 per cent of the population is engaged in agriculture, 31 per cent of the gross domestic product is attributable to agricultural production, and 71 per cent of the total value of exports is earned by the sale of agricultural products. And in Thailand agriculture virtually everywhere means rice. This is the chief support of the self-sufficient subsistence farmer, who still predominates in agriculture, especially in areas inaccessible to modern transport. Even in those areas where there are plantations or where other cash crops are grown, the farmer usually raises rice as well for his own family needs. Rice production for the last five years has averaged 12 million tons, and Thailand has alternated with the United States as the world's principal exporter.

In Thailand rice production is relatively inefficient and yields are rather low (around 1,600 pounds per acre national average), although this is less true for the Central Plains area (1,780), where mechanization, fertilizers, insecticides, and better grades of seeds are more widely used in the large-scale commercial enterprises. These average yields compare with 4,820 per acre in Japan and 4,190 in the United States, on the one hand, and 1,520 in India. For the most part only a single rice crop is grown each year, although irrigation is now beginning to encourage the planting of a second crop. The quality of the rice is high, however, and it has a premium reputation on the world market.

Rubber, corn, kenaf, jute, and tapioca (cassava) are also grown commercially, largely for export. Rubber, which is primarily a family-farm rather than a plantation enterprise, has been an important commercial crop for many years. Production is mostly on a small scale and inefficient, and quality is often relatively poor. Much of the rubber acreage is in old trees which now have low yields and badly need replacing. The other crops, however, are of fairly recent origin, and their rapid spread demonstrates the readiness of the Thai farmer to diversify and move into new kinds of farming if they are shown to be feasible and profitable. Other important crops are cotton, fruit, beans, coconuts, tobacco, kapok, and sugar cane.

Fisheries, primarily in the Gulf of Thailand, are of increasing importance each year as a source of food and exports; the fish catch was 116,000 tons in 1950 and 635,000 tons in 1966. The leading types of catch are mackerel, mollusks, shrimp and prawn, crab, and shark.

Industry is still in its infancy, although there has been considerable ex-

Fish, caught in the seas, rivers, khlongs (canals), ponds, and flooded fields everywhere, provide most of the protein consumed by the Southeast Asian villager and are the principal supplement to his rice diet. Here is a typical net used by fishermen in Thailand.

pansion in recent years. Except for a major tin smelter at Phuket, whose product is mostly exported, most of the industry is targeted on domestic markets. This includes cement, tires and other rubber products, cotton and silk textiles (some of the latter, the renowned "Thai silk," largely for foreign consumption), jute milling, petroleum refining, paper, food, automobile assembly, and modest metallurgical and machine industries. These are heavily concentrated in the Krung Thep area. Japanese, American, and Western European investment has played a significant role in this industrial development, but almost always in conjunction with local investors. In an earlier period, when the impulse was very strong for industrial expansion, the Thai government itself entered the field in a number of enterprises. This proved to be inefficient and unprofitable in most cases, and about ten years ago the government began to encourage private investment, domestic and foreign, and enacted a favorable industrial promotion act.

According to *Asian Industry* (May, 1968), Thailand's prospects for further industrialization are "rosy," based on recent surveys which have discovered sizable quantities of iron ore and new deposits of tin and phosphate rock. To stimulate current exploration for petroleum, the government has offered to enact a Petroleum Mining Act "embodying all the privileges and benefits offered to the mining operators, and a special income-tax law amendment to give statutory shape to a variety of investment and fiscal privileges promised to them."

Plans call for the enlargement of several existing petroleum refineries and the building of new ones to bring refining capacity to about 6 million tons a year, more than enough for the nation's needs "in the near run." This opens up the possibility of establishing petrochemical industries and the manufacture of plastics and fertilizers.

In the early years of this century Thailand established a state railway administration and by the 1940's had completed a network that reached with single-track lines into the north, the northeast (with spurs to Udon Thani and Ubon Ratchathani), Cambodia, and south along the length of the Malay Peninsula into what is now Malaysia. Until recent decades the highway network was very sparce, and it was only in 1958 that a paved highway from Krung Thep finally reached Nakhon Ratchasima and thus connected the northeast with the capital. In the ensuing years, however, paved roads have been rapidly extended to reach the same areas as the railways and beyond, and now form the basis of a satisfactory national highway network. More recently feeder roads have been built into heretofore isolated but often thickly settled rural areas, permitting more subsistence farmers to be in touch with the rest of their countrymen.

Throughout history the waterways of the Central Plains have been prime arteries of commerce. Their total usable length today is 684 miles in the dry season and 1,240 miles in the rainy season, and they are considered to be one of the most complex and intensively used systems in the world. The waterways, consisting of rivers and interconnecting canals, extend at their maximum distance from the sea to Phitsanulok, 300 miles north of Krung Thep. The traffic of the port of Krung Thep–Thon Buri consists mostly of raw and construction materials, rice and corn, and fuel. The barges and boats, which are a never-ending source of fascination to the tourists on the early morning "floating market" tours, carry well over half the cargo moved in central Thailand.

Until the decade of the 1950's electric power was mainly from diesel generators. Since that time there has been a phenomenal increase in power output, sometimes as high as 30 per cent annually, and power grids now extend to most of the densely settled areas of the country. This has been based on both steam electric plants and a number of hydroelectric dams, and, as noted above, there is in prospect an immense expansion of this electric output from the development of the potential of the Lower Basin of the Mekong River. The responsible authorities are now charting Thailand's entry into the nuclear power field as well.

With a predominantly agricultural economy, Thailand finds its principal exports coming from this sector. Out of total exports valued at about $670 million average for the period 1967–69, the largest share ($183 million) comes from rice, while rubber contributes $94 million, corn $76 million, jute and kenaf $40 million, and tapioca products $37 million. The only other significant export is tin, with a 1967–69 average of $81 million. The principal buyer of Thai exports has for many years been Japan, with the United States next, followed by Malaysia, Singapore, and Hong Kong. Thailand each year earns a large and increasing amount of foreign exchange from the tourist traffic. Tourists numbered 225,000 in 1965 and were estimated at nearly 500,000 in 1970. The largest number of tourists from outside the region came from the United States, Western Europe, and Japan, in that order.

In the same period the nation's imports averaged $1,150 million, running far ahead of the value of exports. These imports consisted primarily of machinery, vehicles, fuel and lubricants, and clothing and footwear. They came principally from Japan and the United States, and other important suppliers were West Germany and the United Kingdom. With a considerable trade deficit, Thailand would also have had a deficit in its balance of payments were it not for the tourist trade, foreign investment, military and economic aid (provided largely by the United States), and the expenditures for construction (now considerably reduced) of American military forces as well as for rest and recuperation for soldiers and airmen stationed in Thailand or visiting from Vietnam. As a consequence, the balance of payments has been positive almost up to the present, with 1969 showing the first modest deficit. The nation has thus managed to maintain comfortable gold and foreign-exchange reserves, which will help to cushion the readjustments now anticipated.

In the 1960's Thailand saw a remarkable growth in its economy at rates which are exceptionally high for a developing country. The annual increase in the GNP has exceeded 8.5 per cent each year since 1965, except for 1967, when it fell to just under 5 per cent because of a bad rice harvest.

For an even longer period, the Thai baht has maintained a virtually constant value, both because of the generally prosperous economic situation and because of wise and conservative management of the nation's finances. Economic expansion has also been fostered by the clear government policy of encouraging investment.

The national budget was balanced until about 1966. The increasing expenditures required for social and economic development as well as for internal security and national defense have caused a growing deficit, which reached about 20 per cent in 1969, although, as noted, this has not been seriously inflationary. It is hard to conceive of Thailand's returning to a balanced budget as long as its development needs continue, as they will for some time, and as long as the problems persist of an externally supported insurgency within the country and, just across the frontier, neighbors under communist attack.

focus *on Prospects for the Future*

The uninitiated visitor coming to Krung Thep for the first time may expect to find a quiet, quaint oriental city; instead he encounters a bustling, noisy, crowded twentieth-century commercial metropolis, complete with

TABLE 6.1

MATERIAL QUALITY OF LIFE IN THAILAND, COMPARED WITH
JAPAN, THE UNITED STATES, AND INDIA

	Thailand	Japan	United States	India
Life expectancy (years)	50	71	71	47
Infant mortality (per 1,000 live births)	34	15	22	81
Diet (calories per day per capita)	2,120	2,350	3,200	1,810
Literacy (per cent)	68	98	98	24
Percentage of school-age population in school	53	90	96	45
1969 GDP ($ U.S. per capita)	181	1,420	4,565	105
Consumption of electricity (kwh per capita)	89	2,440	6,614	79
Motor vehicles (per 1,000 people—1967)	8	100	833	1.7
Telephones (per 1,000 people—1967)	3	182	526	2
TV's (per 1,000 people—1967)	.6	192	385	.01
Doctors (per 1,000 people)	.14	1.1	1.4	.21

skyscrapers, luxury hotels, impossible traffic tangles, large universities, ladies in the latest fashions, and evidence everywhere of an active, up-to-date business community. To be sure, the quiet temple compounds, the ubiquitous wats, are still there, but the general impression is that of a world metropolis. Needless to say, this is not typical of Thailand as a whole. While the per capita Gross Domestic Product was $240 in 1966 in the Central Plains, the most prosperous and modern region, where Krung Thep is situated, it was $145 for the nation as a whole, and as low as $75 in the underdeveloped northeast.

Table 6.1 shows some current indices of the level of living or the material quality of life in Thailand as compared with Japan, the United States, and India.

There is an air of optimism in Thailand, and the facts of the economic and political situation seem, generally speaking, to support this, especially if Thailand today is contrasted with the Siam of forty years ago or with many of its neighbors in the region. At the same time there are elements of uncertainty, indeed of danger, which should be taken into account in assessing prospects for the future.

One of the most striking of these is the extremely high rate of population increase. If the present annual 3.3 per cent rate were to continue, the total population (now about 36 million) would climb to 50 million by 1980 and 94 million by the year 2000. This year the government has taken official cognizance of this problem and has begun to make some substantial budgetary provision for programs of education and counseling in family planning. But, even if family planning does become widely accepted, there will still be rapid population expansion, which, even under favorable assumptions of a declining birth rate (presently 45 per 1,000), will bring the total to 48 million by 1980 and 76 million for 2000. What does this mean for Thailand's economic and social development?

For one thing, the supply of unused arable land may be threatened with exhaustion rather soon. Until today Thailand has been an exception among Southeast Asian nations in that there has been little pressure of population on the land—the average number of acres per farm family was about 5.2 in 1963. A landless farmer, if he had initiative and energy, could always find new acreage to bring into cultivation. This era may now be drawing to a close, with predictable economic and social consequences. However, more diversified and intensive agriculture and industrialization should be able to provide some outlet for surplus farm population, and there are government programs designed to help this adjustment and to bring new land into cultivation.

The rapid growth of population means many more mouths to feed; without a rapid increase in rice production the new consumers will make heavy inroads on the rice surplus, which has been the nation's principal source of foreign exchange. Statistically this figures out to an annual increase in domestic consumption of about 2 or 3 per cent, or an increase of some 150,000 tons of milled rice (based on present consumption rates). To some extent this increased domestic consumption may take up what might otherwise become an unmarketable surplus because of the shrinking foreign demand for rice in the areas to which Thailand has customarily exported. Even if a certain balance is achieved in this way, however, it will be at the expense of the considerable foreign-exchange earnings that rice provides today. On the other hand, better seed, fertilizer, and improved water supply will all contribute to higher yields and expanded production, and irrigation projects will also help in this respect.

Another consequence of the rapid rate of population growth is already being felt—there is a smaller percentage of school-age children in school now (about 53 per cent) than ten years ago (about 58 per cent). This is true in spite of a steady (about 15 per cent) annual increase in the education budget, the training of more teachers, and the building of more schools. The demand is running far ahead of supply, and it will be some years before anything like the 1960 level will again be reached, and that by dint of giving education even higher priority in the national budget.

Roads have been built, power dams constructed, TV stations set up in regional centers as well as the capital; the life of the people is changing for the better, albeit slowly. An important advance has been in the field of accessibility. The Accelerated Rural Development and other programs have opened extensive rural areas to the outside world. This has begun to make it possible to bring public services to the villages. In the last years an effective extension program has begun to be organized on a broad scale to help the farmer diversify and improve cultural practices for higher yields and better-quality products and to market his products more advantageously. Credit at reasonable interest rates—an important factor in farm improvement—is available to the well-to-do farmer but is less readily obtainable by the poorer farmer except in a few areas where pilot projects are now getting under way. Land reform has had little relevancy to a discussion of the rural scene in the past, but there are reports of increasing farm tenancy today. The government has in fact a multitude of programs for the improvement of rural life and in recent years has considerably expanded its activities in this field. Changes are slowly taking place. The danger, however, is that the villager will become more aware of the growing disparity between his situation and that of the city-dweller than of the improvement in his own well-being.

The need for modernization is at the heart of many of Thailand's problems, as is true of so many developing countries. This extends to the administration and government of the country as well as the techniques of agriculture, commerce, and industry. Formerly the role of the government was limited, and the greater part of the national economy—made up of self-sufficient farmer-villagers—virtually ran itself. Today the government must be able to act effectively domestically and internationally at various levels to serve the national interest and protect the country from foreign encroachment. Domestically this means that it must be able to demonstrate to the people that it can provide better services and more opportunities to them and their offspring than the communists, who are trying to persuade the Thai people that they offer a better life.

At the level where people have contact with their government, the public official must be seen to be in fact a servant working for the good of the people and not for his own pocketbook, prestige, or pride. One of the most effective instruments to put over this essential philosophy has been the Nai Amphoe (district officer) Academy, which instills in its classes the true spirit of the public servant. That pioneer institution is now about five years old, and the government is beginning to extend the technique to other branches of government, where it is badly needed.

What has been said above should testify sufficiently to the extraordinary needs to be met in agriculture, education, health, and public administration. On the other side of the ledger are the slowly expanding but still strictly limited revenues available to meet these burgeoning needs, to the extent that they are a proper governmental responsibility. Only a well-informed and highly skilled staff for budgeting and planning will be able effectively to relate resources to needs, set priorities, and establish programs that properly interrelate in time and space. The skills are there—Thailand has many talented professionals who have received excellent training, some of it abroad, and who can do the technical job. But as in every government their work must be accepted and related effectively to the policy and decision-making level, where planning is only beginning to play a significant role in the governmental process. Institutions like the Bank of Thailand, the National Economic Development Board, the Budget Bureau, and others are showing the way. Their advice and professional example will no doubt be followed elsewhere.

It will be interesting to see how Thailand comes through this critical period and finds answers, as it has through the past centuries of its independent existence, to such pressing problems. Some of what the West has developed has seemed to the Thais valuable and worth adopting, always with some modification. But other things may not be appropriate, and in those instances modernization of established traditional Thai institutions may serve better.

In June of 1968, a new Constitution was adopted, and under its provisions a Parliament was elected in February of 1969—the first in eleven years. This Constitution was, however, abolished in November, 1971, by a group of military leaders who, at the same time, dissolved Parliament, disbanded the cabinet, and established martial law. It would be best if this event and future developments were studied in terms of what a Southeast Asian culture can devise to meet the needs of the modern world and how well this works in that environment rather than by applying standards of judgment worked out in a very different environment, which have only limited relevance.

The momentous and tragic events unfolding today in Southeast Asia deeply affect Thailand. Externally, there is the war that has been going on in one form or another on the territory of its neighbors to the east (Vietnam, Laos, and Cambodia) since the early 1940's. While the fighting has actually reached Thailand's frontiers only occasionally, the Thais realize that the buffer between them and the communist world of North Vietnam and China may be removed at any time, and that they may be left in direct confrontation with an enemy who has made no secret of his hostility. For this reason Thailand has in a variety of ways recognized its stake in the fighting and has made substantial contributions to the defense of its neighbors.

Like many other independent nations in Southeast Asia, Thailand is confronted at home with a "war of national liberation"—that is, an externally directed and supported insurgency aiming eventually at subverting Thailand's government and substituting one responsive to communist wishes. It is the Thai people who will make the final decision in this contest. Today they overwhelmingly reject the insurgents' efforts to win them over by persuasion or terrorize them into submission. Nevertheless, the insurgents have been able to develop serious pressures locally in the north and northeast, particularly in areas bordering Laos. To deny to the communists the richest prize in Southeast Asia will continue to call for great energy, ingenuity, perseverance, and wisdom on the part of the Thai Government, coupled with continued foreign assistance.

Suggested Readings

DE YOUNG, JOHN E. *Village Life in Modern Thailand.* Berkeley and Los Angeles: University of California Press, 1955. A firsthand account of the daily life of Thai peasant-farmers living outside the big cities; discusses changes and future prospects. Slightly dated.

GOLDSTEIN, SIDNEY. "Urbanization in Thailand, 1947–1967." *Demography,* VIII, no. 2 (May, 1971), pp. 205–23. Assesses changing levels and rates of urbanization in Thailand, compares regional variations, and relates them to selected indicators of economic and demographic development.

JACOBS, NORMAN. *Modernization Without Development: Thailand as an Asian Case Study.* New York: Praeger, 1971.

MUSCAT, ROBERT J. *Development Strategy in Thailand: A Study of Economic Growth.* New York: Praeger, 1966. This study seeks to help planners, technicians, and administrators find a systematic approach to the problem of accelerating the pace of economic growth.

National Economic Development Board. *Evaluation of the First Six Year Plan 1961–66.* Bangkok, 1967.

Royal Thai Survey Department. *Thailand—Natural Resources Atlas.* Krung Thep: Supreme Command Headquarters, 1969.

STERNSTEIN, L. "Aspects of Agricultural Land Tenure in Thailand." *Journal of Tropical Geography,* XXIV (June, 1967), pp. 22–29.

VAN ROY, EDWARD. *Economic Systems of Northern Thailand: Structure and Change.* Ithaca, N.Y.: Cornell University Press, 1971. Conceptual tools and research methods of the economist and anthropologist are used to study non-Western economic systems.

See also Suggested Readings for Part I, pp. 57–59.

7 CAMBODIA

William A. Withington

Physical Setting • *Climate and Vegetation* • *The People* •
Historical Highlights • *Changing Society* • *Economic
Activities* • *Development Plans and the Future* • focus *on
Ethnic Minority Groups,* by Peter A. Poole

On November 9, 1968, the Kingdom of Cambodia, wedged in between
Thailand, Laos, South Vietnam, and the Gulf of Thailand, celebrated
fifteen years of independence after many decades of French control, in-
terrupted only by the Japanese occupation during World War II. Less
than a year and a half later (March, 1970) the kingdom was racked by a
succession of events, beginning with replacement of the government of
Prince Sihanouk by one headed by Cheng Heng as Chief of State and
Lieutenant General Lon Nol as Prime Minister and principal active leader.

By the end of April, 1970, the warfare in neighboring South Vietnam
had spilled over into Cambodia as part of an attempt by both South
Vietnamese and American forces to end the effectiveness of the "sanctuaries"
—areas in the eastern fringes of Cambodia used by North Vietnamese and
the National Liberation Front (Viet Cong) to stockpile equipment and to
rest their forces. One of the many tragic aspects of this enlarged scope of
the now general Indochina War is that age-old antagonisms between the
Khmer people of Cambodia and the Vietnamese were rekindled. Another
is the devastation caused by American and South Vietnamese air attacks
on communist strongholds in Cambodia, which have severely crippled the
economy and have left several hundred thousand people homeless.

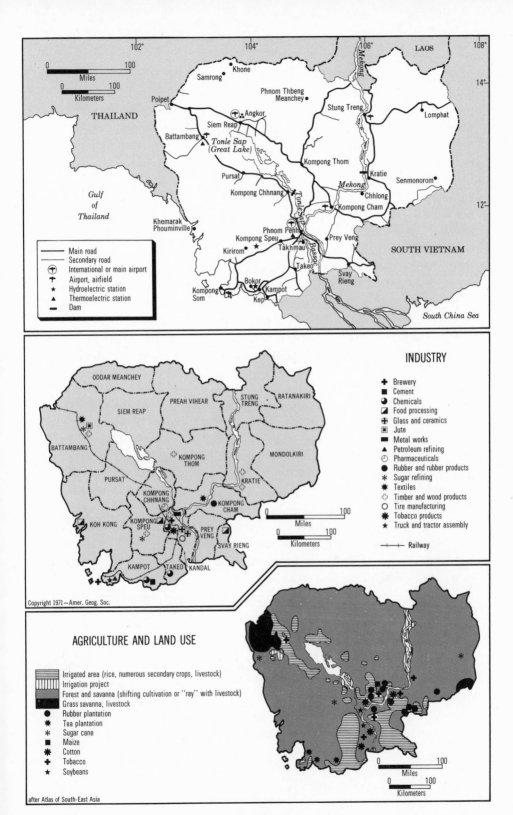

CAMBODIA

Physical Setting

Cambodia, with an area of almost 70,000 square miles (about the size of Missouri), is shaped like an irregular saucer with its densely forested northern, southwestern, and eastern mountainous edges. These areas are occupied by scattered tribes practicing varieties of shifting "slash and burn" or *ray* agriculture. To the southeast, the great Mekong River flows southward out of Laos across the eastern third of Cambodia draining the central lowland, including the huge Tonle Sap Lake, and moves southeastward into South Vietnam and the South China Sea beyond. The central lowland occupies perhaps three fourths of the "Cambodian saucer." The highest elevations in this lowland, other than natural or manmade *phnom* (prominences), are the curving natural levees separating the rivers from their parallel, seasonally flooded plains, known in Cambodia as *beng*.

The Tonle Sap varies greatly in area and depth from season to season, and hence it is surrounded by broad mudflats, fisherman's houses characteristically built on stilts, and fresh-water swamp forests. The lake is reduced to minimum size and depth—1,000 square miles and five feet—after being drained during the dry season from November to April by the Tonle Sap River, which flows southeastward into the Mekong. In late April and May, with the arrival of the rainy season, the Mekong River rises swiftly and reverses the flow of the Tonle Sap River. In succeeding months the lake becomes a vast reservoir as much as 4,000 square miles in area and 50 feet deep. (Plans for the development of the Mekong River Basin may change these conditions considerably in the years to come. See p. 13.) This annual flooding of the Mekong River and the Tonle Sap supplies rich new silt on the plains, reinvigorating the soils for agriculture; it also means large fish catches and permits easy water transportation by lake, river, or canal across much of the lowland.

Climate and Vegetation

A tropical savanna climate, with rainy summers, dry winters, and warm to hot temperatures averaging between 75° and 85°F., is typical of most of the country except at higher elevations. Annual precipitation in the central lowland is less than 60 inches; it may exceed 160 inches in the uplands, particularly along the southfacing slopes overlooking the Gulf of Thailand.

The lower rainfall in the central lowland reflects its protected position; the mountain chains to the southwest and east, including the highlands in Vietnam, block off a significant proportion of the moisture-laden winds from the Gulf of Thailand and the South China Sea.

The climatic conditions of Phnom Penh are representative of most of the interior lowland. The northeast monsoon between November and April, bringing slightly more than one fourth of the annual rainfall, is the dry monsoon season. By contrast, more than two thirds of the yearly precipitation falls between May and October during the southwest or wet monsoon season, when winds bring moisture from the Gulf of Thailand. While both monthly and annual rainfall totals vary greatly from year to year, October, with as much as fifteen inches, is usually the wettest month; January or February, with less than an inch each, the driest. Daily temperature extremes are between 68° and 97°F., the highest temperatures coming in April at the end of the dry season, the lowest in the lowest sun months of December and January.

Forests still cover nearly half of Cambodia. The broadleaf evergreen tropical forests of the southwest, north, and east are most extensive. Tropical deciduous forests occupy broad stretches around the Tonle Sap, the Tonle Sap River, and the Mekong River, but lack such valuable timber species as teak, which are found in nearby Thailand.

At present only 6.5 million acres of Cambodia's 44 million are listed as cultivated. Of the land neither forested nor cultivated, half is in savanna vegetation, a quarter is water-covered, notably by the Tonle Sap, and the remainder is largely swamp.

The People

Cambodia has an estimated 7 million people, whose numbers are rising at a rate of at least 2.2 per cent per year. The vast majority of these people live in villages along the main waterways. The principal settlement zones include the flood plains of the Mekong River downstream from Kratie and of the Tonle Sap and Bassac rivers, the plains fringing the fluctuating shores of the Tonle Sap, and the lowlands along the Gulf of Thailand. Many of the settlements, with ribbon-like patterns and occupying natural levees rising above the Mekong and the many smaller rivers, are known as *chamkar* villages. Most provincial capitals have riverbank sites. Phnom Penh, the national capital, is situated where the Mekong River from the north and the Tonle Sap River from the northwest come together before separating downstream into the parallel more easterly Mekong and westerly Bassac rivers.

Population densities vary widely, being very high in the capital city district of Phnom Penh and extremely low in most peripheral areas. Among the provinces, Kandal on the lower Mekong River had (in the census of 1962) nearly 500 persons per square mile, Takeo about 350, the three southeastern provinces of Kampong Cham, Prey Veng, and Svay Rieng over 200.

Less than 13 per cent of the Cambodians are urban dwellers. In 1970 nearly three fourths of these, about 700,000, lived within the eighteen-square-mile capital city district of Phnom Penh. Since the spread of the Indochina War to Cambodia, refugees from other parts of the country have reportedly swelled Phnom Penh's population to over 1 million. Kompong Som (formerly Sihanoukville) has 40,000 people. Other sizable communities are Battambang (45,000), Kampong Cham (33,000), Pursat (16,000), Kompong Chhnang (15,000), and Kampot (15,000).

About 85 per cent of Cambodia's people are Khmers who practice Theravada Buddhism, the official religion of the state. Khmer is the national language, spoken by nine of every ten people. Although they are still largely farmers living in small villages, the Khmers are increasingly found in the growing urban centers, where educational expansion is beginning to offer new economic opportunities. The two largest minority groups are the 425,000 Chinese and the 300,000–400,000 Vietnamese (for further information on the minority groups, see pp. 112–17).

Historical Highlights

The Khmer Empire evolved on the lower-middle course of the Mekong River and around the Tonle Sap Lake within essentially the present core area of Cambodia. By A.D. 802, the empire was more powerful than the adjacent peoples of Funan and Champa to the south and east in present-day South Vietnam, those of the upper Mekong River in what is now Laos, and the Mons to the west in the central alluvial river plains of today's Thailand.

During the great period of the Khmer Empire, from 802 to 1431, many monumental structures were erected, notably Angkor Wat and Angkor Thom near the northwest end of the Tonle Sap, using local laterite rock from the subsoil overlaid with a more resistant sandstone on which great bas-reliefs were carved. The economic basis for this empire was the fertile soil around the Tonle Sap, which was provided with irrigation water for multiple cropping of wet rice by means of a vast hydraulic reservoir system that maintained a water balance during both wet and dry monsoon periods each year.

The Khmer Empire gradually declined in the late thirteenth and early fourteenth centuries under attacks from the west by the Thai, and in the seventeenth century the Annamese (Vietnamese) came in from the east. The combination of these external attacks, and growing Khmer emphasis on monument building, wars of aggression, and, possibly, serious disease epidemics eventually destroyed the economic and social organization that had maintained the empire for more than 600 years. It was at the end of the empire period, in 1431, that the capital was relocated at the site of modern Phnom Penh.

During the four centuries between the decline of the Khmer Empire and 1863, Cambodia struggled continuously to maintain its identity against the forces of Thailand and Annam. In 1863 France and Cambodia signed an agreement for a French protectorate over Cambodia, confirmed the following year, giving it support against its neighbors. This protectorate continued until 1949, when Cambodia began to assume increasing internal and external responsibilities. Cambodians celebrate their modern independence day on November 9, the day in 1953 when the French transferred control over military powers to the Cambodian Government. By January of 1955, Cambodia had achieved financial and economic independence from France and later that year became a member of the United Nations.

Changing Society

The complex blend of traditional and modern, so characteristic of developing nations, is reflected in Cambodia in the manner in which status is achieved, among other ways.

In rural society, high status is characteristically accorded to monks, important government officials, and wealthy aristocrats. In the larger urban centers, status is now attained not only by religious participation, by political or economic success, or by birth, but also through higher education, which may lead to a responsible position in political, military, religious, or economic affairs. To a limited extent, women, previously barred from temple education conducted by the Buddhist monks, now have greater opportunities through educational and occupational advancement.

Education in Cambodia has expanded rapidly since independence. Previously most education was carried on by Buddhist monks in the temples and temple schools in both the small and large settlements. Even today, for the great majority of the people outside the few larger urban places, the Buddhist monks are the principal transmitters of information. Although inexpensive transistor radios may carry news from outside the local community, Buddhist monks frequently serve as interpreters. Today's 1.2 million students at all levels represent a nearly fourfold increase since 1953, and growing numbers are being educated outside the Buddhist schools as new facilities are completed. More than a million students are in primary schools, nearly 120,000 in secondary schools, and about 18,000 in higher technical or professional schools and universities. All nine of the universities have been established since 1955, most recently in the large provincial capitals of Battambang, Kompong Cham, and Takeo-Kampot. Although about 90 per cent of the people use Khmer as their language, higher education is still conducted primarily in French, and French tends to be the language of those in professional and intellectual activities.

Illiteracy, estimated to be as high as 69 per cent at independence, has been reduced to less than 40 per cent among those fifteen years and older. This striking reduction reflects the government's great emphasis on public education, both at the younger levels and in adult education programs: In recent years, close to a fourth of Cambodia's annual budget has been spent each year on education. This educational "revolution" is not without its problems. The greater mobility of the more educated people is reflected in the rapid increase in population in Phnom Penh and several other urban centers. Many school graduates are unprepared or unwilling to work in technical and blue-collar jobs. Although independence brought a need for more indigenous people in government positions, the numbers of those graduating from secondary and higher institutions far exceed the available openings, resulting in considerable under- and unemployment. This educational elite, not fully employed, apparently provided one of the pressures leading to the March, 1970, change in government.

Economic Activities

Despite large percentage increases in most other activities, agriculture is still the predominant source of livelihood among Cambodians, about 70 per cent of whom are engaged in farming. Development projects have helped to raise the amount of land under cultivation to about 6.5 million acres, out of at least 20 million acres estimated to be cultivable.

The Phnom Penh focus together with the downstream areas along the Mekong and Bassac rivers in the southwest are the most diversified and intensively cultivated part of the nation's cropland. In addition to irrigated and floating rice, maize (corn), soybeans, cotton, tobacco, and sugar cane are important crops, along with the raising of considerable numbers of livestock. A second agricultural region extends along both sides of the Mekong River and several of its tributaries northeast of Phnom Penh, including the rubber-growing *terres rouges* (red soils) areas of Kompong Cham. Crop and livestock diversity is considerable but less widespread than in the downstream region. The third major agricultural region is the "rice bowl" around the Tonle Sap and to the northwest in Battambang Province. The most extensive irrigation works in Cambodia help to make this the most productive rice-growing section of the region and country. Some livestock is also raised here. The fourth and by far the smallest agricultural area consists of the coastal lowlands and adjacent mountain slopes inland from the Gulf of Thailand in the south around Kampot. Some rice and pepper are grown in the coastal lowlands, while pepper and tea plantations are found on the mountain slopes above.

The annual rice harvest now totals about 3.25 million tons, of which one tenth is usually available for export. The relatively low population densities and low-intensity agricultural methods are reflected in the fact that at most only about 10 per cent of the land is used to grow a second rice crop under irrigation during the dry season, and up to 25 per cent of the rice land lies unused each year.

Most Cambodians grow rice on plots averaging about ten acres, although along the river banks, or *chamkar,* where land is more valuable, the typical farm is only about three acres. The average rice yield throughout the country is no more than 1,000 pounds per acre, below the yields of South Vietnam or Thailand but above those of Laos. The chamkar zones provide the chief areas for intensification through increased double-cropping of rice along with other areas of controlled irrigation.

Natural rubber is normally produced on a series of large plantations occupying over 126,000 acres, mainly in the red-soil area of Kompong Cham or in immediately adjacent areas on both sides of the Mekong River. Most of the land devoted to rubber is in a few large French-owned estates which use Vietnamese workers. In recent years the annual production of natural rubber had risen to nearly 59,000 tons (double the preindependence levels of 1953), all but 10,000 tons being exported. American and South Vietnamese air attacks have, however, crippled the rubber industry; only one of the plantations is currently in operation.

Maize occupies as much as 250,000 acres of land, most of it along the Mekong River in the south. Higher grades of maize are raised for export, lower grades for domestic consumption. Annual production has fluctuated in recent years between a peak of 204,000 tons in 1963–64 and only 140,000 tons in 1968; about two fifths is exported. A variety of other crops, including groundnuts (peanuts), greens beans, and soybeans, are grown along the lower Mekong in the same general areas as maize. Commercial market gardening of vegetables and fruit is expanding to meet the needs of the urban populations.

Other kinds of farm production in the lowland areas include the raising of livestock for draft, meat, or export. Among the livestock are nearly 2.3 million cattle, over 1 million pigs, and about 860,000 water buffalo. Tobacco grown mainly for the domestic market, has an annual production of about 12,000 tons, mainly from areas along the lower and middle Mekong River and the west. Fiber crops include cotton used for the sarong-like *sampot*; jute, manufactured into sacking or twine; and ramie, used for fishnets.

In the limited Gulf of Thailand lowlands and on the nearby slopes of the Elephant Mountains small pepper, tea, and coffee farms represent almost the only plantation production other than that of natural rubber. Efforts are being made to increase the quality of these crops and to encourage family-type farm production. Most farmers in Cambodia own their own land and have, by Asian standards, rather high capital investments in the form of livestock and various kinds of farm equipment (valued at between $600 and $1,000). In addition, almost all rural families now own a bicycle for local transportation.

Fishing is second only to rice farming as a means of livelihood. Each year more than 160,000 tons of fish are caught in Cambodia's rivers, the Tonle Sap, and the Gulf of Thailand. Most farmers are part-time fishermen, thus helping to provide animal protein in an otherwise largely vegetable diet. The principal concentration of full-time fishermen is along the shores of the Tonle Sap, where at least 25,000 people, mainly Vietnamese, live in stilt houses or floating villages.

Cambodia may well have the greatest fresh-water fishery resources in Southeast Asia, but recent official figures on the fish catch show a decline from such causes as overfishing, silting, and ecological changes in plant life in the rivers or the Tonle Sap, and possibly underreported inland and ocean catches. Over 60 per cent of the total catch is used in the form of dried fish, *prahoc* (fish paste), or *tuk trey*, a strong, pungent sauce made from putrefied fish. Trawling and other methods are used along the coast of the Gulf of Thailand.

Even though Cambodia has considerable forests, its lumber industry is relatively small. The alternating wet and dry seasons plus the widespread practice of slash-and-burn agriculture in upland forest areas result in woodlands more sparse and of poorer quality than in many other parts of Southeast Asia. Of the 385,000 cubic yards of timber cut annually, nearly two thirds are exported, although increasing quantities of plywood and paper are being made locally.

Ancient temples, palaces, and other monuments attest to the abundance of laterite and sandstone rock, and to the durability of the latter. Mining currently yields phosphate rock, limestone, salt, semiprecious stone, and some gold. Some other minerals are known to exist but are not mined in significant quantities.

Cambodia's largest industries are the processing of agricultural products and the making of handicraft goods. Rice milling and the weaving of the cotton sampot lead in the number of establishments and workers and the value of output. As many as 100,000 people work in handicraft industries, while about 10,000 are in the more modern factory industries that are beginning to diversify Cambodia's manufacturing. The concentration of modern plants is greatest in Phnom Penh, but provincial capitals and other large urban centers have recently established some factories, including textile mills, palm and cane-sugar refineries, a cement works in the Kampot area, tire manufacturing at Takhmau, distilleries (particularly at Phnom Penh and Kompong Som), assembly plants for motor vehicles including tractors, an oil refinery, and a paper mill at Chhlong using bamboo and rice straw. Associated with both increased urbanization and industrial expansion, electric-power capacity has risen almost sixfold since 1953, from about 11,000 kilowatts to nearly 70,000 in 1970.

Historically and today, waterways provide a principal means of transport; nearly 900 miles of rivers and canals are navigable in the wet season. Phnom Penh is an international port on the Mekong River but is limited to vessels of no more than 4,000 tons. Free transit on the lower Mekong River is guaranteed by treaty, but the combination of uncertain relations with South Vietnam and years of warfare in that state led Cambodia to develop its own Gulf of Thailand ports, particularly the deepwater port of Kompong Som. A highway built in 1959 with American aid and a railway of 175 miles (nearing completion in late 1971) link Kompong Som and Phnom Penh, and a railway connects the capital city to Poipet and the Thailand railway network 240 miles away.

The network of highways has expanded considerably in the postindependence years, linking Phnom Penh with provincial capitals and other centers as well as with surrounding nations. Main routes, largely paved, total 2,170 miles; another 6,770 miles of dirt roads or tracks are usable at least part of the year by motor vehicles. The Asian Highway system in Cambodia comes in from Thailand at Poipet and goes to Phnom Penh via Pursat south of the Tonle Sap or via Siem Reap north of the lake. From Phnom Penh this highway branches out—northward along the Mekong River into Laos, eastward to Saigon in South Vietnam, and southward to Kompong Som on the Gulf of Thailand.

International air traffic focuses primarily at Phnom Penh and Siem Reap (near Angkor). Four national airports serve Battambang, Kompong Som, Kompong Cham, and Stung Treng, and at least twenty-one smaller provincial airfields are usable by medium and smaller craft. Telecommunications are limited to the main urban centers. Most of the nearly 6,000 telephones, together with the one television station and 20,000 sets, are in the capital city area.

The principal exports of Cambodia are rice (45 per cent by value), rubber (40 in prewar days), and various fruits and vegetables (10). Maize, forestry products, live animals, fishery products, and pepper are other exports of note. So far the export of manufactured goods is limited to small quantities of automobile tires. France and associated African states, eastern and southern Asian nations, Europe, and the United States are the main destinations for Cambodian exports. Leading imports are motor vehicles and petroleum, textiles, vegetables fibers, iron and steel, industrial equipment, and chemical and pharmaceutical products. The chief sources of imports are France, the United Kingdom, Japan, Hong Kong, the People's Republic of China, Singapore, and the United States.

Development Plans and the Future

Since 1953, Cambodia has had three official plans: a Two-Year Plan (1956–57); a First Five-Year Plan (1960–64); and a Second Five-Year Plan, inaugurated in 1968. As a result of the two earlier plans, the Gross National Product increased at an annual rate of about 4 per cent, well above the estimated 2.2 per cent rate of population increase per year. Both internal investment and external aid in various forms have been devoted primarily to the development of production facilities; communications, transportation, and power infrastructure; and social needs, particularly educational and health facilities. In the field of production, there are now 13 state enterprises, 29 mixed or joint enterprises with both state and private capital involved, and 3,200 small to medium-sized private enterprises.

To offset adverse conditions, such as droughts, raw-material shortages, and related economic problems, in mid-1969 the government took steps to encourage foreign investment and expand production. These steps included a 12.5 per cent devaluation of the riel to increase the value of foreign money, regulations to exempt foreign investors from taxes on profits and guarantees against nationalization, and an austerity program to emphasize development schemes directly boosting national output.

During most of the period since independence, Cambodia has sought foreign assistance in forms compatible with its unaligned foreign policy. Gifts, loans, or "no strings attached" foreign aid have come from as many as twenty countries, including France, the People's Republic of China, the

Courtesy United Nations

Building trades students operate a cement mixer to make foundation pillars for a new building at the Center for Technical Staff Training and Increased Productivity near Phnom Penh, Cambodia. The Center was set up in 1962 to meet the demand for skilled workers posed by the First and Second Five-Year Plans (1960–64 and 1968–72). It received $635,000 in aid from the United Nations, plus $312,500 for scholarships. It offers courses in general mechanics, electrical engineering, building trades, and automobile and diesel maintenance and repair.

Soviet Union, the United States, both West and East Germany, Yugoslavia, and Czechoslovakia. Other nations, participating through the United Nations in the Mekong River Basin Development Plan, are providing funds for dams or other facilities (see Chap. 2).

Cambodia, located in the midst of the monsoon Asian crescent, which is the world's most densely populated area, still has considerable room for growth. Its population density of 93 persons per square mile, though considerably above the 57.5 figure of the United States, is still much lower than that of the other Southeast Asian nations, except for landlocked Laos.

Population growth and increasing urbanization in the near future seem likely to be sources of strength rather than problems as in some of the more densely peopled Southeast Asian areas. Much currently unused land is cultivable, and further extension of controlled irrigation acreages, double-cropping, and use of improved seed stocks and fertilizers should greatly increase production levels. With an improved and expanded transportation network, not only agricultural but also fishery, forestry, and mineral resources could be more effectively utilized. Within recent years, Phnom Penh and many of the provincial capitals have been in stages of transition from enlarged market towns to increasingly diversified urban centers of commerce, manufacturing, administration, and higher education. Others, some of them completely new communities, serve as vital links to the outside world, as tourist resorts, or as new industrial centers.

Until April, 1970, Cambodia managed to avoid the political and military struggles that have plagued nearby South Vietnam and Laos in recent years. The question of noninvolvement was a sensitive one, for Cambodia has had a relatively limited military establishment with which to deal with external or internal enemies. Now that it has been drawn directly into the enlarged Indochina conflict, future development trends are uncertain; but, in the long run, despite its comparatively small size, Cambodia appears to have most of the resources—physical, social, cultural, and economic—needed to become one of the more prosperous nations of Southeast Asia.

focus *on Ethnic Minority Groups*—Peter A. Poole

The presence of a variety of ethnic minority groups in Cambodia—and of Cambodian (and other) minorities in South Vietnam, Laos, and Thailand—has been a source of friction between these countries for hundreds of years. Some minority groups live by raising illegal crops, such as opium, and by smuggling goods across poorly policed borders, and government efforts to control these activities may seem like unwarranted interference in their traditional way of life. Other groups, such as the Chinese, have shown a talent for economic enterprise which gives them a great deal of influence in the countries where they reside and is often resented by the rest of the local population. Furthermore, the Cambodian, Lao, and Thai governments have each expressed concern, at various times, that the Hanoi or Saigon authorities would gain control over Vietnamese minorities living in their countries and use this influence for subversive purposes. With such possibilities for social and political friction inherent in the presence of so many minorities, the wonder is that the different peoples of Indochina actually do live together peacefully much of the time.

Ethnically, the population of Cambodia, which reached 7 million in 1970, is more homogeneous than that of South Vietnam, Laos, or Thailand (85 per cent of the people are of predominantly Khmer stock), and a certain amount of intermarriage has taken place, providing a range of variations in the predominant physical type which is most noticeable in urban areas.

The Vietnamese

There has long been a fear among Cambodians that Vietnam would annex their country and permanently submerge the Khmer people and culture. This fear has been reinforced by the presence of between 300,000 and 400,000 Vietnamese in Cambodia, most of whom make few concessions in the way of adopting Cambodian dress, language, or culture. Earlier generations of many Vietnamese families now living in Cambodia moved there to work for the French colonial government or French commercial firms, which generally preferred to hire them rather than Cambodians. Many have made a comfortable place for themselves as merchants, tradesmen, doctors, teachers, landowners, farmers, or plantation workers. Although the exact numbers are not known, a large percentage of the Vietnamese in Cambodia are baptized Catholics, and a considerable number attend mass regularly. Religion, therefore, tends to set them apart from the predominantly Buddhist Cambodians.

In March, 1970, the Cambodian leaders (including Lon Nol and Sirik Matak) who removed Prince Sihanouk from power charged that the former ruler had been too lenient in allowing Vietnamese communists to use the eastern border areas of the country for military bases. Vietnamese civilians living in Cambodia were accused of being actual or potential agents of the Vietnamese communist forces. As a result of these charges, according to press reports, many of the Vietnamese people in Cambodia were dispossessed of their property and forced to move to crowded refugee centers. Thousands were voluntarily evacuated to South Vietnam, and several hundred were killed under circumstances that suggested they had been massacred by Khmer soldiers or civilians.

Press reports indicate that the worst excesses against the Vietnamese minority in Cambodia were curtailed by Lon Nol's government a few weeks after it overthrew Prince Sihanouk. But there were continued reports of looting by South Vietnamese soldiers who had been sent to aid Cambodia, and in 1971 reportedly some 200,000 ethnic Vietnamese were evacuated to South Vietnam. All in all, the events that followed the March, 1970, coup greatly intensified the bitterness that has long existed between the Cambodian and Vietnamese people.

The term Khmer Krom literally means "Lowland Cambodian" and is used by Cambodian officials to describe the Cambodian minority in South Vietnam, the last remnant of Cambodia's once dominant position in the Mekong Delta region. The status of this minority group has been a source of friction and controversy in Cambodian–South Vietnamese relations since 1954. The Cambodian Government has insisted on the right of the Khmer Krom to preserve their ethnic identity by practicing their own form of Buddhism and by running schools in which the Cambodian language is taught. The South Vietnamese Government seems to acknowledge this right, although it regards all persons born in South Vietnam as Vietnamese nationals. Prince Sihanouk and other Cambodian leaders have, in the past, accused Saigon of practicing "genocide" against the Khmer Krom by forcing them to serve in the South Vietnamese armed forces and by destroying their homes and pagodas in the course of military operations against the Viet Cong. After the March coup, several thousand Khmer Krom soldiers who had been trained by the United States in South Vietnam were airlifted to Phnom Penh to help the Cambodian Army fight the Vietnamese communists.

The term Khmer Loeu (literally "Upland Cambodian") has been used by Cambodian officials to describe the various tribal peoples, numbering more than 40,000, who live mainly in the northeastern provinces in semi-isolation from the country's main population centers. Many of these tribal people are related to the dominant Khmer group, but only a few speak Cambodian and understand the concepts of nationhood and Buddhism that bind the Cambodian people together. Most of them are animists and live by hunting and slash-and-burn farming; in general, they look to their village headman as the main souce of authority.

In April, 1970, the Vietnamese communists launched a series af attacks against Cambodian Army posts in the northeastern provinces. Shortly after this, the Cambodian Government evacuated all of its forces from the northeast to concentrate on defending the central part of the country. This left the Khmer Loeu with no protection from roving bands of Vietnamese communists, who were believed to be trying to form the tribesmen into antigovernment guerrilla units.

The Chinese

According to a recent study, about 425,000 people in Cambodia may be considered "Chinese" because they participate in some form of Chinese voluntary association. They are concentrated mainly in Phnom Penh and smaller urban areas throughout the country, although there are several thousand Chinese farmers in the province of Battambang; in Kampot and other southeastern provinces they are an important rural minority.

Large numbers of ethnic Chinese are voluntarily integrating into the Khmer population. Male Cambodians who belong to the bureaucratic elite often choose a bride from a wealthy Chinese or Sino-Cambodian merchant family. By learning the Cambodian language, adopting the Khmer form of Buddhism, and intermarrying with Cambodians, the descendants of Chinese are gradually finding a place even in the highest ranks of Cambodian society.

Some reporters believe that the majority of the Chinese in Cambodia are pro-Peking, but after the March coup and the persecution of the Vietnamese minority many of them flew Cambodian flags from their houses and otherwise tried to display their support for the Lon Nol government.

Although the Vietnamese and Chinese in Cambodia resemble each other physically and both are distinct from the ethnic Khmers, differences in dress and language make them fairly easy to tell apart. The capital city of Phnom Penh is roughly divided into one third Cambodians, one third Chinese, and one third Vietnamese—with most trades and commercial activity dominated by the latter two groups. Intermarriage between members of the Chinese and Vietnamese communities is relatively uncommon, in part because of religious differences.

Chinese influence has so far reached Cambodia mainly by sea. The country has no common border with China and has not known the type of overland invasion and occupation by Chinese soldiers and officials that transformed Vietnam into a little replica of Chinese society during the first millennium of the Christian era. This probably explains why the Cambodian people and their leaders have seemed to fear the People's Republic of China less than either North or South Vietnam. Indeed, during the 1960's, Prince Sihanouk sought Chinese arms and diplomatic support to ward off the aggressive moves that he claimed Krung Thep (Bangkok), Saigon, and Washington were constantly planning against Cambodia.

After the March, 1970, coup, Sihanouk sought Peking's aid in his bid to regain power. China's leaders responded cautiously. Although they granted Sihanouk political asylum and access to their communications media, they maintained an embassy in Phnom Penh and withheld recognition of Sihanouk's government-in-exile until after U.S. forces crossed the Cambodian border in early May.

The Thais and Other Groups

An estimated 400,000 Cambodians live in eastern Thailand, and about 20,000 Thais (Siamese) live in western Cambodia. The majority of these people have long been settled in their present districts, and there appears to be less friction between Cambodians and Thais on a personal level than between Cambodians and Vietnamese. The Siamese Government exercised suzerainty over what are now Battambang and Siem Reap provinces during most of the nineteenth century and again (with Japan's help) during World War II. But Thai administrative control did not involve any concentrated effort to displace Cambodian culture (as happened under Vietnamese suzerainty in eastern Cambodia). Thais and Cambodians practice virtually the same rites of Theravada Buddhism, and their alphabets and many other aspects of their cultures are similar.

After the March, 1970, coup, the Thai Government moved much more cautiously than Saigon to aid Lon Nol's regime. The Thais were reportedly concerned that China—and perhaps North Vietnam—might be provoked into increasing their support of insurgents in northeastern Thailand if Thai regular army troops moved into Cambodia. Therefore, the Thai Government recruited several thousand ethnic Khmers in Thailand, as well as some Thai volunteers, and began training them for service in Cambodia.

There are believed to be only about 5,000 Lao in Cambodia and perhaps an equally small number of Cambodians in Laos. Contact between the two nations has been limited by the difficulty of navigating the middle reaches of the Mekong River. Although the French built a road connecting Laos and Cambodia, both kingdoms have greater need for communication with Thailand and Vietnam than with each other.

Several even smaller Asian minority groups add to the distinctly cosmopolitan character of Phnom Penh and other Cambodian towns. These include the Indians and Pakistanis, who are active in commerce and money-lending (but on a much smaller scale than the Chinese community). The Mons, an ancient Buddhist people renowned for their artistry, provide a weak cultural link between Cambodia and Burma. The Chams, a Muslim remnant of the once great kingdom of Champa (in what is now Vietnam), are a living reminder to the Khmers of the results of Vietnamese expansionism.

Ironically, Cambodia's semipermanent European community (which is mainly French) increased after Cambodia achieved independence. Since the colonial link was cut with comparatively little bitterness, independent Cambodia has been hospitable to French teachers, businessmen, and "experts" in a wide range of activities. French advisers sat in every ministry; French teachers played a major role in the school system; French rubber plantations provided Cambodia with one of its main export crops. Restaurants, hotels, clubs, shops, and other services operated by Frenchmen added to the charm and comfort of Phnom Penh and some of the smaller towns. However, the new Cambodian leaders have looked to the United States, rather than to France, as their major patron.

Many of Cambodia's most serious social and political problems are related, at least indirectly, to the presence of ethnic minority groups in Cambodia or of Khmer minorities in adjacent countries. This pattern repeats itself throughout Southeast Asia. In order to survive and regain control over all of Cambodia's provinces the government will have to excercise exceptional care in dealing with its neighbors and with minority groups inside the nation's borders.

Suggested Readings

American University. *Area Handbook for Cambodia.* Washington, D.C.: U.S. Government Printing Office, 1968. A comprehensive analysis of social, economic, and political aspects of the area and its national security.

EBHIHARA, MAY. "Khmer." In Frank M. Lebar *et al., Ethnic Groups of Mainland Southeast Asia.* New Haven, Conn.: Human Relations Area Files, 1964, pp. 98–105. Miss Ebhihara lived in a Cambodian village and observed its life closely. Other sections describe the role of ethnic minority groups in Cambodia.

Kirk, Donald. "Cambodia's Economic Crisis." *Asian Survey*, XI, no. 3 (March, 1971), pp. 238–55. Analyzes some of the factors in the nation's current economic dependence on foreign largesse.

Leifer, Michael. *Cambodia: The Search for Security.* New York: Praeger, 1967. A good background for understanding current events in Cambodia.

Poole, Peter A. *Cambodia's Quest for Survival.* New York: American-Asian Educational Exchange, 1969. A monograph discussing some of Cambodia's current problems.

Steinberg, David J. *Cambodia: Its People, Its Society, Its Culture.* New Haven, Conn.: Human Relations Area Files, 1959. Somewhat dated but useful overview of Cambodian society and economy.

Willmott, William E. *The Chinese in Cambodia.* Vancouver: University of British Columbia Press, 1967. An important study of one of the two largest ethnic minority groups in Cambodia.

See also Suggested Readings for Part I, pp. 57–59.

8 LAOS

Leonard Unger *

The Physical Setting• The Economy • Transportation •
The People

Because it has been the fate of Laos to suffer as a battleground in recent years, most people now know at least that it is a country in Southeast Asia; but only a few are aware of who lives there, what the country is like, and how the people make a living.

Contrary to much off-hand newspaper comment, Laos is not a new creation. It has a history dating back, in written records, to the fourteenth century, when there was a kingdom, centered sometimes in Luang Prabang and sometimes in Vientiane, that ruled over the Lao people in the upper Mekong Basin. In succeeding centuries this kingdom was on occasion partitioned and often threatened by the Thai kingdoms to the west and south and by the Vietnamese to the east, but, until the French established their colonial rule at the close of the nineteenth century, there were always one or several independent Lao entities. In 1949, Laos achieved nominal independence from French rule, and in 1954 full independence. However, hopes for the peace and prosperity that were to come with freedom have been shattered by the efforts of communist groups to impose their system on the Lao people. And, even since the signing of the Geneva Accords (July 23, 1962), the outlook has been dim. Fighting in many parts of the country has gravely disrupted life over large areas, devastating farm lands, forests, roads, and villages and swelling the ranks of refugees to a number currently estimated to be in excess of 250,000.

* When the original version of this article was written in 1963–64, the Honorable Leonard Unger was U.S. Ambassador to Laos. When this revised edition went to press, he was U.S. Ambassador to Thailand.

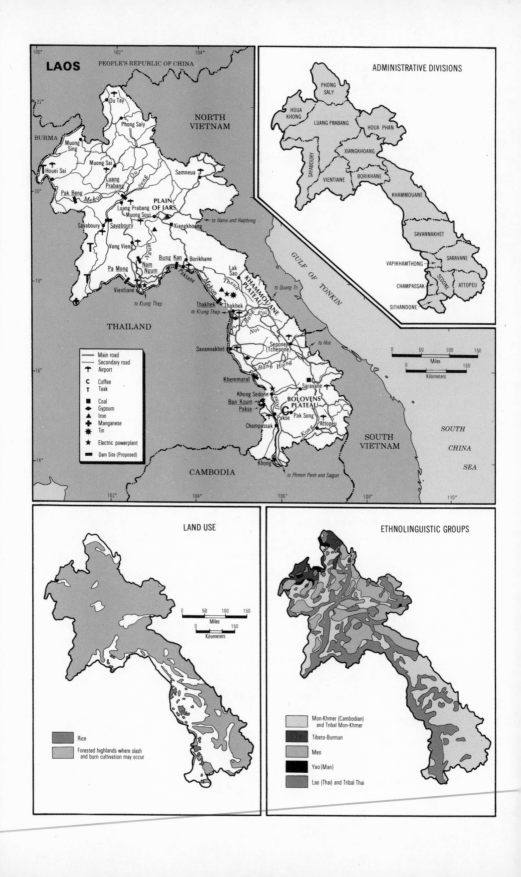

LAOS

PEOPLE'S REPUBLIC OF CHINA

NORTH VIETNAM

BURMA

Ou Tay
Phong Saly
Muong Sing
Houei Sai
Muong Sai
Samneua
Luang
Prabang
Pak Beng
Luang Prabang
PLAIN
OF JARS
Muong Soui
Sayaboury
Sayaboury
Xiangkhoang
to Hanoi and Haiphong

THAILAND

Vang Vieng
Pa Mong
Nam
Ngum
Bung Kan
Borikhane
Vientiane
to Krung Thep

Lak
Sao
KHAMMOUANE
PLATEAU
to Quang Tri

Thakhek
Thakhek
to Krung Thep

GULF OF TONKIN

Savannakhet
Sepone
(Tchepone)
to Hue

Khemmarat
Saravane
Khong Sedone
Ban Koum
Pakse
Pakse
BOLOVENS
PLATEAU
Pak Song
Champassak
Attopeu

SOUTH
VIETNAM

CAMBODIA

Khong
to Phnom Penh and Saigon

SOUTH
CHINA
SEA

Legend:
— Main road
— Secondary road
Airport
C Coffee
T Teak
■ Coal
Gypsum
▲ Iron
Manganese
✱ Tin
★ Electric powerplant
▬ Dam Site (Proposed)

ADMINISTRATIVE DIVISIONS

PHONG
SALY
HOUA
KHONG
LUANG PRABANG
HOUA PHAN
SAYABOURY
XIANGKHOANG
VIENTIANE
BORIKHANE
KHAMMOUANE
SAVANNAKHET
VAPIKHAMTHONG
SARAVANE
SEDONE
CHAMPASSAK
ATTOPEU
SITHANDONE

0   50   100   150
Miles
0   150
Kilometers

LAND USE

0   50   100   150
Miles
0   150
Kilometers

Rice
Forested highlands where slash
and burn cultivation may occur

ETHNOLINGUISTIC GROUPS

Mon-Khmer (Cambodian)
and Tribal Mon-Khmer
Tibeto-Burman
Meo
Yao (Man)
Lao (Thai) and Tribal Thai

Why has this kingdom, which lacks strategic resources of any kind, been a focus of such struggle?

Its location undoubtedly is part of the answer. Laos shares borders with Burma, Thailand, Cambodia, South Vietnam, North Vietnam, and the People's Republic of China. An underpopulated area such as Laos offers a natural avenue for southward expansion of communist Chinese domination or even conquest. Thus far the People's Republic of China has limited its overt influence mainly to a road-building effort in the north. The North Vietnamese, on the other hand, while perhaps regarding Laos as potential space for future expansion, today view it primarily as an indispensable means of access to South Vietnam and Cambodia.

In a period of regional conflict, Laos's neighbors give it attention far beyond that dictated by the nation's meager resources and population. Similarly, Laos has attracted attention and aid from distant powers sympathetic to or allied with its neighbors.

The Physical Setting

Laos is the land of the Mekong, the mighty river that rises in Tibet and flows 2,600 miles to the South China Sea just south of Saigon. All of the kingdom lies in the Mekong Basin except the extreme northeast. Almost without exception, the developed areas are along or fairly close to the river.

The lowlands of Laos, mostly alluvial, bordering the Mekong and its principal tributaries, are extensive in the south around Pakse, Champassak, and Savannakhet, and more limited in the vicinity of Thakhek and Paksane. There is also an important plain surrounding the capital city of Vientiane and along the lower reaches of the Ngum. North of this the Mekong itself is still flowing for the most part through a deep valley, and along its banks there are only occasional small, isolated lowlands, such as that around the royal capital of Luang Prabang.

The mountains of Laos, rising abruptly everywhere around these plains, are mainly of three types: long, folded ridges; karstic ranges; and basaltic outflow plateaus. South of about 18° N., the principal folded ridges run northwest-southeast and are continuous, except for a few major gaps, along the Laos-Vietnam border. In the north, they crisscross virtually the entire country in a confusion of trends, but mostly northeast-southwest. This rugged terrain discourages settlement except by the more hardy hill tribes.

The karstic ranges, some scattered among the northern mountains and some in belts of their own, present a fantastic landscape of almost bare, gray, vertical cliffs, flat-floored valleys, and sharp peaks and pinnacles that are serious barriers to travel and, again, discourage settlement. These ranges are most prominent in a wide belt running parallel to the Mekong north and east of Thakhek, then swinging southeast into Vietnam at about latitude 17°.

There are also several intermontane plateaus which, by their elevation and difficulty of access, are set off from the plains, such as the Kham-mouane Plateau, the most extensive, and the Plain of Jars, which forms the central part of the Plateau of Xiangkhoang.

The Bolovens Plateau in the south and a smaller one to the east of it are both supported by a thick basaltic flow. Atop the plateau (maximum elevation, 4,800 feet), the topography is relatively level or rolling, and this, combined with rich volcanic soil, ample rainfall, and moderate temper-atures, provides an environment quite favorable to a varied agriculture.

The climate of Laos is everywhere tropical, of the monsoon type, with distinct seasons: wet (May or June to October), cool (November to Febru-ary), and hot (March to May). In the two dry seasons, for at least four successive months the rainfall remains under two inches (except on the Bolovens) and under one inch in many lowlands; but rainfall is every-where sufficient for rice cultivation. Temperatures are highest toward the end of the hot season, just before the monsoon rains begin; in Vientiane one may experience several weeks with daily maxima approaching 100°F. During January, on the other hand, nighttime temperatures may drop into the mid-40's, although the days are sunny and warm. Frost is unknown on the lowlands.

As would be expected, the climate in the plateau and mountain areas is characterized by lower temperatures and, usually, higher rainfall. On the Plain of Jars, for example, the temperature falls below freezing on occasional nights during the cool season; on the Bolovens, at Pak Song, the minimum on record is 34°F. and the annual rainfall is the highest recorded in Laos, approximately 155 inches.

The natural vegetation of Laos is forest, varying from open, savanna-type forest in the drier areas to the much denser, quasi-rainforest generally on mountain slopes or at higher elevations, where rainfall is more abun-dant. In the north and at high elevations there are some pines and warm temperate outliers such as oaks.

Very little is known about what lies beneath the surface in Laos. Tin is present and exploited (578 tons of 50 per cent tin concentrate produced in 1965; 1,262 tons in 1969). Gypsum, salt, and limestone are also extracted. Two promising deposits of iron ore have been found. Petroleum may exist under some of the lowlands, which represent an extension of the Korat Plateau in Thailand, but this remains to be proved. Some maps show other mineral occurrences, including copper, coal, lead, manganese, and gold, particularly in the north, but accurate information about them is not available.

Electric power now serves only a small proportion of the population; however, major increases in power production are taking place with the development of the country's very large hydroelectric potential. Under the auspices of the Mekong Committee, several dams and power plants are being considered. A dam and hydroelectric plant are under construction on the Ngum River in Vientiane Province. This hydroelectric complex will have an initial capacity of 30,000 kw and an ultimate capacity of 135,000 kw. Construction has been underway since 1968; completion of the project is scheduled for early 1972. A study of the feasibility of damming the Mekong River at Pa Mong has been completed. If the decision is made to construct this dam twenty-five miles upstream from Vientiane, the benefits that will be derived are immense—4.8 million kw of power capacity, plus water to irrigate 4 million acres in Laos and Thailand.

The Economy

It would not be an oversimplification to say that rice is the economy of Laos. Rice is far and away the most important article in the diet, and rice milling is the country's main industry. Farmers and their families make up 80 to 85 per cent of the nation's population, and the great majority of them produce rice, at least for their own subsistence but often also for sale in the towns and cities. Nevertheless, not more than 60 per cent of the people in areas under Royal Lao Government control grow the food they eat.

In Laos rice is of two kinds: wet rice (mostly glutinous), raised on some 185,000 acres in the lowlands in *na* (diked, flat fields), which are irrigated, generally by natural flooding; and upland rice, raised in *hai* (fields above the flooding level, often on hill slopes), where, because of rotation, larger areas are used and yields are lower. Yields of even the lowland rice in the early 1960's averaged only 500 to 600 pounds per acre, the lowest yields in all monsoon Asia. Since about 1966, however, rice production has increased steadily: 487,000 tons (1967), 514,000 (1968), 537,000 (1969), 550,000

In many parts of Southeast Asia, methods of farming and processing food have changed but little over the centuries. In Laotian homes that lack rice mills, mortar combinations like the one shown above are used to pound rice.

(1970 estimate). Credit for this growth goes to improved strains, use of fertilizer, and more modern techniques.

Opportunities that exist in some areas for a second crop per year are not exploited. Today, in fact, Laos must import rice, whereas natural conditions suggest that it should be at least a modest exporter. To be sure, the local demand is constantly increasing, because the total population and that of the cities are increasing rapidly. A more salient explanation of the deficiency, however, lies in the number of men who for so many years have been absorbed in the army, coupled with insecurity in some rural areas as a result of war and political strife, and the difficulties of moving the crop to the markets in many places where producton could be expanded. Also, heavy dependence on outside aid has perhaps seriously disrupted habits of self-sufficiency.

Although rice dominates in agriculture, other food crops are produced in areas where rice does not do well. The alternate food crops are sweet potatoes and corn, both grown mostly in the rugged northern uplands inhabited by tribes such as the Meo and Yao, to whom rice is not an indispensable food. This is the well-known slash-and-burn type of shifting cultivation, where a small plot in the forest is cut and burned and a crop is planted in the ashes, sometimes under a few remaining sentinel trees. For two or three years this same plot is cultivated and then abandoned to the forest. When all the land within a certain radius of a village has been thus exploited, the entire village moves to a new spot. In addition to food crops, opium is grown on these hillside and mountaintop plots, supplying a sizable cash income, particularly to the Meo.

Vegetables, pimentos, red peppers, and a few fruits, such as bananas, pineapples, pomelos (resembling grapefruits), and mangos, are grown throughout the country, usually in or around the villages. About 60 per cent of all the vegetables for sale in the Vientiane market are now grown in Laos, an increase of 40 per cent over the past eight years. Cotton is also widely grown (production about 2,500 tons in 1968), although nowhere on a large scale, and its destination is generally the handloom still found in almost every village dwelling.

During the French regime a few coffee plantations were developed, chiefly on the Bolovens Plateau, but since independence many of these have been abandoned. Coffee production reached about 3,500 tons in 1968. Rubber has been planted on a small scale in the south, and tobacco, grown sometimes as a commercial plantation crop (around Vientiane) but also on farms, including the upland *hai*, provides the raw material for one of Laos's few industries, cigarette-making. Cardamom is another crop, mostly grown commercially on the Bolovens.

In this simple economy the rivers, ponds, and forests yield many of the essentials of life. Fish, eaten most often as a sauce to flavor the sticky rice, provide the principal protein in the diet. Wood and, above all, bamboo provide construction materials and the basis for virtually all implements. Also from the forests, which cover half the country's area, come charcoal and small quantities of products, such as benzoin and stick-lac, wood-oil for lighting, food plants and roots, and tropical hardwoods, of which teak is the best known and most sought-after in world markets.

War and insecurity have reduced livestock production to a point where it barely suffices for local needs. Pigs and poultry are numerous in the villages. Elephants today are used for transport only in the extreme south and in the north, particularly in Sayaboury Province.

Industry in the modern sense hardly exists, other than the rice mills, many sawmills, a cement plant (not yet in operation), building materials plants, shoe factories, three cigarette factories, and a soft-drink bottling plant. Lime-burning, brick-making, and charcoal-burning, however, are widespread. And in virtually every village there are skilled craftsmen working with wood, bamboo, silver, iron, cotton, silk, and the varied fibers found in the jungle.

With such an economy, Laos obviously has little to export. In value, tin is at the head of the list, followed by lumber and forest products, and green coffee. Total exports, however, earned only $2 million for Laos in 1969. Malaysia and Singapore (destination of the tin ore) have been the principal customers, followed by Thailand, Hong Kong, South Vietnam, and France.

Imports are chiefly minerals (petroleum, primarily), manufactured goods (textiles, machinery, vehicles, processed foods), chemicals, metals and their products, and even meat and vegetables. These totaled about $42 million in 1969, coming mainly from Thailand (food), Indonesia (petroleum), the United States, Japan, and France (manufactured goods).

It is apparent that Laos faces a severe deficit in its balance of payments; without substantial foreign aid, the country cannot sustain its economy, underdeveloped as it is. In 1969, 67 per cent of the nation's imports were financed by a commodity import program of the United States and by the Foreign Exchange Operations Fund (FEOF), which was established in 1964, on the recommendation of the International Monetary Fund, by the United States, Great Britain, France, and Australia, and joined in 1965 by Japan. The Royal Lao Government civilian budget deficit is covered for the most part by FEOF. Since 1964, FEOF has played the key role in the economy of Laos by stabilizing the exchange rate, neutralizing the inflationary impact of the government's large budgetary deficits, and creating economic conditions that favor a modest rate of growth even under the stresses of war. Even with a return to peace and considerable economic development, however, it will be some time before Laos's deficit can be overcome.

The internal economic and financial situation is equally grave. The GNP in 1968 was estimated at $188 million. Revenues are limited by the very low per capita average income, estimated at $66 a year, and by deficiencies in the fiscal administration, complicated by the insecurity and inaccessibility of many areas, while expenses are exceptionally high because of the military burden which the government must bear if it is to maintain independence. Per capita income in the monetized sector is estimated at $180 per year; in the nonmonetized village economy it is estimated at $55.

Transportation

There are few nations today so deficient in modern transport as Laos. This is a land without railroads. The road network currently under control of the Royal Lao Government consists of 487 miles of asphalt, 1,542 miles of gravel or laterite, which are all-weather roads, and 1,943 miles of earth roads, which can be traveled in the dry season only. The roads leading east through central Laos to Vietnam are closed. Route 13 is now asphalt-surfaced from the Cambodian border to Savannakhet; from Savannakhet north, with the exception of small stretches in the vicinty of Thakhek and Vientiane, the road is surfaced with laterite. The 249-mile stretch of Route 13 north from Vientiane to Luang Prabang (which by 1965 had deteriorated in many places to a footpath through the jungle) has been rebulit and is now open to traffic.

The Mekong ties together virtually all the larger towns and most thickly populated areas via pirogue, but it is useful for transport by larger craft only over certain stretches, notably Khong-Pakse, Savannakhet-Vientiane, Vientiane–Luang Prabang. Travel elsewhere proceeds by oxcart, jeep, or heavy truck during the dry season over many local roads, which may lie under water when the rains come; or the elephant is called into service. In remoter rural areas travel is largely by foot.

A new day is fast arriving, however, and the Lao are jumping from the Middle Ages into the modern era by turning to the airplane to knit their country together. Statistics are unavailable, but it seems safe to say that a substantial majority of persons setting out from Vientiane today to visit some other part of the country will travel by air. Although there is no great movement of heavy goods within the country, a significant share of the freight that does move is also carried by air.

The People

Laos in 1971 has an estimated population of about 3 million people. The figure remains an estimate, for no formal census has been taken. Of these 3 million, about 1.7 million live in that part of the nation under control of the Royal Lao Government; of these, about 1.2 million live in rural areas and engage in subsistence agriculture, and about 500,000 live in places where economic activity is largely monetized. Among the 1.2 million people of the subsistence economy, there are more than 250,000 refugees who are dependent in varying degrees on the government for support.

The population is estimated to be growing at an average rate of 2.6 per cent per year. The birth rate is placed at 47 per 1,000 and the death rate at 23 per 1,000, with life expectancy between thirty-five and forty years. Population density is estimated at 30 per square mile, compared with 264 in South Vietnam and 57.5 in the United States. About 20 per cent of the people are literate. Of the school-age population (six to four-teen) in that part of Laos controlled by the Royal Lao Government, 58 per cent are enrolled in public and private schools.

The war has brought about significant shifts in the population and has produced a tight labor market in the urban centers. Population is increasing in the towns (the annual rate is 10 per cent in Vientiane, 7.5 per cent in urban areas generally) and in the monetized sector (6.3 per cent). A 1966 census of the city of Vientiane placed the population at 132,000; in 1970, it was placed at nearly 200,000. Of the other principal cities, Luang Prabang has a population of 23,000 (1967); Savannakhet, 36,000 (1967); and Pakse, 35,000 (1968). These cities are all provincial capitals which also serve as modest commercial centers, although none has any industry to speak of.

The area of well-settled lowlands along the Mekong is also the home of the Lao people, who, together with the Thai groups, make up the greater part of the population, some 2 million. The Lao cling to the valley—to the areas of wet rice—departing any distance from the master stream only to follow up the valleys of tributaries, notably the Ou, Ngum, Done, and Kong. Their close relatives, the Thai, who in Laos still live for the most part in tribal organization, make up less than one quarter of the 2 million and live in more remote areas.

The second major group, commonly called *Kha*, or slave, more recently called *Lao Theung*, meaning upland Lao, number some 380,000. This group includes a great variety of tribes and peoples, most of whom live on a primitive scale as hunters and gatherers. The third major group, the Meo and Yao, numbering about 260,000, live on mountaintops and high slopes, rarely below 3,600 feet, away from heat and malaria. Most of them practice shifting cultivation, growing upland rice, corn, some vegetables, sweet potatoes, tobacco, and frequently opium. Of these last two major groups, over 100,000 are today counted among the refugees.

As everywhere else in Southeast Asia, the Chinese, mainly in the towns, are merchants and rice-millers. Here, however, they run into sharp competition from the Vietnamese who came into Laos either for trade or as lower-level civil servants under French rule. All told, the Chinese number about 60,000 and the Vietnamese about 30,000.

In Vientiane and to some extent in the few other large towns, there is national political awareness and some active participation in a money economy, but in the much more extensive village areas, most people still live in a self-contained communal pattern, where money, machines, mass media, and other manifestations of modern ways make little impact; the focus of life is the Buddhist wat. And beyond these lowland villages lie the yet more remote tribal people who have little consciousness of an entity called Laos and tend to resent the lowlanders who try periodically to impose Lao institutions.

With time these disparate elements may be cemented together into a nation, despite the rugged topography and thick forests, but at the moment the skills and capital required to build the infrastructure essential for such unification and for the introduction of even a modest measure of modernization are not available. Further development will require foreign aid.

The tragedy of Laos is that, instead of being able to concentrate on constructive activity, it has suffered from civil strife and foreign intervention almost from the day of independence. Energies that should have gone into development have been devoted instead to national survival. Let us hope that before too long the Lao will be left in peace to tackle the task of building their own nation.

Suggested Readings

American University. *Area Handbook for Laos.* Washington, D.C.: U.S. Government Printing Office, 1967. A comprehensive analysis of social, political, and economic aspects of Laos and its national security.

DOMMEN, ARTHUR J. *Conflict in Laos: The Politics of Neutralization,* rev. ed. New York: Praeger, 1971. Deals in great detail with the period 1954–64 spanning the two Geneva conferences and more recent events.

HALPERN, JOEL M. *Economy and Society of Laos: A Brief History,* Southeast Asia Studies: Monograph Series no. 5. New Haven, Conn.: Yale University Press, 1964. An integrated socio-economic view of northern and central Laos; good background material.

———. *Government, Politics and Social Structure in Laos: A Study of Tra-*

dition and Innovation, Southeast Asa Studies: Monograph Series no. 4, New Haven, Conn.: Yale University Press, 1964.

———. "Laos: Future Prospects and Their Limitations." *Asian Survey,* VI, no. 1 (Jan., 1966), pp. 59–65. Briefly discusses some of the crucial factors shaping the future of Laos.

LaBar, F. M. and Adrienne Suddard, eds. *Laos: Its People, Its Society, Its Culture.* New Haven, Conn.: Human Relation Area Files Press, 1963. A thorough, if somewhat dated, study of the Lao and their culture, with an extensive bibliography.

See also Suggested Readings for Part I, pp. 57–59.

9 VIETNAM*

The People • Monsoon Lands • Farming and Fishing • North Vietnam • South Vietnam • focus on Land Reform in South Vietnam, by Roy L. Prosterman

In A.D. 939, after more than eight centuries of Chinese control, Vietnam gained its freedom. Since then, it has often been a nominal vassal of Chinese rulers; in addition, its written script and educational system (both used until the twentieth century), its agricultural and artisanal techniques, and its system of government have all been adapted from Chinese models. Nevertheless, the Vietnamese have retained their national characteristics, and ethnically they are a strikingly homogenous people.

French interest in Vietnam grew out of missionary contacts dating back to the sixteenth century. Between 1862 and 1884, through a series of treaties, France established a protectorate over Tonkin and Annam and annexed Cochin China; shortly thereafter all three became part of the French colony of Indochina.

The French remained in control of Vietnam until it was conquered by Japan in 1940. During the period of Japanese occupation, a coalition of nationalist, revolutionary, and communist organizations was formed, the Vietminh League. When Japan surrendered in 1945, at the end of World War II, the Vietminh set up a republic known as Vietnam, which included Tonkin, Annam, and Cochin China. However, the French quickly re-established themselves in Cochin China, and in subsequent negotiations France and the Vietminh failed to reach agreement. The following year the disagreements led to war, which ended in 1954 with a Vietminh victory over the French Army.

In accordance with the agreement signed in Geneva that same year, Vietnam was divided into two zones roughly at the 17th parallel, pending general elections designed to bring about unification. The elections were

* Parts of this article are based on material from a 1965 issue of *focus.*

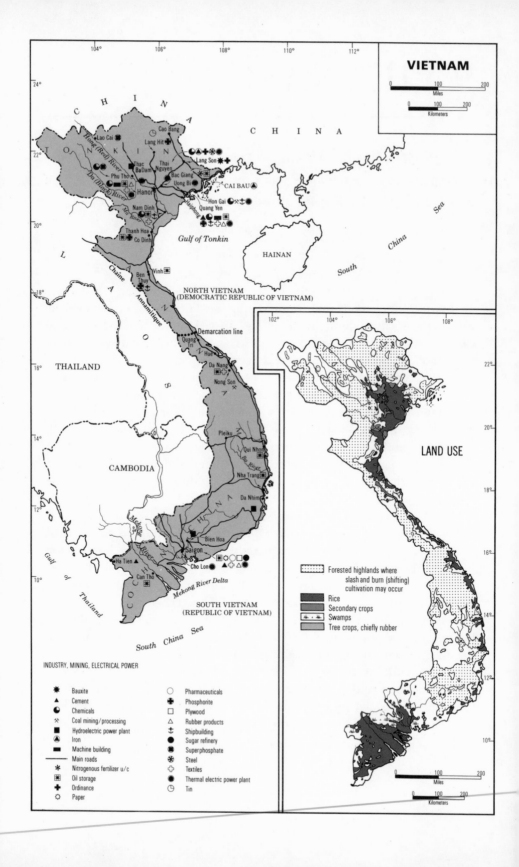

VIETNAM

0   100   200
Miles

0   100   200
Kilometers

C H I N A

C H I N A

TONKIN

Lao Cai
Hong (Red) River
Da (Black) River
Cao Bang
Lang Hit
Lang Son
Thac Ba Dam
Thai Nguyen
Phu Tho
Bac Giang
Uong Bi
CAI BAU
Hanoi
Haiphong
Hon Gai
Quang Yen
Nam Dinh
Ma River
Thanh Hoa
Co Dinh

Gulf of Tonkin

HAINAN

South China Sea

Ben Thuy
Vinh

NORTH VIETNAM
(DEMOCRATIC REPUBLIC OF VIETNAM)

Chaine Annamitique

L   A   O   S

Demarcation line
Quang Tri
Hue
Da Nang
Nong Son

THAILAND

Pleiku

A   N   N   A   M

Qui Nhon
Ba River
Nha Trang

CAMBODIA

Da Nhim

Mekong River
Bien Hoa
Saigon
Cho Lon
Ha Tien
Can Tho
Mekong River Delta

C   O   C   H   I   N   C   H   I   N   A

SOUTH VIETNAM
(REPUBLIC OF VIETNAM)

Gulf of Thailand

South China Sea

LAND USE

Forested highlands where
slash and burn (shifting)
cultivation may occur

Rice

Secondary crops

Swamps

Tree crops, chiefly rubber

0   100   200
Miles

0   100   200
Kilometers

INDUSTRY, MINING, ELECTRICAL POWER

✳ Bauxite
▲ Cement
◗ Chemicals
✕ Coal mining/processing
■ Hydroelectric power plant
◭ Iron
▬ Machine building
— Main roads
✳ Nitrogenous fertilizer u/c
⊞ Oil storage
✚ Ordinance
✿ Paper

○ Pharmaceuticals
✚ Phosphorite
□ Plywood
△ Rubber products
⚓ Shipbuilding
● Sugar refinery
◉ Superphosphate
✳ Steel
♧ Textiles
◉ Thermal electric power plant
◷ Tin

never held. Today, North Vietnam (Democratic Republic of Vietnam) and South Vietnam (Republic of Vietnam) are separate nations, engaged in still another bloody war.

At issue is the fundamental organization of society. Communist North Vietnam, with huge amounts of military equipment and economic aid supplied by the Soviet Union, plus some from the People's Republic of China, has sought to "liberate" the people in South Vietnam. The government of South Vietnam, with massive U.S. military assistance, including equipment and troops, and billions of dollars of economic aid, has struggled to thwart both attacks from the communist North and the efforts of those in South Vietnam who either sympathize with the communists or seek a greater voice in shaping the policies of the South Vietnamese Government and a more equitable distribution of wealth. (For additional information on some of the basic factors leading to the conflict, see pp. 143–50.)

Attempts to end the war through peace talks in Paris, begun in 1968, so far have been unsuccessful. From time to time there are indications that concrete results may be forthcoming, but meanwhile fighting continues in South Vietnam. At present, through a process known as "Vietnamization," U.S. troops are gradually being withdrawn as South Vietnam assumes greater military responsibility. By October, 1971, the U.S. military force in South Vietnam was down to 202,000 men from its high of more than 540,000 in 1969.

In area, the Democratic Republic of Vietnam is slightly smaller than the Republic of Vietnam (63,344 square miles versus 66,263); in population it is somewhat larger (22.1 million versus 18.4 million). The majority of Vietnamese in both North and South derive their subsistence from farming and fishing and speak the same language. Traditionally they have practiced a form of Buddhism with some elements of Confucianism and Taoism, all derived from China.

The People

About 85 per cent of the people in North and South Vietnam are Vietnamese, most of them living in lowland villages. In the South, power at the village level has been in the hands of government-appointed village chiefs, who were usually more interested in pleasing the central government than in looking after the villagers' interests. Only very recently has a system of village elections been instituted, making the village chief directly responsible to the villagers. This may go a long way toward eliminating corruption at the local level and improving the lot of the average villager. It should also decrease the relative power of the small elite group of professionals, wealthy landowners, government officials, and military officers, who are largely urban dwellers. The largest minority in the South are the Chinese; they are most active in trade and commerce. In the North the communist government introduced measures to eliminate the traditional socio-economic structure, the gap between rich and poor, the Confucian-based family, and the prevailing religious beliefs. A general "social transformation" struck at the fabric of society, and many members of the elite fled to the South, were removed from their positions, or were killed. At present the social hierarchy is dominated by Communist party officials and party members.

The mountainous interior of both South and North Vietnam is inhabited chiefly by *montagnards* (mountain people), who have intermingled little with other groups. In the South they occupy the highland area of the Chaîne Annamitique, from the Mekong Delta to the 17th parallel, and from Bien Hoa to Hue. This group resembles the modern Indonesians, with some Mongoloid elements acquired through intermarriage. The northern *montagnards* are divided into three subgroups based on language patterns—the Thai-Kadai, the Sino-Tibetan, and the Austroasiatic. They inhabit two autonomous regions—the Tay Bac, south and west of the Hong River (Red) in the mountains bordering Laos and China, and the Viet Bac, northeast of the Hong River near the mountains bordering China.

Monsoon Lands

The rainfall regimes in both the South and the North are markedly influenced by the shifting monsoon winds, but variations in climate are also, of course, caused by differences in latitude, elevation, configuration of land, and distance from the sea. In both areas, most of the rain comes with the summer monsoon winds originating in the Indian Ocean.

In the southern lowland, Saigon, for instance, has an annual rainfall averaging 80 inches, most of which falls between April and October; winters tend to be somewhat dry. The average temperature ranges are small: between 80°F. and 86°F. There is no frost.

In the northern lowland, around Hanoi, the climate, although monsoonal, is humid subtropical, with hot summers. The range in temperatures is much greater than in the South because of the higher latitude and the resultant more pronounced seasons, but here also frost is unknown. Hanoi has a January average of 63°, a July average of 85°. The rainfall is about 72 inches a year, and there is no dry period in winter. Rainfall is also relatively abundant in the interior highlands, but winters are dry and temperatures are lower than in the lowlands.

Along the coastal plain of Annam the northeast monsoons predominate in winter, the southeast trade winds in summer. As a result, rainfall is fairly evenly distributed through the year, but the maximum is in late summer and early autumn during the period of tropical typhoons. Moist air rising and cooling as it approaches the Chaîne Annamitique brings heavy orographic rainfall to the area around Hue, for example, which has an average of 116 inches a year. Farther south, in the rain-shadow area near the Mekong Delta, the average drops to less than 40 inches. Temperatures along the Annam coast average between 60° and 75°.

Farming and Fishing

Subsistence farming, mainly for home consumption, forms the basis of the Vietnamese economy. Rice is the main crop; under peaceful conditions it occupies about 80 per cent of the total cultivated land, and most of the labor force is engaged in its cultivation. The growing of wet rice is concentrated in the rich alluvial areas of the Hong River Delta, the Mekong Delta, and the coastal lowlands of Annam; dry rice is raised on the upland slopes of the interior.

Because rice needs a great deal of water, most farmers grow their biggest crop during the summer rains. But it is also grown in winter where precipitation is adequate or where irrigation is practiced. Interculture (the young rice shoots are set out in the fields in between the plants with maturing grains) is quite common. In the most favored places, three crops a year are produced.

Fresh and dried fish and fish sauces are major items of the diet; they are the principal source of animal protein supplementing the largely vegetarian fare. Fresh-water fish come from the rivers and canals (many families live on the water in floating houses); pisciculture is practiced in rice fields and the innumerable ponds surrounding villages. Offshore fishing is common along the entire coast, and it is the chief occupation in many villages on the Tonkin and northern Annam coasts. Most of the fishing equipment does not permit long journeys: At night, fishing craft (both sampans and junks) are drawn up on the sandy beaches. There is, however, in the far south, some deep-sea fishing on sturdy junks.

North Vietnam

Most of North Vietnam is mountainous or hilly, and about half is forest-covered. The Tonkin lowland is extremely flat, almost entirely built up of alluvium from the Hong River (and the river is indeed red, about the color of tomato soup) and its tributaries. The delta, only a few feet above sea level, is the most productive part of this lowland; all of it is arable. However, flood prevention has always been a serious problem.

The river's flow varies enormously according to the season. Over the past 2,000 years many dikes and canals have been built to contain the Hong River and drain off its flood waters. In 1925, the existing works were united in a single network, which provided effective control, but the river bed, confined between dikes, quickly silted up. At present in some places the high-water mark is 25 feet above the level of the surrounding countryside, and occasionally, as in 1945 and again in 1971, catastrophic floods occur.

The great majority of the people in North Vietnam live in the Tonkin lowland and make their living by farming. Rural densities here reach 2,200 people per square mile and even 4,000 in the best areas of recent alluvium and where improved water management ensures adequate irrigation and protection from floods.

Rice planted in small patches (usually less than a quarter-acre in size) occupies 80 per cent of the cultivated area. Most of the rest is devoted to sugar cane, cotton, tea, corn, sweet potatoes, manioc, and various other vegetables and fruits. Much of the farm work is done by hand, with the help of water buffaloes and oxen, in spite of recent efforts to increase mechanization. But in many other ways the communist regime has brought radical changes.

Before World War II, the great majority of farmers in North Vietnam were tenants or small landowners. They were perpetually burdened with crushing debts and had to pay 40–60 per cent of the yearly harvest for rent or as interest on debts. The communist government's program to redistribute land, especially to the landless laborer and the poor farmer, thus gained considerable support. By 1956 the intital and most difficult phase of its land-reform program had been completed. Following the example of the Chinese communists, the rural population was divided into five groups: landlords, rich peasants, middle peasants, poor peasants, and landless farm workers. Land was virtually confiscated from the first two categories and distributed to the last two. As a result, all peasants own the land they farm. Although the average holding is small (about one-third of an acre per person), on balance, the redistribution of land has probably provided a stimulus to increase farm production.

Once the distribution of land had been carried out, farmers were encouraged to form mutual aid teams and then agricultural cooperatives, as in China. By 1969, 95 per cent of all farm families had become members of "high rank" cooperatives, in which all the means of production, including the land, are owned in common. According to available reports, the farmers are better off than before. But reports also indicate that there is still considerable opposition to the concept of collectivization and a rather widespread tendency to disregard government orders whenever possible. (One should keep in mind that even today the average North Vietnamese has a per capita income of less than $100 per year.)

Because the North never produced enough rice for the needs of its population, it used to import rice from the South, which had a surplus. Deprived of this source of food since the war, the government has attempted to increase local production by the use of more efficient farming techniques and by extending the area under cultivation in both the lowlands and the uplands. According to North Vietnamese figures, rice acreage increased by 17 per cent between 1939 and 1956 and average yields per acre increased from 28 to 38 bushels. Now some 5 million tons of rice are produced in a good year, enough to feed the population on the basis of the official ration of 660 pounds per person per year. In a bad year, however, the rice ration has to be reduced. In recent years, when farms and factories have been repeatedly damaged by bombings, and a large proportion of men and women have been engaged in the war effort, the official ration has occasionally dropped to 330 pounds per year, while students and soldiers received about 400 and 530 pounds, respectively. The goal of the current Five-Year Plan apparently is to increase annual production to 7 million tons, enough to keep pace with the rapidly growing population (some 3 per cent per year); but more widespread use of improved seeds and much greater use of fertilizers will be needed if production and productivity are to be raised enough to achieve this goal.

The string of lowlands along the Annam coast are miniature replicas of the Tonkin Plain. Their fertile alluvium, brought down by rivers rising in the Chaîne Annamitique, is excellent rice land, and rice occupies about 80 per cent of the cultivated area.

In the sparsely populated uplands of the North (and also in the South), most farmers grow wet rice on the valley floors and lower slopes; higher up, most practice a system of shifting cultivation, raising dry rice, corn and other vegetables, and cattle.

Until the end of the nineteenth century, northern Vietnam had a self-sufficient regional economy based on subsistence agriculture and rural handicraft industries. Under French control this rural economy was progressively disrupted. France's colonial policy, like most colonial policies, was aimed at supplying manufactured goods in exchange for raw materials produced cheaply by local labor under European management. Industrialization in Vietnam did not begin until the last two decades of French rule, and many of the hydraulic installations, mines, and factories established during this period were damaged by the war of independence.

One of the basic goals of the communist government's first economic plan (1958–60) was to replace private ownership in industry by a centrally planned economic structure and to expand and diversify basic manufacturing. By the end of 1960, nine tenths of the industry and commerce and four fifths of the transport were state owned and operated. During the first Five-Year Plan (1960–65), industrial production increased rapidly, especially in iron and steel, fuel, engineering, metallurgy, and chemicals. The manufacture of consumer goods, such as textiles, also increased; at the same time, greater output of agricultural raw materials for industry was encouraged. Since then, reliable statistics have been unavailable, but there is considerable evidence that, despite the ravages of war, industrial production has continued to expand.

North Vietnam's mineral resources are among the richest in Southeast Asia and have been an asset in the industrialization program. The best coal is mined north of the Hong River in the Quang Yen and the Hon Gai anthracite fields, which were producing some 3.3 million tons in the mid-1960's. Not only is its caloric value high, but it is accessible and near the thermal plants and factories of the Hanoi-Haiphong industrial region. Output is currently sufficient to meet domestic needs and permit export of about 1 million tons a year, mostly to Asian markets, which has helped reduce the huge trade deficit.

Other mineral deposits include iron ore near Thai Nguyen and on the island of Cai Bau, and tin and chromite. Phosphates have been found, especially at Lao Cai, and are being developed in response to the rising demand for chemical fertilizers. There are also minor deposits of gold, silver, lead, zinc, uranium, nickel, cobalt, tungsten, bauxite, antimony, and managanese.

The largest industrial complex, at Thai Nguyen, includes an integrated iron and steel plant, a steel-rolling mill, and piping and cable workshops. The fertilizer industry has grown considerably. Output rose to about 180,000 tons in 1964 and is probably much greater today, since the government has placed such emphasis on increasing crop yields. Other factories are making machine tools, farm implements, bicycles, and kitchen utensils.

After minerals, food processing and textiles are the most important industries. Numerous rice mills, sugar refineries, tea factories, fish canneries, plants to process cassava, soybeans, and vegetables, and a distillery have been established near producing areas or in the major cities. The textile industry includes a cotton combine at Nam Dinh, a fully automated, 50,000-spindled textile mill in Hanoi, and many dyeing and weaving shops that have been organized into cooperatives. The emphasis has been on small workshops that can produce needed manufactured goods without large capital investment. Where there were only about 40 industrial enterprises in 1955, there were 1,200 in 1965. Handicrafts also contributed to the consumer goods available, and artisans have been encouraged to improve the quality of their work and their productivity so as to cut down on imports. Besides traditional items such as pottery, baskets, and textiles, craftsmen are making farm tools, carts, boats, and simple machines. Most of the larger factories have been established with machinery, equipment, and technical assistance supplied by the Soviet Union. China has helped to build new plants in Haiphong and Hanoi to produce electric lamps, rubber goods, enamelware, soap, matches, cigarettes, and knitwear. The East Germans have helped with a glassworks, the Czechs with a plywood plant, the Poles with a sugar refinery.

The output of electric power reached 550 million kwh in 1964, but it has apparently dropped since then because of frequent air attacks that damaged the new electrical plant at Uong Bi and the Thac Ba dam and hydroelectric station.

The ambitious industrial expansion program has been hampered by the war and, in spite of much aid from communist friends, by lack of sufficient capital and technical skill. Nevertheless, the North Vietnamese have succeeded in laying the foundations of an industrial economy, which should help to raise the standard of living when peace is restored.

South Vietnam

Traditionally, the southern part of Vietnam was considered to be richer than the North, not because of any great industrial output, but because it produced a surplus of rice. During the 1946–54 war, vast areas of rice land reverted to swamp, much of which remained unrehabilitated for more than a decade. Nor did the proposed land-reform program make much headway.

It was to have consisted of four stages: (1) reduction of farm rents to 15–25 per cent of the value of the annual rice crop; (2) granting of credit at annual rates of not more than 6 per cent; (3) redistribution to cultivators of 500,000 acres of government land; and (4) limitation of individual holdings of rice land to 247 acres, compulsory sale to the government of the excess, and resale of this land to cultivators on a deferred-payment basis. Some progress was made, but, as of 1967, two out of three farmers in South Vietnam did not own the land they worked and paid rents and interest on debts that left them barely enough to survive. (For additional information on current land reform in South Vietnam, see pp. 143–50.)

Most of the cultivated land in South Vietnam is in the large fertile delta of the Mekong River and around Saigon, and nine tenths of this is planted in rice, which is watered by the summer monsoon and the subsequent floods and by irrigation canals. Most of the farm work is done by hand and by draft animals. The farms and rice fields are much larger than in the North and more suitable for mechanized equipment; double-cropping, on the other hand, is less common than in the North because of the winter dry season.

Before the war the South was a major exporter of rice, but by the mid-1960's large amounts had to be imported (about 700,000 tons per year). Production is now rising, however, and self-sufficiency is expected by 1972. This remarkable recovery in spite of the continuing war can be traced to a government decision in the late 1960's to raise the official price of rice in the cities. This greatly increased the amount the farmers received for their crop. Farmers who had resisted innovations and had been uninterested in raising anything above their own needs suddenly became aware of the possibilities of improved techniques and better market conditions. Large numbers of them shifted away from subsistence farming toward surplus production. The more enterprising ones began to use the new high-yield rice seeds developed by the International Rice Research Institute in the Philippines (see p. 215). By late 1968 thousands of farmers who had used the new seeds had increased yields by 100 per cent or more. With rising incomes, they could afford to buy new farm tools, more fertilizers and pesticides, and small gasoline engines to run irrigation pumps and boats. Today, tens of thousands of farmers in South Vietnam are using the new rice seeds, and more than 1,000 agricultural technicians who have studied at the National Rice Training Institute are now returning to their villages to train other farmers. The popular term for the new grain is "Honda rice," for, among other benefits, the income from the sale of the surplus production is often used to buy a Japanese Honda motorcycle.

Once peace is restored and funds become available for drainage and irrigation programs and resettlement of the hundreds of thousands of war refugees, several million acres of unused land can be put into production. Also, the Mekong Valley scheme (see pp. 13–29) promises to supply enough water in the Delta during the dry winter season to grow two or three crops of rice a year instead of one. South Vietnam could also raise a variety of other food crops for export. It could, in fact, become a prime source of food for the undernourished millions of South and Southeast Asia.

The second most valuable crop in South Vietnam has been rubber, grown mainly on plantations that were established during French rule, with French capital. The French also provided the roads and railroads needed to get the produce to the coast for shipment overseas. The plantations were run by Europeans, who were paid European-scale salaries; the labor was provided by Vietnamese, paid Vietnamese-scale salaries. More than 80 per cent of the rubber was exported, and it was the chief source of foreign exchange earned. Defoliation by aerial spraying to reduce cover for enemy troops and other dislocations resulting from the war (such as labor and transport shortages) have greatly reduced output. But,

Van Bucher/Photo Researchers, Inc.

Motor bikes, a symbol of newly acquired wealth in South Vietnam and many other less-developed nations, jam the parking area in this mile-long park that cuts through Saigon's main shopping district.

once rural security is re-established, new trees can be planted and damaged ones restored, production methods modernized, and roads rebuilt. Rubber should then again be a major source of export revenue and also provide a valuable raw material for local industries.

Other plantation crops include tea, tobacco, and coffee, grown in the uplands along with bamboo, cinnamon, timber, vegetable dyes, raw silk, and vegetables. Sugar cane, peanuts, corn, and copra are also grown, and there is some cattle-raising.

South Vietnam has few mineral deposits other than a small coal field near Da Nang, a gold mine, and silica in the white sands along the coast, which is used for glass-making. Power for industry now comes mainly from diesel and thermal installations, imported petroleum, and a few hydroelectric stations. A large hydroelectric plant with a yearly capacity of 800 million kwh is, however, under construction on the Da Nhim River, and the Mekong offers a vast potential for the future. Also, recent geological reports indicate the existence of petroleum deposits in the Mekong Delta and offshore. Some eighteen oil companies—including three Vietnamese—have formally requested permission to explore for oil in South Vietnam. According to some experts, these coastal waters may contain as much as 25 per cent of Southeast Asia's reserves.

There is practically no heavy industry. Most of the manufacturing industries are concentrated in the Saigon–Cho Lon region, and they are mainly consumer-oriented. They include food processing, cotton spinning and weaving, the manufacture of paper and other wood products, rubber tires, tobacco products, cement, soap, paint, glassware, pottery, and gunny bags. There are also plants making articles in plastic and aluminum and assembling radios, motor scooters, bicycles, and sewing machines.

The fastest growing industry is textiles, developed with the help of technicians from Taiwan and capital from the United States. By the mid-1960's some 20,000 looms had been installed, most of them electrically operated. The capacity of the existing gunny-bag mill is being increased, and a new mill is to be built with Italian capital, so as to increase production to 9 million rice and sugar bags a year, enough for local needs. West Germany has agreed to help South Vietnam establish a plywood factory, and several other friendly nations have offered to aid in the reconstruction of damaged plants and the establishment of new industries to produce items that are now imported.

Foreign aid will also be needed to repair and extend the transport network, rebuild schools and houses, improve sewage systems, increase the supply of power, raise agricultural production, and generally reconstruct the economy to provide additional jobs for the refugees, for the young men now in the armed forces, for the urban unemployed, and for the large numbers who will be entering the labor force in the coming decade. Specialized educational programs will be needed to improve the productive capacity of the young in both agriculture and industry. Inflation will have to be curtailed, imports drastically decreased, and exports greatly increased. Also, effective measures to limit the growth of population will be needed if the South Vietnamese are to maintain or improve their standard of living. A more equitable and efficient system of taxation is also essential if the gap between urban and rural populations is to decrease and the majority of the people are to benefit from future economic growth.

All this hinges on the outcome of the war and the degree to which the government can establish a viable political system and, particularly, on the degree to which this system enlists the villagers' enthusiasm and support for economic and social innovations. It also hinges on whether the government can expand exports sufficiently to become independent of foreign aid.

focus *on Land Reform in South Vietnam* *
—Roy L. Prosterman

Whatever else has happened in South Vietnam since the bloody 1968 Tet offensive from the North, some profound changes have been wrought in the countryside by the Thieu government.

A system of village elections has taken most of the power out of the hands of the old gentry-landlord group and put it in the hands of the tenants, smallholders, and *petit bourgeois.*

A program to arm the farmers has transferred much of the burden of the fighting from regular army (ARVN) strangers billeted in the villages, who often abused their power, to "Regional Force," "Popular Force," and "People's Self-Defense Force" units drawn from the villages themselves.

A program has been launched to attract at least half a million refugees and urban immigrants back to the villages.

The villages continue to hold three fifths of South Vietnam's population and to be vital to communist military and political planning; therefore, measures that profoundly affect the village have a great bearing on resolution of the conflict. Only strong local support for the government can

* Portions of this article appeared in *The Wall Street Journal,* Feb. 5, 1971, and in *Asian Survey,* Aug., 1970.

make "Vietnamization" a realistic prospect. Such support may also provide new leverage for achieving a political solution of the conflict at the Paris peace talks.

Of the reform measures, probably the most profound and central is the land-reform program. South Vietnam has had one of the highest rates of tenant farming in the world, and it has long been clear to most informed observers that the land problem is at the root of the Vietnamese conflict. During the critical period of the early 1960's, the Agricultural Census of South Vietnam (1960–61) indicated that only 257,000 of the 1,175,000 Mekong Delta farming families—22 per cent—owned all the land they worked. Their average holding was four and a half acres. Another 334,-000 families (28.5 per cent of the total) tilled an average mixed-tenure holding of six acres, four of which were rented, while 521,000 families (roughly 44 per cent) farmed an average of three and a half acres of land that was *totally* rented. Thus, in the Delta, more than seven farming families out of ten were substantially dependent on tenant farming. A Stanford Research Institute field work study of Vietnamese land tenure carried out for the U.S. Agency for International Development (AID) in late 1967 confirmed the continuing predominance of tenant farming. In its percentage of landlessness, the Mekong Delta thus qualified as one of the five worst areas of the world—along with Java (Indonesia), northeastern Brazil, the eastern tier of the Indian subcontinent (West Bengal, East Pakistan, and the contiguous parts of India), and the Huk country of central Luzon (Philippines)—and equaled or exceeded prerevolutionary China, Russia, and Cuba.

As the 1967 field work confirmed in detail, to be a tenant in the Mekong Delta meant paying an average of 34 per cent of the crop in rent to a landlord who supplied no inputs or support of any description; existing on the land as a tenant at the landlord's will or on a year-to-year basis; bearing the predominant risk of a crop failure, with the rent still due; and having virtually no disposable surplus after paying the rent. The Vietnamese field interviewers found that landownership was named five times more frequently than physical security as a matter of crucial concern. If tenants wanted to borrow, interest rates ranged from 60 per cent to 120 per cent *per year.*

The tenants' situation has been no better in the central lowlands. As the 1960–61 Agricultural Census showed, the typical family—403,000 out of 695,000—lived on a two-acre farm, one acre of which was rented. About 74,000 families held rented land only, their average holding being one and one tenth acres. Rents on the tenanted or sharecropped portion of lands in the central lowlands generally have averaged 50 per cent of the gross crop, although here the actual crop was the measure more often than an estimate made in advance. Security of tenure, however, was nonexistent here as in the Mekong Delta.

The Vietnamese situation was, statistically at least, as impressive and fully as explosive as that among the landless peasants of prerevolutionary Russia, China, or Cuba (where promises of land had played a crucial role, although ultimately followed by collectivization). Indeed, the Vietminh, in the war against the French, had made highly effective promises of land. By the time the Geneva Conference was convened in 1954, the Vietminh ruled 60 to 90 per cent of what is now South Vietnam. Support by the rural population accounted in substantial part for the crucial advantage that enabled the Vietminh to overcome the superior arms and manpower of the French.

As long ago as 1945, the Vietminh had enforced strict limitations on rent and interest rates in areas they controlled. Lands held by the French, communal lands, and the lands of "traitors" were confiscated and given to the poorer farmers. Beginning in 1953, the Vietminh undertook the second, more sweeping phase of their land-reform program, under a classification system similar to that which had been employed by the communist Chinese (landlord, rich peasant, middle peasant, poor peasant, and landless farm worker). In its first stage of implementation, this system was aimed at taking land from the first two groups and giving it to the last two. Wherever it was applied, the program utterly transformed the village social structure.

The sad history of the post-1954 years can be sketched only briefly here. In North Vietnam, the reform moved to a stage featuring bloody village "trials" of the landlords and—very broadly defined—rich peasants (100,000 died, according to the best estimates) and then to collectivization. In South Vietnam, President Ngo Dinh Diem missed the chance to carry out a competitive democratic land reform, on models such as those of Mexico, Japan, Taiwan, Bolivia, and South Korea (all of which had inaugurated sweeping land reforms before 1954). President Eisenhower urged land reform and other basic reforms upon Diem, but, unfortunately, this pressure was not translated into an effective reform program. Instead, under cover of a "rent-control" law dutifully approved by U.S. advisers, the Diem regime set about restoring the landlords to the countryside in the 1957–59 period. It is already becoming clear that this "negative" land-reform program (which affected the peasantry far more widely and profoundly than any of Diem's political repressions) was the key factor that laid the groundwork for the renewal of the conflict. Once it had acquiesed to Diem's downgrading of land reform, the U.S. aid mission had great difficulty in recognizing and conceding its blunder. Indeed, a report by a U.S. House of Representatives foreign operations subcommittee issued in March, 1968, roundly criticized the U.S. aid mission for failing to give strong support to land-reform measures.

Robert Sansom, a young member of Presidential assistant Henry Kissinger's staff, wrote in 1970: "The Americans offered the peasant a constitution; the Viet Cong offered him his land and with it the right to survive." All through the mid-1960's, the United States tinkered with the creation of a Western-style political structure in South Vietnam, while the Viet Cong dealt with the basic grievance of the population: land.

In addition to the "rent-control" program, Diem adopted an extremely mild law providing for the acquisition and redistribution of large holdings. The law allowed retention of 247 acres, eventually raised to 284 in most cases—a figure at least thirty times greater than the "retention limits" in the successful Asian land-reform programs of Japan, South Korea, and Taiwan. The acquisition program also suffered from multiple administrative defects. This part of Diem's program ground to a final halt in 1961, having provided benefits for only one out of ten tenant families. Provincial and local officials were allowed to retain and rent out the best of the acquired lands, which had been bought by the French Government from the former French landlords and given to Diem for distribution to the peasantry.

This left two sizable groups that identified the communists with land reform and the government in the South with the interests of the landed oligarchy. As many as one million peasants who had remained under Vietminh control even in Diem's heyday continued to live under the economic and social transformations wrought by "first-stage" (that is, precollectivization) communist land reform. The great mass of tenant farmers returned to Diem's control; most of them not only gained no benefits from his laws but actually found the government re-establishing a relationship that the Vietminh previously sundered. In the circumstances, it seemed not only logical but virtually inevitable that the Viet Cong should become the active successors of the Vietminh, building popular support throughout the countryside with the promise of maintaining and extending the Vietminh land reforms.

The consequences of this neglect, and of allowing the Viet Cong to proclaim themselves the party of agrarian reform, were grave. For it is deeply rooted rural support that gave the Vietnamese conflict the very strong "insurrection" or "civil war" flavor that it retained despite the highly publicized infusions of manpower from the North beginning in 1965. Indications of this support are not hard to find. In March, 1968, the *New York Times* noted that over long periods the Viet Cong had been able to recruit 7,000 men a month, with a 1967 low point of 3,500 men a month. Lieutenant Colonel William Corson, former head of the Marines' Combined Action Platoons (CAP) program, writing in the summer of 1968, noted that three fifths of these Viet Cong recruits could be regarded as volunteers or "soft-sell" enlistees. The common appeal in wide areas where Viet Cong land reform was in effect was "The movement has given you land; give us your son."

At least well into 1969, more than half of the communist-directed troops were native South Vietnamese. Villagers acted as porters for the communists, buried their supplies, gave them "safe houses," offered intelligence, set booby traps, and stood silently by as U.S. patrols walked into them. Even North Vietnamese main-force units were helpless in the populated areas unless peasants brought in and buried their supplies in advance and then kept quiet about the location of the depots.

Even before the 1968 Tet offensive, President Nguyen Van Thieu had indicated deep concern about the bearing of the land problem on the conflict. At that stage, landlords were still riding in on jeeps with ARVN to reassert their rights to lands in newly "secured" villages. Needless to say, this gave the farmers a perspective on "security" very different from the ARVN view. But Tet, the start of the U.S. scale-down, and U.S. political turmoil all served to sharpen Thieu's concern to get the farmers actively on his side. Thieu also had the results of the Stanford Research Institute project, showing the central role of the land issue.

He had, as well, the historical examples of completed communist land reforms versus completed democratic land reforms. For the bizarre reality, of course, is that, while the communists have successfully billed themselves in Vietnam (and elsewhere) as "land reformers," collectivization, which has been the universal "second stage" of communist land reform, has been vastly distasteful to the farmers and in most cases has failed to increase output. But the major noncommunist land reforms of this century (in Mexico, Japan, South Korea, Taiwan, Bolivia, and Iran, in that chronological order, perhaps soon to be followed by Peru) have led to large increases in agricultural production and have furnished a bulwark of political stability—including helping to defeat attempts to start guerrilla movements in Bolivia and South Korea by depriving the would-be revolutionaries of their "gut" issue. Narrower land reforms aimed at landless peasants who were supporting insurgencies in Malaysia and Venezuela have had the same stabilizing effect.

The first signs of real movement toward a competitive program came when Thieu, speaking to a gathering of provincial land-affairs officials at the National Agrarian Reform Congress on January 18, 1968, just before the Tet offensive, stated: "In the Social Reconstruction mission, land reform, as is natural, has to be placed on the top line. . . . Nevertheless, we must bravely acknowledge that until now the results obtained are lowest in consideration of the goal and its requirements."

Beginning in late 1968, Thieu proceeded to put into operation a series of broad reforms aimed at winning over the farmers. By early 1970, village elections had given the tenant farmers a three-to-one edge over the landlords in village council representation. A half million peasants were armed to serve in and around their own villages in the Regional Force, Popular Force, and People's Self-Defense Force units. Most important in kindling a new motivation to support Saigon, land reform began.

In September, 1968, the government declared that the process by which landlords evicted occupants and collected rents in newly "secured" areas would be ended. This declaration was followed by three administrative actions: (1) an order, issued in November, 1968, prohibiting officials or soldiers in newly secured villages from reinstalling landlords or helping to collect rents; (2) a circular of February, 1969, extending the prohibition to the private landlords themselves and making it effective until February, 1970; and (3) a circular issued in April, 1970, making the earlier prohibitions country-wide, apparently in anticipation that landlords in more secure areas might try to evict tenants and resume personal occupation in contemplation of further land-reform measures. In some villages, newly established Popular Force units chased out returning landlords at gunpoint.

The provisions of all these decrees were simple and sweeping, violations were by their nature highly public, publicity was widespread, and the word was out that the government meant business. Consequently violations were few. "Negative" land reform, at least, was dead.

The positive program got under way in earnest in mid-1969 with a decree providing for the universal free distribution of government-owned lands to the occupants, under a highly simplified title-granting procedure. As of today, close to 400,000 acres of these government lands (about one twelfth of the cultivated acreage in the country) have been distributed to over 100,000 families. The bulk of choice former French-owned lands have now been taken away from the provincial and local officials who were renting them out and distributed to the tenants farming them.

The biggest piece of the program, the Land-to-the-Tiller Bill, was submitted to the National Assembly in July, 1969. After an eight-month fight against landlord interests and Thieu's political opponents, the bill was passed in March, 1970, in virtually its original form. The widely publicized measure was proclaimed by Thieu on March 26, 1970, and the date was declared a national holiday.

This program calls for the free distribution of substantially all privately owned land that is not owner-cultivated. As in the case of government-owned land, the recipients are to be the tenant farmers who presently work it, and the parcels distributed are to be the ones presently worked. Thus the measure avoids virtually all of the administrative problems, and the loopholes for corruption, that traditional programs might have encountered. There is no picking and choosing among landlords or measuring the quantity of their tenanted land, since all the tenanted land is affected. There is no picking and choosing among tenants, since all present occupants are benefited. No surveyors are needed (aerial photos of the existing rice fields are used), and no payment is collected.

After minimal gearing up, distribution started in late August, 1970, and by March, 1971, final titles had been granted on 525,000 acres to 162,000 families. Title issuance is now approaching the rate of 2,000 a day.

Together, the government land and the Land-to-the-Tiller distributions have benefited nearly one third of all tenant farmers (representing 1.6 million people), and about one fifth of the cultivated land in the country has been distributed. By the end of 1971, a total of over a half million titles will have been issued, and by mid-1972 nearly all the 800,000 families who made their living as tenant farmers in 1968 (the others having fled to the cities or become refugees) will have become owner-cultivators. By then three fifths of all the cultivated land in South Vietnam will have been distributed. Many refugee families will also be resettled on abandoned or government-owned lands in the Delta on the same terms.

The cost of all this—or at least 95 per cent of it, excluding a fringe of high-priced lands along the coast that may or may not be taken—will be about $400 million in cash and bonds. This figure, representing the full value of the land, is equal to the cost of about five days of the war during its 1968–69 peak. The Nixon Administration has agreed to furnish $140 million of this amount in commodity support if Congress approves, and Congress has now approved the initial requests totaling $40 million.

Thus, for the first time, the government of South Vietnam is striking at the roots of Viet Cong rural support, at the single issue that, over the years, has motivated large numbers of peasants to support the Viet Cong in manifold ways and many more to be at best apathetic toward Saigon. The results thus far are encouraging in terms of both political and military impact.

It is to be hoped that, as a result of the Vietnam war, the United States will come to understand more fully the relationship between land-tenure grievances and insurgency and will reorder the priorities of its aid programs to such nations as Brazil, India, and the Philippines.

Suggested Readings

American University. *Area Handbook for North Vietnam; Area Handbook for South Vietnam.* Washington, D.C.: U.S. Government Printing Office, 1967. Comprehensive studies of social, political, and economic aspects of the areas and their national security.

Council on Vietnamese Studies *et al.* "Vietnam: Politics, Land Reform, and Development in the Countryside." *Asian Survey,* X, no. 8 (Aug., 1970). A symposium issue with papers from the Council's conference at Asia House in New York, April, 1970.

Joint Development Group. *The Postwar Development of the Republic of Vietnam: Policies and Programs.* New York: Praeger, 1970. Comprehensive and specific programs for the development and reconstruction of postwar South Vietnam.

MOLE, ROBERT L. *The Montagnards of South Vietnam: A Study of Nine Tribes.* Rutland, Vt.: Tuttle, 1970. An analysis of varying political and social structures, religions, and economic activities of nine Montagnard tribes.

New York *Times. The Pentagon Papers.* New York: Bantam, 1971. Excerpts from a Pentagon study of American participation in the Vietnam war.

PROSTERMAN, ROY L. "Land Reform in South Vietnam: A Proposal for Turning the Tables on the Viet Cong." *Cornell Law Review,* LIII, no. 1 (Nov., 1967). Contains the initial recommendation for the sweeping and simplified approach that the Thieu government ultimately adopted.

SANSOM, ROBERT. *The Economics of Insurgency.* Cambridge, Mass.: MIT

Press, 1970. A discussion of the rural Vietnamese economy by a member of Henry Kissinger's staff.

Stanford Research Institute. *Land Reform in Vietnam*. Menlo Park, Calif.: 1968. A comprehensive work analyzing land ownership, tenurial relationships, and government measures to change the land-tenure structure in South Vietnam, prepared for the Republic of Vietnam and the U.S. Agency for International Development.

"Vietnam's Postwar Development: A Symposium." *Asian Survey*, XI, no. 4 (April, 1971). Topical papers considering South Vietnam's postwar economic and political problems.

See also Suggested Readings for Part I, pp. 57–59.

10 MALAYSIA

Kenneth Thompson

*A Humid Land • The People • Farming, Fishing, and
Forestry • Mines and Manufacturing • Recent Tensions •
Questions for the Future*

Until quite recently the term Malaysia was used to signify the British-
ruled Malay Peninsula together with the island groups extending from
Sumatra to the Moluccas. Now the Federation of Malaysia, or simply
Malaysia, consists of the southern part of the Malay Peninsula (excluding
Singapore) and the former British Borneo colonies of Sarawak and Sabah.

Politically and economically the federation is dominated by its mainland
component, the peninsula. Indeed, the Malay Peninsula has long occupied an important place in world affairs—more important than its
small size might perhaps suggest. In prehistoric times it was a physical
and cultural link between mainland Asia and the islands to the southeast. It later became the home of advanced civilizations, such as the
eighth-century Sri Vijaya Buddhist Empire and the fourteenth-century
Javanese Hindu Empire known as Majapahit. During the following centuries, its inhabitants were converted to Islam, and the peninsula became
a center for the dissemination of this religion throughout Southeast Asia.
In the colonial era it became a great commercial outpost for a succession
of European nations.

The first Europeans to come were the Portuguese (1511), seeking the
riches of the Spice Islands. They captured the port of Malacca, strategically located for control of the trade between the Indian Ocean and the
West and the South China Sea and the East. This base flourished until
1641, when the Portuguese were ousted by the Dutch. Under their rule
the port's prosperity declined: They were commercially active in South-

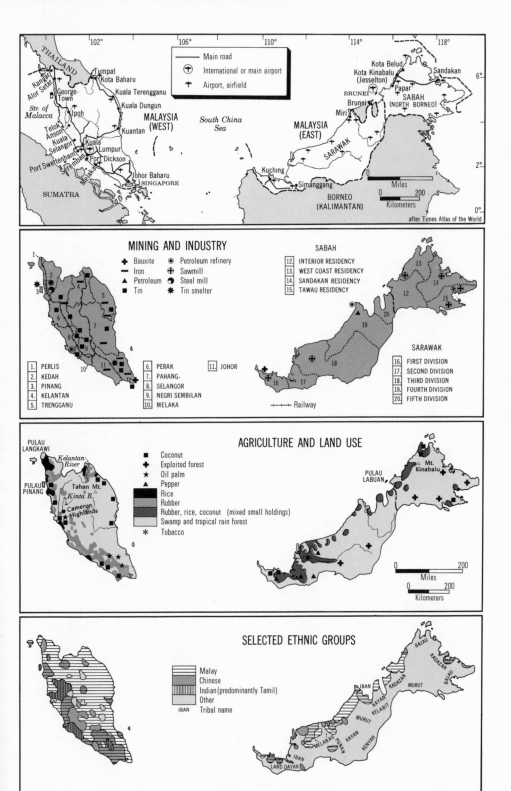

MALAYSIA

east Asia, but concentrated their trade at Batavia (now Djakarta), Java.

Next on the scene were the British. Their first foothold was established in 1786, at Pinang (Penang). In 1819 the intrepid empire-builder Thomas Stamford Raffles founded Singapore on an island just south of the tip of the peninsula. Five years later the British took over Malacca and, in the course of the following decades, gradually instituted protectorates over the several small sultanates in the main river valleys of the peninsula. Perak, Selangor, and Negri Sembilan were acquired in 1874, Pahang in 1888, Perlis Kedah, Kelantan, and Trengganu in 1909, and Johor in 1914. British control over this conglomeration of states began to be surrendered in 1957, when the independent Federation of Malaya (consisting of the peninsula territories) came into being. In 1963, Singapore, British North Borneo (Sabah), and Sarawak joined with the Federation of Malaya to form Malaysia. Brunei declined to join the new federation at the outset and Singapore withdrew in 1965. The rationale behind the establishment of an enlarged federation of former British territories was the expectation that the weak units would draw strength from the association. Time alone will tell whether this was shrewdly planned decolonization or merely a political delaying action.

A Humid Land

Stretching between latitudes 1° and 7° N., Malaysia's two parts—mainland West Malaysia and insular East Malaysia—are separated by about 400 miles of South China Sea at their closest. Together, they cover some 128,400 square miles of lush, humid land. West Malaysia is the smaller component of the nation, with 50,800 square miles.

The landscape is essentially one of hills and alluvial lowlands bordering extensive interior uplands. In West Malaysia the uplands culminate in Tahan Mountain (7,186 feet) and in East Malaysia in Mount Kinabalu (13,455 feet), the loftiest peak in Southeast Asia. But most of the country is below the 3,000-foot level, and the highlands generally represent a less serious obstacle to travel than do the dense forests or tracts of swamp.

Because of its location, close to the equator, its marine setting, and its generally low elevations, Malaysia has constantly high temperatures and copious rainfall. Shade temperatures average between 70° and 90° F., with only slight seasonal and daily variations, except, of course, in the highlands, where much greater extremes occur. Rainfall varies considerably but is everywhere abundant: even the driest places average 65 inches annually, most of the lowlands get about 100 inches, and parts of Sarawak average 160. Not infrequently fantastically heavy rains bring disastrous floods that destroy crops and turn roads into rivers. In Trengganu, 15½ inches of rain fell in a single day about fifty years ago, and the total for that month was more than six feet!

Although Malaysia forms part of monsoon Asia, the typical monsoon rhythm of winds and rain is not so pronounced here as in countries to the north. The northeast monsoon, from November to March, does bring strong winds and heavy rains to the eastern coast of the peninsula, but the full force of the southwest monsoon, from June to September, is usually broken by the island of Sumatra, and winds and rain are light. Away from the east coast, the heaviest rains occur during the transition periods of April–May and October–November. Humidities remain uncomfortably high for most of the year.

In the hothouse atmosphere of the lowlands the vegetation is naturally luxuriant tropical rainforest, with towering trees, well over 100 feet high, topped by a thick green canopy laced with great climbing plants and studded with brilliant flowers. Despite considerable cutting in the more accessible areas, especially the western and northern parts of the peninsula, nearly three fourths of the nation is still forested.

The People

Although during the past century a large number of immigrants have come in, attracted by job opportunities in the rubber plantations and tin mines, Malaysia is relatively sparsely peopled and living standards are much higher than in most Asian nations. The total population, estimated at nearly 11 million in 1970, consists of Malays (about 45 per cent), Chinese (about 35 per cent), and Indians and Pakistanis (about 9 per cent). The Malaysian population is increasing rapidly; at present rates it will double in twenty-five years.

The Malays are mostly in West Malaysia, especially in the rural areas, and they consider themselves the indigenous people, although most of them are descendants of fairly recent immigrants from what is now Indonesia. The Malays are Muslims (Sunni) in religion and have their own language, Malay, which is now the national language. It is hoped that spreading use of a single national language will have a unifying effect on the nation's diverse population, but many of the non-Malays have been slow to adopt it. Except for the many Malays employed in government service, Malays have generally remained aloof from wage-earning, preferring their traditional rural occupations, such as rice and coconut growing and fishing.

China and what is now Malaysia have had contacts for centuries, but the Chinese were not numerous in Malaysia until recently. Mostly Cantonese-speaking from the south, the Chinese brought with them Confucianism and a myriad of associations, secret societies, and guilds. The Chinese dominate commercial activities and provide most of the workers in the tin and manufacturing industries. They are also numerous on rubber and pineapple estates and in truck farming. Most Chinese in Malaysia are urban dwellers. Regarded as transients by themselves and their Malay neighbors until recently, the Chinese formed, and continue to form, a distinct and exclusive community.

The other substantial minority group in Malaysia, nearly all in West Malaysia, is composed of comparatively recent immigrants mainly from South India and Pakistan. Like the Chinese, they form a distinctly alien group, but in contrast to the Chinese they have achieved only modest economic power and work chiefly as laborers.

In East Malaysia Malays are a minority (somewhat over 13 per cent) and Chinese make up nearly 30 per cent of the population. The most numerous group (some 300,000) are the Iban (Sea Dayak), settled mainly along the coasts and rivers of Sarawak. The Iban, who traditionally lived in communal longhouses, used to be notorious for their weird and barbaric custom of headhunting, which had a minor renaissance during World War II. The other major indigenous group in Sarawak is the Melanau, considerably influenced by the Malays and converted to Islam. Sabah's most important indigenous group is the Kadazan, a lowland rice-growing people. Other groups in Sabah are the cattle-raising Bajau on the coasts and the relatively primitive and reclusive Murut of the interior.

With so many diverse ethnic and linguistic groups, Malaysia's educational system has been under considerable strain. Since confederation the movement has been toward academic centralization and away from the nineteenth-century school system organized along ethnic-cultural lines —Malay, Chinese, English, and Tamil (Indian). With the institution of Malay as the national language, it became the main language in education, with English second. Resistance among the Chinese is strong because their children are thus forced to be trilingual if they are to maintain cultural ties and also advance in Malay society. Chinese schools still exist, but the government is making vigorous efforts to increase assimila-

Malaysia is establishing large-scale land-settlement and development schemes to bring unexploited land into production, increase employment opportunities, and diversify crops so as to broaden the base for exports and reduce imports. Oil palm beans, pictured above, are one of the new products being grown for export.

tion through government grants that require adoption of the national language and adherence to the national syllabus. These efforts have been stepped up since 1968, when the government alleged that Chinese propaganda was being disseminated through the Chinese schools. The conflict over education continues to be a major divisive factor in Malaysian society.

Farming, Fishing, and Forestry

Agriculture is the mainstay of the Malaysian economy and supports more than half the total labor force. Agricultural workers, however, generate only slightly more than one third the value of the national product. This disproportion is less pronounced than in many other Southeast Asian nations and suggests a relatively prosperous agriculture. Farming is dominated by the production of industrial crops for export, principally rubber and oil palm.

About 40 per cent of the world's natural rubber comes from Malaysia. Rubber cultivation was introduced in 1877 from Brazil via Kew Gardens, in England. Approximately two thirds of all cultivated land in the country is now devoted to rubber, on both large estates and small holdings. Of the 4.5 million acres of rubber, about half are in estates, usually managed by British or Chinese with Indian labor, where every operation is done in the latest scientific manner—from planting, to first tapping when the tree is seven years old, to the making of rubber sheet, to the final sorting. The small producer—most often a Chinese or Malay family—is beginning to threaten the primacy of the estates, but these still produce more rubber, of better quality, than do the small holdings.

Oil-palm production has increased greatly in recent years, with most of the acreage located in Johor, Selangor, and Perak (West Malaysia). Because the crop is bulky and requires prompt and relatively complicated processing at or near the production site, the oil palm industry is very largely an estate operation.

Compared to some other areas of Southeast Asia, the copra and coconut oil industry has remained small. Even so, the coconut is the most widely grown industrial crop after rubber. The main coconut-growing areas are along the western coast of West Malaysia, production is largely in the hands of small holders, and most of the copra and oil is used locally.

Pineapples are one of the few commercial crops that can be grown on peaty soils, with which Malaysia is well provided. Production of canned and fresh pineapple, mainly for export, is from estates and small holdings operated by Chinese, mainly in western Johor. Other cash crops include tea, produced on estates chiefly in the highlands of Pahang, West Malaysia. Tobacco, pepper, and abaca (a fiber) are other minor cash crops.

Emphasis on cash crops for export leaves Malaysia deficient in food-stuffs. Rice, the main food grain, is grown on alluvial lowlands through-out the country, especially the northwestern coastal plain and the Kelan-tan Delta of West Malaysia. About 20 per cent of the rice crop is grown in East Malaysia, especially in southern Sarawak. Rice growing is largely in the hands of Malay small holders; the milling and marketing are Chinese monopolies. The undesirability of heavy dependence on rice im-ports, chiefly from Thailand, has been acknowledged by the Malaysian Government for some time. Attempts to increase rice production through such measures as subsidies; improvements in drainage, water, and fertilizer use; double-cropping; the use of high-yielding seeds; and land-tenure reform have met with only limited success. Malaysia continues to be an

Courtesy United Nations

Studies of food consumption in Malaysia reveal that the average diet is seriously deficient in some important nutrients. To improve the quantity and variety of locally grown food, the government has embarked on an agricultural development program. In the Food Technology Research and Development Centre, established with the assistance of various United Nations agencies, students are learning mod-ern methods of handling, storing, processing, and marketing local foods.

importer of rice, and Malaysian rice-production costs are about double those of Thailand and Burma. Other food crops include tapioca, sweet potatoes, sago, sugar cane, corn, peanuts, vegetables, fruits, and spices.

Livestock play a small role in the farm economy, principally because local fodder is scarce. Hogs, raised mainly by Chinese, are the most numerous; buffalo, used as draft animals, are a common sight in the rice fields, as are goats and chickens everywhere. Cattle are raised in many areas.

The second staple in the Malaysian diet is fish. Every river and stream is fished, and fish culture is widespread. Along the coasts of the South China Sea fishing is the prime occupation in many small villages, but dependence on traditional methods has kept catches relatively small and restricted to local markets. Modern commercialized fisheries based on ports along the western coast of West Malaysia, together with more recent developments in Sabah, provide most of the nation's fish, mainly mackerel, whitebait, and prawns.

Much of Malaysia is covered with tropical rainforest. Marketable tree species are rather few and hard to find among the dozens of unwanted ones, but operations are being modernized, and the industry is rapidly gaining importance in the economy; it also now ranks as the third largest foreign-exchange earner. About 25 per cent of the world's supply of tropical hardwoods, mainly Dipterocarps, comes from Malaysia. Lumber is produced in all parts of the country, but especially in Sabah, where it is a major source of revenue.

Mines and Manufacturing

Tin has been mined for centuries in the Malay Peninsula, attracting both Chinese and European entrepreneurs and Chinese and Indian laborers. During the latter part of the nineteenth century, thousands of Chinese entered Malaysia to fill the demand for labor created by the burgeoning tin industry. Although large producers dominate the tin mining industry, the vast majority of mines are actually very small operations, generally run by Chinese. This overwhelming Chinese presence, which has now permeated all economic spheres, has contributed to intense rivalries among the major ethnic groups. But, on the other hand, both tin and rubber have contributed greatly to economic development. The lucrative trade in both has filled the treasury coffers and provided funds to build the basic infrastructure, including a good transport system. West Malaysia currently accounts for about 40 per cent of the world output of tin, with well over half coming from the Kinta Valley, the greatest tin field in the world.

Apart from tin, Malaysia's mineral resources appear to be modest. Iron ore occurs in various areas, with production mainly from Trengganu, Kelantan, Perak, and Pahang. Since there is only a small iron and steel industry, nearly all the ore is exported, the chief customer being Japan. Bauxite, the ore of aluminum, is produced in Johor and Sarawak. There is a small production of petroleum in East Malaysia, and there are hopes of making significant offshore discoveries of oil. Other minerals, produced in small quantities, include gold and some coal. The area is well endowed with clay, limestone, sand, and stone for use in pottery, glass, and construction materials. The Mamut copper mine in Sabah, which will be opened in 1972, has an estimated reserve of 75 million tons.

Only a modest amount of hydroelectric power is generated (chiefly in the Cameron Highland), but the nation's many rivers offer excellent possibilities for the future, and plans are under way to make more use of this potential.

Beyond the processing of tin, rubber, pineapples, copra, palm oil, rice, lumber, and such, there is relatively little industry. Thus far the Malaysian economy has been based mainly on export agriculture and commerce. There are, however, a growing number of factories, including steel plants, cement plants, oil refineries, and several producing electrical equipment. Mining and agricultural machinery, transport equipment, construction materials, and metal products are manufactured. Numerous plants, mainly in West Malaysia, are engaged in making a wide variety of consumer goods of the simpler types. The Klang Valley from Kuala Lumpur (the national capital) to Port Swettenham is the greatest manufacturing center and is becoming an urban-industrial complex.

In recent years the Malaysian Government has attempted to encourage the growth and diversification of manufacturing through various tax incentives. It is emphasizing particularly the establishment of factories to make goods that are now imported so as to reduce the amount of money spent abroad and simultaneously increase the amount available for local development projects. Current plans also offer encouragement to industries that require little capital investment *and* generate employment opportunities. The present rate of unemployment in the nation as a whole is unacceptably high, about 9 per cent, and the problem is especially acute among the fifteen-to-twenty-five age group, where unrest and alienation are most likely to occur. A third objective of the government is to bring small industries and industrial training centers to towns and rural areas so as to increase employment opportunities among the "have-not" Malays, many of whom have lacked incentives and skills to enter the labor market. It is true that in practically every town and village men and women make silverware, baskets, mats, and clothing and other handicrafts, but with rising incomes more and more people are demanding products of modern industry such as bicycles, cars, and radios.

Export revenues are derived largely from rubber and tin, some 45 and 23 per cent, respectively, in 1970. Other exports include food, beverages, and tobacco; copra and coconut oil; palm oil and kernels. Imports consist mainly of rice and other foods, mineral fuels, textiles, machinery, and vehicles. Malaysia's leading trading partners are Singapore, Japan, and Great Britain.

Recent Tensions

Perhaps most valuable among British accomplishments in the lands that now make up West Malaysia, besides the large-scale development of rubber and other commercial crops and of tin mining, was the creation of an effective, integrated transport system. Railroads and roads were built to link producing areas with urban centers and ports that developed as a result. This, more than anything else, promoted unification of government services and of the area into a single political and economic unit.

British rule may also be held responsible, however, for laying the foundations of some of the nation's most serious problems. It tended to favor Malayans: Tax moneys were lavished on Malay social services, only Malayans could advance in government service, and much of the best farm land was reserved for them. Recent immigrants, such as Chinese and Indians, received comparatively little official attention, and scant effort was made to assimilate them as citizens. They established their own schools and preserved their economic, linguistic, religious, cultural, and ethnic distinctiveness. This governmental rejection reflected a Malayan antipathy toward the immigrants, which led, in the 1930's, to enactment of restrictive immigration laws. There was a Malayan fear that the Chinese immigrants would eventually swamp them in their own country by sheer numbers. This long-standing racial ill-will became acute under the Japanese occupation during World War II, when the two principal groups generally took opposing positions.

Considerable tension continues today. The present Constitution appears to do less than justice to the Chinese and Indian elements: Malay is the official language and Islam the national religion. During the 1960's there were frequent outbreaks of strife, including riots in May, 1969, in which nearly 200 persons died. At the time some sober observers believed that this presaged the end of Malaysia. Since then the government has been following a moderate and conciliatory policy in the critical areas of citizenship and "nationalization" of minority cultural institutions, particularly schools. It is also attempting to reduce the gap between the small affluent group, many of whom are Chinese engaged in mining, industry, and commerce, and the large have-not group, many of whom are Malay farmers. Efforts on behalf of the Malays include a variety of rural development schemes aimed at improving farming methods to raise productivity and extending educational and training facilities to increase job opportunities.

Unfortunately, Malaysia has also endured considerable political strife, both internal and external, since 1948. In West Malaysia, communists (mainly Chinese) were in armed revolt, engaging in murderous and destructive raids, slashing rubber trees, and carrying out other types of sabotage. Communist terrorists, waging a guerrilla campaign from the forests, at one time came close to producing chaos. Extensive military countermeasures were required to restore some measure of peace. Later, a far-reaching program was initiated for the resettlement of several hundred thousand Chinese in newly built communities, each provided with shopping areas, vegetable gardens, schools, dispensaries, and other local facilities. Although the danger of revolutionary communism is now much diminished, it is still a consideration that cannot be ignored.

Questions for the Future

The biggest question for the future of Malaysia concerns the very survival of the federation. The ethnic-cultural diversity of the nation, particularly its division into two contrasting major communities, Malay and Chinese, and the lack of affinity between West and East Malaysia cause many to doubt that this assemblage of peoples and cultures constitutes a viable political unit. Malaysia is now entering the critical maturation phase of its development, but it does so with a remarkable record of successes. It was able to withstand the internal threat of communist subversion during the "Emergency" (begun in 1948 and ceremonially ended in 1960) and the pressures resulting from Indonesia's "confrontation" during 1963–66. Despite the often conflicting aspirations of the Chinese, who largely control economic power, and the Malays, who remain predominant in political affairs, overt large-scale hostilities have been relatively rare in recent years. Equally significant is the continued economic growth of the nation, which has now raised its per capita income to one of the highest levels in Asia.

Economic problems remain, of course, including the old concern about agriculture's narrow commercial basis for export markets. Apart from considerable success with oil palm, agricultural diversification programs have made only limited progress. Diversification is sought by some Malaysians as a means of reducing present dependence on imported food supplies. It is also considered desirable to break away from the current reliance on rubber. The government is offering attractive financial incentives to encourage the setting up of plants to produce crumb rubber, which brings higher prices than sheet rubber and also larger returns to the producer. But the demand for natural rubber may be seriously affected by development of alternative materials. And what effects will these materials have on rubber prices? Changes in this technology could precipitate economic disaster. Similarly, disaster could strike as a result of the increasing use and development of tin substitutes, although this seems less likely than the gradual exhaustion of tin-ore reserves.

Despite such problems, however, Malaysia has better grounds for optimism than the other newly independent nations of Southeast Asia. It is richly endowed by nature; it is not overcrowded; it benefits from decades of investment, not only in agriculture and industry, but also in education, transportation, the civil service, and in all the other features essential to continued economic and social evolution.

Suggested Readings

American University. *Area Handbook for Malaysia and Singapore.* Washington, D.C.: U.S. Government Printing Office, 1965. A comprehensive study of social, political, and economic aspects of the area and its national security.

BAHRIN, TUNKU SHAMSUL. "A Preliminary Study of the Fringe Alienation Schemes in West Malaysia." *Journal of Tropical Geography,* XXVIII (June, 1969), pp. 75–83. Discusses the goals and relative success of these schemes.

GULLICK, J. M. *Malaysia.* New York: Praeger, 1969. Traces the history of

Malaya, Singapore, and the Borneo territories and examines some current political, social, and economic problems of Malaysia.

GUNGWU, WANG, ed. *Malaysia: A Survey.* New York: Praeger, 1964. Discusses the natural and human structure of Malaysia, its history, society and culture, economy, politics and government, and position in a changing world.

HO, ROBERT. "Rice Production in Malaya: A Review of Problems and Prospects." *Journal of Tropical Geography,* XXIX (Dec., 1969), pp. 21–32. An attempt to determine the planned and longer-term prospects of the West Malaysian rice industry.

JAIN, RAVINDRA K. *South Indians on the Plantation Frontier in Malaya.* New Haven, Conn.: Yale University Press, 1970. This discussion of the changing influence of social strata is valuable in studying the evolution of similar societies elsewhere in the less developed nations.

Malaysia: Official Year Book, 1969. Malaysia: Government Press, 1971. A reference work prepared by the Malaysian Ministry of Information and Culture, with the cooperation of many other government departments and national organizations.

OOI JIN-BEE. *Land, People, and Economy in Malaya.* London: Longmans, 1963. Deals with the physical environment; the evolution, distribution, and composition of the population; and economic patterns and prospects.

See also Suggested Readings for Part I, pp. 57–59, and Suggested Readings: Singapore, pp. 183–84.

11 SINGAPORE

Yue-man Yeung *

*Historical Background • Man and Land • Urban Growth •
Economic Boom • The Jurong Industrial Estate • The Port •
The Social and Cultural Fronts • focus on Public
Housing and Urban Renewal*

With pomp and ceremony, Singapore recently observed the 150th anniversary of its founding by Sir Thomas Stamford Raffles. As a sovereign independent republic, however, it is only six years old. The island nation's modicum of natural resources, limited land area, and large and powerful neighbors gave many a pessimist doubts about its future. But as a result of determined and well-guided efforts, the republic is now riding the crest of a period of prosperity. The annual per capita income reached S$2,437 (U.S. $812) in 1969, second only to Japan in Asia. There is a steady flow of foreign capital into the country, and trade and exports continue to increase. Steadily and visibly, the various social programs have also been bearing fruit. The success story began in 1959 with the ascent of the present People's Action Party (PAP) government to power.

Historical Background

Ancient Singapura—the Lion City—was given its name by a prince of the Sumatra-based Srivijaya Empire. Its fortunes waxed and waned with the battles fought among the feuding princes, but it could not vie with the then flourishing Malacca. Modern Singapore dates from February 6,

* Thanks are due to Professors Norton Ginsburg and Ooi Jin-Bee for helpful comments on this article.

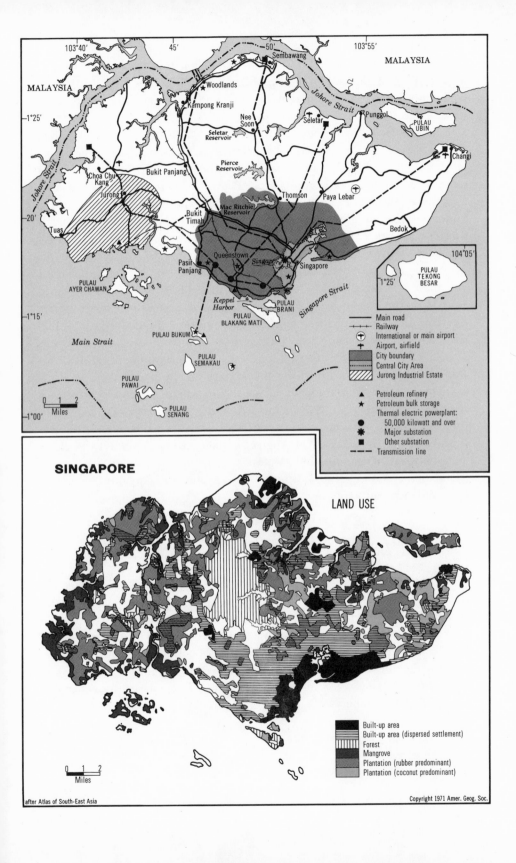

103°40' 45' 50' 103°55'

MALAYSIA

MALAYSIA

Sembawang

Woodlands

Kampong Kranji

1°25'

Nee Soon

Seletar

Punggol

PULAU UBIN

Seletar Reservoir

Pierce Reservoir

Changi

Choa Chu Kang

Bukit Panjang

Johore Strait

Thomson

Paya Lebar

Jurong

20'

Mac Ritchie Reservoir

Bukit Timah

Tuas

Bedok

104°05'

Queenstown

Singapore R.

Singapore

PULAU TEKONG BESAR

1°25'

Pasir Panjang

PULAU AYER CHAWAN

Keppel Harbor

PULAU BRANI

Singapore Strait

1°15'

PULAU BLAKANG MATI

Main Strait

PULAU BUKUM

Main road

Railway

International or main airport

PULAU SEMAKAU

Airport, airfield

City boundary

Central City Area

Jurong Industrial Estate

PULAU PAWAI

0 1 2

Miles

Petroleum refinery

Petroleum bulk storage

Thermal electric powerplant:

1°00'

PULAU SENANG

● 50,000 kilowatt and over

✳ Major substation

■ Other substation

--- Transmission line

SINGAPORE

LAND USE

Built-up area

Built-up area (dispersed settlement)

Forest

Mangrove

Plantation (rubber predominant)

Plantation (coconut predominant)

0 1 2

Miles

1819, when far-sighted Lord Raffles concluded a historic treaty with the Temenggong of Johore (Johor) establishing a trading post on the island on behalf of Britain. This initiated an era of rapid population growth and trade expansion.

Strategically located between the South China Sea and the Indian Ocean, Singapore was envisioned by Raffles as a trading post of great potential. The combination of a stable government and a thriving entrepôt trade soon attracted immigrants from China in large numbers, and also, to a lesser degree, from India. In 1824 Singapore became part of the Straits Settlements, along with Penang (Pinang) and Malacca. Before long, it overtook the others in population and economic emportance. When British influence was extended to the Malay Peninsula in 1867, the Straits Settlements became a colony. British rule continued uninterruptedly until Singapore was conquered by the Japanese in 1942. With the end of World War II in the Pacific in 1945, Singapore passed into British hands again, but this time in a changed anticolonial political climate. With a predominant Chinese majority, Singapore was separately governed as a British Crown Colony, and did not join the Federation of Malaya for fear of arousing opposition from the Malays on the peninsula.

Internal self-rule was achieved in 1959, when Singapore became a state. On September 16, 1963, it merged with Malaya, Sarawak, and Sabah to form the Federation of Malaysia. For Singapore the experience was short-lived and traumatic. On August 9, 1965, owing to underlying cleavages between Singapore and Malaysia ranging over many issues, the island state was separated from Malaysia and subsequently became a fully independent republic.

Man and Land

Singapore, lying seventy-seven miles north of the equator and at the extremity of the Malay Peninsula, is one of the smallest nations on earth. It has 225 square miles of land, 8 per cent of which is made up of sixty-two smaller islands, still as yet relatively undeveloped. In general the land is low-lying, with few striking topographical features. Bukit Timah, the highest point on the island, reaches to only 581 feet. More conspicuous perhaps are man-made features. Three large water bodies, used for water conservation and recreation, dominate the center of the island.

The geologic structure of the main island exhibits a clear-cut threefold division. The western section, of Triassic sedimentary strata, is bordered by a sizable batholithic granite intrusion that forms the present topographically conspicuous central part. The eastern third, geologically the youngest, is a raised marine platform formed by semiconsolidated, waterborne materials, and now heavily incised by small streams. Several low hills dot this little-varied landscape.

Climatically, Singapore is characterized by the usual equatorial uniformity. Temperature regimes demonstrate little annual, seasonal, or diurnal variation, resulting in a monotonously hot and humid climate. The mean annual temperature is 80°F., with an insignificant range of less than four degrees. In spite of these averages, one must not overlook the areal differences in sunshine and solar radiation, causing notably dissimilar microclimatic types in urban as well as rural areas. The rainfall averages 95.7 inches per year, but yearly fluctuations are considerable.

The chief asset of the physical environment does not lie in the land itself, nor in the occurrence of significant mineral resources. Rather, the natural endowment hinges on locational attributes, in relation both to other parts of the world and to a natural deep-water harbor: Whoever controls Singapore controls the Straits and the trade route between India and China.

Another asset that Singapore can claim is its people. Its 2.1 million inhabitants, largely of Chinese origin, have inherited from their immigrant forefathers qualities of resilience, determination, and industry. On the other hand, both in outlook and characteristics, the present population differs markedly from the past.

For a long time, the population of Singapore and Malaya was unsettled and transient. Immigrants from China and India came to seek their fortune and had little desire to make the Nanyang region (the "Southern Seas") their permanent home. In those days Singapore gained more from migration surplus than from natural increase. The sex ratio of the population was skewed, with a sizable surplus of males over females. Most of these early settlers were poor and illiterate; some even "sold" themselves for the passage money to Singapore. With dedication and a capacity for hard work, some became millionaires, but the majority stayed poverty-stricken for generations.

After 1930, the inflow of men was restricted, in an attempt to improve the sex balance. In 1938, however, a quota of 500 a month for female immigrants also was imposed. By 1969 the sex distribution was 1,065 males per 1,000 females. After World War II the population became more stable. A steadily larger proportion of the people are now locally born, and the population has become increasingly youthful. In 1966, 44 per cent of the people were under fifteen years old, 51 per cent were between fifteen and nineteen, and only 5 per cent were sixty or over. At the same time, literacy has improved immensely. In 1969, one quarter of the entire population was in school.

The convergence, in Singapore, of historical migrational streams of people from three major culture blocs of Asia has resulted in a multi-racial population, whose characteristics have remained more or less unchanged to this day. According to the 1970 census, the percentage distribution of ethnic groups is as follows: Chinese, 76.2; Malays, 15; Indians and Pakistanis, 7; and others, 1.8. True, cultural diversity can enrich the daily life and character of a society, but it also can be a cause of political agitation and a source of difficulty for development policies.

With more stringent regulations governing immigration, population growth after the war and in the past ten years in particular was due mainly to natural increase. In this regard, a recent precipitous decline in fertility is most noteworthy. Primarily as a result of attitudinal changes and an intensified family-planning campaign, the crude birth rate fell from 42.7 per thousand in 1957 to 23.8 in 1968, and the rate of natural increase from 35.3 per thousand to 18.2. Consequently, the annual growth rate of population plunged from an alarming 4.4 per cent in 1957 to a manageable 1.5 per cent in 1970.

Urban Growth

Urban Singapore comprises 50 square miles, of which 3.2 square miles form the earliest developed and most congested central city area. Rural Singapore occupies only 175 square miles. However, the once favored distinction between "Singapore Town" and "Singapore Country" is gradually being replaced by a concept whereby the whole island is regarded as an urban complex. State and city or regional planning has gained currency since planning within the sole confines of the urban unit is no longer compatible with contemporary ideas.

Initially, urban development in Singapore followed orderly lines, as envisaged by Raffles. The results of his decision to delineate expansive areas for government use near the Singapore River and, to a lesser extent, to promote residential separation according to ethnic stock can still be seen in today's cityscape. For instance, imposing government buildings and the *padang* (literally, the field) north of the river still constitute a conspicuous and impressive portion of the skyline viewed from the sea. With regard to ethnic segregation, the heretofore identifiable groupings based on occupation, religion, and language or dialect have been increasingly blurred by modernizing and integrative tendencies.

For a long time after Raffles' era, haphazard urban growth was the order of the day. After what is now the central city area was laid out and built up, there was a considerable lag before urban development was extended to other parts of the island. Instead of a horizontal spread of the city commensurate with population growth, most of the immigrants throughout the nineteenth century converged on the congested urban area centering on the river. The result was one of the worst urban slums in the world. It was only after World War II, but especially since 1959, that slum clearance was pursued with vigor and success. By degrees, urban growth took on patterns in keeping with modern town-planning principles and in consideration of city-country relationships.

The most significant advance in urban development was the adoption in 1958 of a Master Plan which was a statutory, as distinguished from an advisory, document to guide future urban growth. It was to be revised and brought up to date every five years. Although this plan has served to direct and control development, it has outgrown its usefulness in the face of rapidly changing conditions, and a more flexible planning process is being sought.

Since September, 1967, Singapore has been benefiting in its urban-renewal and development program from the professional and technical expertise as well as financial assistance of the United Nations. Proposals have been advanced for long-term and island-wide development. Of five development concepts proposed, the United Nations Review Panel has recently endorsed the so-called Ring Plan, involving a bus- or rail-based mass rapid-transit system for the internal circulation of an anticipated 4 million people by 1992. Air traffic is expected to increase with the advent of the jumbo jets, and the plan recommends the construction of a second and a third airstrip at Changi, in the extreme east of the island. As regards urban growth, the plan calls for a first-priority, western-corridor extension to Jurong, followed by development toward the east. After 1982, development will proceed northward along major arteries of Woodlands and Thomson to meet emerging industrial complexes at Seleter, Sembawang, and possibly Woodlands.

At present urban redevelopment is taking place rapidly in the central city area. With the tendency for new construction to favor buildings thirty and more stories high, this old part of Singapore is rapidly changing beyond recognition. To expedite and encourage private development, the government in February, 1970, "decontrolled" eighty acres of land in the central city area, which had been under rent control since 1947. If this experiment works smoothly, more areas in the city center are likely to be similarly released for speedier redevelopment.

Economic Boom

Since 1968 Singapore has experienced an economic boom of unprecedented magnitude, which has astounded and inspired Singaporeans. So encouraging was the picture that the 1970 Budget Speech did not include any important new taxes. Economic development stemmed from three sources: industry, trade, and tourism. This did not come about overnight but is the deserved outcome of a full decade of painstaking planning and hard work.

When the PAP came to power in 1959, it was already obvious that, with a serious unemployment problem and thousands more entering the labor market each year, Singapore had to diversify its economic base by strengthening its entrepôt trade on the one hand and industrializing on the other. The expansion of employment opportunities was a stated goal of the First Development Plan, 1961–64. In fact, the unemployment problem, still not solved, almost overshadowed all other considerations in the planning and execution of development strategies. Currently unemployment stands at about 60,000, representing nearly 6 per cent of the labor force. However, the recent slowing down of the rate of population increase, coupled with an accelerated program of industrialization, holds promise for fuller employment in the future.

As a first step toward planned and orderly economic growth, the Economic Development Board was established in August, 1961, to direct and shape industrialization programs. It charted industrial sites at Jurong, Kallang Basin, Tanglin Halt, Kampong Ampat, Kallang Park, Tanjong Rhu, Tiong Bahru, Red Hill, and Kranji, all of which have since been taken over for management by the newly formed Jurong Town Corporation. To intensify the industrial drive, the Development Bank of Singapore and the International Trading Company Ltd. (Intraco) were established in 1968. A public company, the former is entrusted with the task of stimulating industrial development by providing loans for new industries and for modernizing and expanding existing ones. Intraco, a part-government and part-private trading organization, is devoted primarily to boosting the export drive.

The benefits of this promotion and planning within and outside Singapore are now being seen. Among them are an influx of foreign capital to finance a rapidly increasing number of industries, foreign or jointly owned. Thus far, much of this foreign investment has concentrated on petroleum and related industries, electronics, shipbuilding, and food and beverages, although the 1967 list of declared pioneer industries totaled 109, covering 395 products. Heading the list of foreign investors was Britain, followed by the United States and Japan.

Despite the inability of the newly established industries to absorb all the unemployed, the surge in manufacturing activities has gone far toward alleviating the problem. The annual number of jobs in the manufacturing sector increased from 5,000 in the period 1963–67 to about 15,000 in 1968–70. The number of people employed in this sector increased from 25,600 in 1959 to 89,800. Many of these improvements were attributable

Courtesy Ministry of Culture, Singapore

Chevrolet, Ford, Vauxhall, Morris, Renault, Mercedes Benz, and Volkswagen, among others, now have local assembly plants in Singapore. Automobile assembly not only is a major developing industry but is of great benefit to a host of related industries because locally produced tires, batteries, interior trimmings, and the like are used. In the decade 1959–69, private motor-car ownership more than doubled, rising to 130,088.

to the mushrooming of pioneer firms, which increased from only seven in 1961, when the vigorous industrial program began, to 236 (in production) at the beginning of 1970. They employed 35,000 workers as against 241 in 1961, and the value of output jumped from S$36 million to S$1,226 million over the same period. And these statistics have been notably bettered in the period since 1968.

Trade, unlike manufacturing, has had its ups and downs. It often fell prey to external political exigencies not within the control of the government. Rather than a de-emphasis on the entrepôt trade, which has always been the lifeblood of Singapore's economy, the over-all trade orientation maintained its traditional importing functions for the region, with new stress on export-oriented, locally made goods. Singapore-made products for export soared in value from S$179.1 million in 1961 to more than S$760 million in 1970. The entrepôt trade continues to be very healthy. In 1967, 54 per cent of the total imports were re-exported, consisting mainly of rubber, petroleum, coffee, sawn timber, and pepper. In that year, Singapore's trade with Malaysia accounted for 27.5 per cent of the total, and other leading Asian trading partners contributed another 22.5 per cent; major developed countries accounted for 23 per cent. Considering both imports and exports, the principal trading partners were Malaysia, Japan, Great Britain, and the People's Republic of China, in that order.

The current hotel construction boom reflects the actual and projected tourist increase; thirty or so hotels are still under construction. In 1968, a total of 298,535 visitors arrived (primarily by air) as compared with 90,871 in 1964. The number reached 360,000 in 1969 and is estimated to reach 800,000 by 1975. In view of a likely overcapacity of hotel rooms, hotels ceased to have pioneer status in late 1969. Mindful of the positive role of tourism in the economy, the Tourist Promotion Board has been stepping up its promotion campaigns overseas. At the same time, attempts are being made or planned to provide more tourist attractions at home.

The Jurong Industrial Estate

A large unproductive swamp at Jurong in west Singapore has been converted into a modern industrial park, which has become the showpiece-of industrial Singapore. Its present area of 7,340 acres is undergoing a second phase of expansion, which will add another 6,000 acres. In mid-

1970 there were more than 255 factories in production, with another 60 in various stages of construction.

The Jurong experiment provides a classic example of central planning and government initiative in blueprinting, swamp reclamation, laying of infrastructure, and setting of development policies and priorities. Land is leased at annual rentals amounting to 6 per cent of its land value for periods ranging from thirty to sixty years. To speed development and save time for local and foreign investors, standard factory buildings have been designed and built by the Jurong Town Corporation and are available for either sale or rental.

Until recently the major problem faced by industries in Jurong was a shortage of workers, who preferred jobs in more centrally located factories. The introduction of better bus services and the planning and gradual implementation of social amenities, including a 900-acre park, have greatly improved the situation. In 1968 there were 4,600 units of low-cost public housing for workers, 90 per cent of them occupied. More are under construction. Including dependents, the resident population in Jurong exceeded 16,000 in 1970.

The Port

For decades, the prosperity of Singapore has been inextricably linked with that of the port. Endowed with naturally deep water, a sheltered location, and freedom from typhoons, Keppel Harbor has been growing in strength since Singapore's founding. By the turn of the century, Singapore was already the seventh largest port in the world in shipping tonnage. In 1968 it outplaced London as the fourth, and at the current rate of expansion it is expected soon to replace Yokohama as the third.

The present flourishing port activities are in part related to the upswing of shipbuilding and ship-repairing industries thanks to the Singapore-based international petroleum explorations taking place in the region, and in part to the conversion of British military shipyards to commercial enterprises. In addition, because of the recent increased volume of trade, more ships are using the port facilities. With the present trend in world shipping in favor of bigger and faster ships, Singapore's share in shipping is going to be enlarged, not diminished. In anticipation of a busy container traffic, a container complex is being built in the East Lagoon in the three-mile deep-water wharf area of the Keppel. Jurong, too, has 3,000 feet of deep-water wharves with facilities for bulk cargo handling. Although the container berth is scheduled for completion only in 1972, the use of temporary facilities enabled more than 6,000 containers to be moved in 1970. The cargo tonnage increased by over 150 per cent between 1960 and 1970. To cope with the increasing traffic and for greater efficiency, the port has recently started operating on a round-the-clock, three-shift system. The turn-around time of a ship averages three days. Thus human endeavor, together with a favorable climate permitting year-round operation, accounts for the large volume of shipping that Singapore is physically able to handle.

The Social and Cultural Fronts

Unlike many governments in the less developed world, PAP is gradually realizing its election slogans. The government's achievements in terms of housing, education, and medical care in the last decade have gone far toward building the kind of society pledged. This should evoke no surprise, for in the First and Second Development Plants social development had a share of 32–40 per cent of the nation's budget.

With the political battle won in 1959, the PAP government has been concentrating, along with strengthening the economy, on social transformation and cultural integration. In these tasks, education has played a vital role.

There are four official languages: Malay, Chinese, Tamil, and English. The education policy ensures parity of treatment for these four streams of education. Parents are free to choose any medium of instruction for their children, and all streams share a common education structure and syllabus. The major shortcoming of the education system before 1969, however, lay in the disharmony between the goals of education and the needs of society. In that year 86 per cent of the pupils were in academic schools, while technical and vocational schools had 14 per cent. As a consequence, school-leavers every year enlarged the pool of unemployed seeking chiefly white-collar jobs, while skilled and semiskilled jobs created by the new industries went short of labor. So acute has been the shortage of skilled labor that the government recently offered Hong Kong workers favorable terms of employment, and even eventual citizenship, as inducements.

To redress the imbalance of emphasis in education, attention is now being focused on technical education. The entire policy has been streamlined, and it is anticipated that starting in 1972 the ratio of school-leavers from the academic stream to the technical-vocational stream will be reduced, from 6:1 in 1968, to 1:2. The PAP government aims to build a nation based on multiracialism. Efforts are being made to foster a sense of common purpose and objectives. Toward this end, the national education policy is complemented by the work of the Ministry of Culture.

By force of circumstances occasioned by the impending British military withdrawal, Singapore has been diverting a substantial part of its national resources toward the building of a citizens' armed force. The National Service was inaugurated in 1967, whereby citizens reaching eighteen years of age are called up for two years' service. By 1971 Singapore expects to have 45,000 trained men in service or in reserve for the defense of the country.

It is clear from the foregoing that, despite adversities, the 1960's have been a decade of success for Singapore in both economic and social terms. While the dynamics of change have been generated from within and without, decisions on the shape and direction of this transformation lie solely in the hands of Singaporeans. Given the momentum of growth and barring direct external intervention, the future looks bright for the 1970's and beyond.

focus *on Public Housing and Urban Renewal*

Of all the factors that have helped modernize and modify the city-state of Singapore, none has been more spectacular and pervasive than public housing and urban renewal, both the responsibility of the Housing and Development Board. The allied problems of shelter and slum formation had contributed to social malaise under the colonial administration since the middle of the nineteenth century. The path toward a solution of these urban ailments was not found until after 1959. In execution, public housing predated urban renewal.

The Housing Problem

Rapid population increase unaccompanied by housing programs in the late nineteenth and early twentieth centuries created problems of overcrowding and congestion which worsened over the years. Whatever new housing was built outside the central city area was for the affluent, leaving the bulk of the population cramped in the city core.

Even after the turn of the century the colonial government contributed little to solving the shelter problem, although one report after another on the housing situation was prepared. Finally, as an emergency measure, rent control was imposed with enactment of the 1917 Ordinance. Once constituted, this supposedly short-term palliative hardened into permanency. From 1917 there have been repeated changes and amendments to the original ordinance, but rent control has remained a salient factor of land use and urban development in Singapore.

After World War II, the immediate and longer-term effect of a 1947 Control of Rent Ordinance, which is still in effect, was to protect tenants at the expense of landlords. Unable to recoup market value for their properties, landlords were willing to let their premises lapse into disrepair until they deteriorated to a stage unfit for human habitation. The result has been an agonizing delay in urban redevelopment, whereby obsolete nineteenth-century structures were allowed to deteriorate further. Only belatedly in 1970, with a partial "decontrol" of the central city area, was there any sign of a departure from this long-standing restrictive measure.

Courtesy Yue-man Yeung

To break the monotonous repetition of building forms, Toa Payoh, the newest and largest of Singapore's satellite towns, reflects a judicious attempt to vary building height and to include structural and landscaping improvements. When fully completed, Toa Payoh will have 36,000 dwelling units and will house 200,000 people.

Early Efforts

Acting on a 1918 Housing Commission report, the Singapore Improvement Trust (SIT) was established in 1927 by the Singapore Improvement Ordinance. Limited in legal power and financial backing, SIT has the primary functions of constructing back lanes and working for the general improvement of the city. In terms of housing, its commitments were confined to housing low-income groups rendered homeless by improvement or sanitary schemes. But, because of shortsighted planning, the houses constructed (mostly in Tiong Bahru) were beyond the budget range of these groups.

SIT managed to complete 2,049 apartments before World War II started, a meager production that did little to alleviate the housing crisis. Lacking whole-hearted official support, SIT failed to meet its responsibilities in two respects: The housing provided was both insufficient and too expensive.

The postwar record of SIT was slightly better. On the recommendation of the 1947 report of the Housing Committee, it became the agency responsible for public housing for low-income groups. In the years 1947–59 the Trust had to its credit 23,019 units of low-cost housing and shops. This was still critically short of demand, which was estimated to be five times as large. A viable solution to the housing famine was not yet in sight.

New Thinking and Approaches

The tremendous population pressure in the postwar period swelled the housing problem in the central city area to critical dimensions. At the time it came to power in 1959, the PAP government was faced with the staggering problem of finding decent shelter for 250,000 slum dwellers and a somewhat larger number of squatters.

Although a heartening departure was made shortly before SIT's dissolution, the majority of the dwelling units consisted of low-rise, three-story buildings. Such structures were insufficient to cope with the large number of people waiting to be rehoused. The Housing and Development Board, which was set up to supersede the Trust in 1960, instead adopted a bold and imaginative approach. It chose to mass-produce high-rise, high-density structures on sites generally within a five-mile perimeter from the city center and sufficiently far away from built-up areas to effect a decentralization of population.

Originally the magnitude of the problem aroused skepticism in many quarters. It was estimated that in the following ten years, a total of 147,000 new homes would be necessary to meet the existing deficiency due to overcrowding in urban areas, central city area redevelopment, and the natural increase of population. Granted that the private sector would provide 2,500 units a year, there remained a balance of 11,500 units to be supplied by the government. Accordingly, two Five-Year Plans were drafted, covering the periods 1960–65 and 1965–70.

The first Development Plan called for the construction of 51,000 apartments in five years at a total cost of S$194 million. At the end of 1965, 54,530 units had been completed, exceeding the target by more than 3,500 units. A similar level of activity was maintained during the second Plan period. By the beginning of 1970, the total number of dwelling units under the Board's management reached 125,000, housing 650,000–700,000 people, or about one third of the total population. Thus public housing generated physical and social changes within a short time span which affected a large proportion of the population. The full impact of these changes on the ecological and social structures is yet to be assessed.

The guiding principle of public housing upheld by the Board has been the neighborhood concept. Initially developed and implemented in Europe, the concept has been given enough flexibility and adaptation to suit this Asian society. Each neighborhood, according to local practice, is composed of 1,000–5,000 families each averaging five to six persons and is intended to be a self-contained entity with sufficient facilities for shopping, schooling, and medical care so that many of the day-to-day activities can be performed within it. Where three neighborhoods are close together, a town center is built to provide additional facilities such as department stores, theaters, and a post office.

Notwithstanding these achievements in the field of public housing, much remains to be done. The 1966 Sample Household Survey showed that 60 per cent of the population was still living in makeshift housing or in substandard permanent structures. The Board aims at eventually housing 75 per cent of the population.

The Third Five-Year Plan

In view of this demand for better shelter and in keeping with the accelerated urban-renewal program in the central city area, the Third Five-

Year Plan (1970–75), which is now in operation, sets the even higher target of building 100,000 units at a cost of S$600 million. The average rate of construction will be 20,000 units a year, which will quicken the tempo of construction by 50–60 per cent.

Apart from improvements in the environmental and structural qualities of the new estates, a major feature of the Plan is to step up home-ownership. At present, about 23,000 flats have been sold, representing some 20 per cent of the total housing stock under the Board's management. Incentives, such as the use of the Central Provident Fund, no down payment for existing tenants wishing to buy, and extension of the loan repayment period, have been offered, in the hope that 40–50 per cent of the flat-dwellers will be homeowners at the end of 1975. The public is said to have reacted favorably to the new move; 5,700 applicants were on the waiting list for flat purchase in early 1970, exceeding all previous records since the home-ownership scheme was introduced in 1964.

In the face of rising costs in labor and construction as well as a dwindling of the Board's stock of "empty" land, an essential task for the Board in the next few years is to battle for the maintenance of the existing standard rentals, which for the past ten years have been fixed at S$20, S$40, and S$60 per month for one-, two-, and three-bedroom apartments, respectively. On the average, these rents make up about 15 per cent of the family income in each case. Past experience has shown that the public prefers roomier, though more expensive, flats. This is particularly true of those who intend to purchase their apartment. In fulfilling this need, the Board will have to tread the path warily so as to avoid competition with private developers, who have repeatedly been assured that the Board will continue to be a social service, not a private enterprise.

With regard to the construction programs, the Plan will finish the nearly completed satellite towns in Toa Payoh and Queenstown before embarking on more ambitious and grander ventures. Except for Telok Blangah, which will stretch on either side of scenic Mount Faber and which is near the city center, the towns are to be located at some distance from the center. Bedok, to be raised from reclaimed land and cut terrace, is about six miles east of the city core, and Woodlands is just to the south of the causeway that connects the republic with West Malaysia.

Urban Renewal

The urban-renewal program in Singapore, which has proceeded with relative smoothness and success, drives home a well-known but often ill-observed rule–that is, adequate housing alternatives, normally in the form of public housing, must be available before redevelopment can be undertaken. Thus, in spite of early preparations for redevelopment of the central city area, the program was only in full swing after the U.N. teams had made their recommendations and after a public housing "breakthrough" was attained about 1965.

Like urban-renewal projects elsewhere, the Singapore scheme focuses on the central city area, which occupies about 1.2 per cent of the total land but contains as much as 15–20 per cent of the population. A large proportion of the properties here are "shophouses" of mid-nineteenth-century vintage, ranging from 15 to 20 feet wide and 100 to 200 feet deep. Shophouses are a characteristic Chinese house form, in which the ground level is used for business purposes while the upper floors, usually one or two in Singapore, are devoted to residential uses. The back portions of the ground floor are also used as living quarters, and it is not uncommon for at least part of the shop area to be similarly used after business hours. Although shophouses are still ubiquitous in the city, their gradual replacement by other house forms in the central city area as well as in other parts of the city has resulted in their lessened importance as part of the composite townscape. Generally speaking, shophouses in the central city area are associated with substandard and dilapidated housing conditions, roads too narrow for the dense traffic, and insufficient public utilities. Nothing short of comprehensive replanning and redevelopment employing modern town-planning principles and techniques is likely to promise long-term and lasting benefits. This is what Singapore has attempted.

The central city area has been taken in its entirety and has been planned as a whole and in parts. The area has been divided into seventeen precincts on either side of the Singapore River, named in accordance with priority of development. Precincts North I and South I, for instance, are now near their final stages, whereas land acquisition and other preparatory work is in progress in other precincts. Since June, 1967, when the first sale of land got under way, the private sector has poured S$300 million into the redevelopment schemes. Direct employment arising from these investments has been estimated to be in the neighborhood of 20,000. Investments deriving from the recent third sale of land more than doubled the first two sales. The role of the government is to "acquire and assemble land, clear land of encumbrances, comprehensively plan the area, and provide the essential infrastructure, including public housing."

Efficacious urban renewal hinges on the coordination and cooperation of many related government departments. In Singapore, the Urban Renewal Department is part of the Housing and Development Board, and as such it maintains close liaison with the Public Works Department and the Planning Department, all of which are, for administrative efficiency, under the control of the Ministry of Law and National Development.

In line with the over-all policy to attract foreign investment and create more employment opportunities, the government has recently provided for a more flexible legislative framework to speed up urban renewal in the city core. Amendments to the Recovery of Possession of Controlled Premises (Special Provisions) Bill of 1968, the Land Acquisition Act of 1964, and the most recent "decontrol" measure are also intended for the good of the private sector.

So far the project has been making steady progress. There has been little resistance among affected families and businesses to be relocated in public-housing estates. The necessary rapport between the private sector and the government is maintained for new developments. The official approach is not an overemphasis on economic-based, tax-generating projects at the expense of social welfare considerations but a balance between these two viewpoints. The government envisages the program as a concerted enterprise whose benefits go not only to the private and public sectors but to the rich and the poor as well.

It is too early to measure the success of the urban-renewal program, but whatever is accomplished the city core will look radically different. If we consider the present trend of development, it seems safe to speculate that the central city area of future Singapore is going to be a bustling center of economy activity and population concentration. Other cities charged with the task of revitalizing their city cores, in both the less developed and the more developed world, may find a message in this experiment.

Suggested Readings

HUGHES, HELEN, and YOU POH-SENG, eds. *Foreign Investment and Industrialisation in Singapore.* Madison: University of Wisconsin Press, 1969. Presents in broad perspective the investment picture by major countries. Gives greater emphasis to foreign investment than industrialization but provides a useful overview linking both.

NEVILLE, WARWICK. "Singapore: Ethnic Diversity and Its Implications."

Annals of the Association of American Geographers, LVI, no. 2 (June, 1966), pp. 236–53. An account of the characteristics of Singapore's plural population and attendant political and development ramifications.

OOI JIN-BEE and CHIANG HAI DING, eds. *Modern Singapore*. Singapore: University of Singapore Press, 1969. A collection of papers covering socio-economic, demographic, political, and other aspects.

OSHIMA, HARRY T. "Growth and Unemployment in Singapore." *Malayan Economic Review*, XII, no. 2 (Oct., 1967), pp. 32–58. The best statement on the unemployment problem to date.

PEARSON, H. F. *Singapore: A Popular History, 1819–1960*. Singapore: Eastern University Press, 1961. Simple and concise history up to 1960.

Singapore Housing and Development Board. *Homes for the People: 50,000 up*. Singapore, 1965. A complete review of the work of HDB up to 1965 with a historical survey of the housing problem.

WIKKRAMETELIKE, R. "Focus on Singapore, 1964." *Journal of Tropical Geography*, XX (1965), pp. 73–83. An account of the changing landscape of Singapore, illustrated with air photographs.

YOU, POH SENG, *et al. Singapore Sample Household Survey, 1966*, Report no. 1. Ministry of National Development and Economic Research Center. Singapore: University of Singapore, 1967. Island-wide statistics on population and housing after the 1957 Census and before results of the 1970 Census were available.

See also Suggested Readings for Part I, pp. 57–59, and Suggested Readings: Malaysia, pp. 164–65.

12 INDONESIA

William A. Withington

*Landscape and Climate • Cultural Diversity • Population
Distribution • Agriculture: Methods and Problems • Fishing,
Forestry, and Mining • Manufacturing, Transport, and
Communications • focus on the Population Crisis and
Economic Development*

During the 1960's, the Republic of Indonesia, like many other less developed nations, passed through a transition period—at times painful—from "first generation" to "second generation" leadership. The shift in power began with an unsuccessful *coup d'état* in late September, 1965, which was quelled by the commander of Djakarta's Strategic Reserve, General Suharto. The general emerged from the event a major national and military leader. By the following March, President Sukarno had granted Suharto wide-ranging powers, and two years later General Suharto became the second President of Indonesia. Since then he has pursued the difficult task of trying to unite this highly diversified nation while seeking solutions to its problems of inflation, heavy foreign debts, and basic economic and political evolution.

In both area and population, the Republic of Indonesia is the largest nation of Southeast Asia. With a land area of 736,000 square miles, it is three times the size of either Thailand or Burma, the next largest states. Its population is 124 million; only the People's Republic of China, India, the Soviet Union, and the United States have more people; and only Pakistan, Japan, and Brazil have populations close to this in size.

Indonesia encompasses more than 3,000 islands which extend over 3,300 miles from northwesternmost Sumatra to southeasternmost West Irian

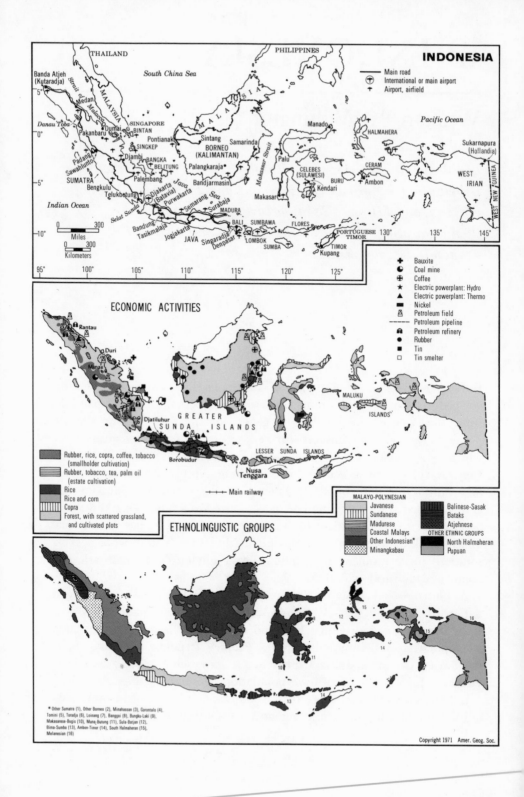

(Irian Barat) and straddle the equator between 6° N. and 11° S. In length and breadth its land and water extent almost matches that of the co-terminous United States.

During the late glacial times of the Pleistocene, the islands, formed of the ancient rocks of the Sunda Shelf in the west and the Sahul Shelf in the southeast, were much more extensive and provided an almost continuous land bridge for the dispersal between Asia and Australia of animals, plants, and early man. More recently, a succession of peoples, cultures, religions, and political influences have come in from Asia, Australia, the Philippines, and particularly the Indian Ocean area—India, Ceylon, Arabia —and Europe. The islands remain a crossroads today, for many of the world's major sea and air routes pass through them or along their margins.

Landscape and Climate

One of the earth's principal zones of instability extends through the Indonesian archipelago in a broad east-west arc. The most fertile soils of Indonesia are in this volcanic zone, and the alluvial soils of many of the river valleys and coastal plains are derived from it. Elsewhere, soils formed from limestone rocks or former coral reefs provide limited fertile areas. Borneo (Kalimantan), which lies outside the zone of recent volcanism, has some of the nation's least productive soils.

Indonesia's equatorial and transitional location between Asia and Australia produces locally diversified climatic conditions. The complex interpenetration of land and water, which gives rise to onshore and offshore daily winds, mitigates the characteristically hot and humid equatorial temperatures on all but the largest islands. Varied exposure and elevation provide additional climatic diversity: Most islands have mountains or highlands rising to several thousand feet in elevation, and many upland agricultural settlements and resort areas are much cooler than nearby lowlands. Seasonal wind patterns and pressure systems are also significant factors in producing a varied climate. The west monsoon of October through March comes from the northeast but curves, as it swings across the equator, to become a westerly air flow from the Indian Ocean. It brings, for most of Indonesia, the highest rainfall totals. The east monsoon of April through September is a southeasterly or southerly flow of dry air from Australia and its fringing waters, which provides little moisture to most of southern Indonesia.

In general, climate and vegetation are transitional from west and northwest to east and southeast. A tropical rainforest climate, with more than eighty inches of annual rainfall and high temperatures and humidities, characterizes most of the large western and northern islands and Sumatra, Borneo, and Celebes (Sulawesi), much of western Java, the central and northern Maluku Islands, and most of West Irian. In these areas water is plentiful for irrigation, domestic and industrial use, river transportation on the larger streams, and hydroelectric power. In east Java, the southeastern islands, and southern West Irian, the annual dry season is more pronounced, and the climate becomes tropical savanna in type.

The ratio of relatively dry to relatively wet months is of vital importance for vegetation and agriculture in an equatorial area. Where there are three or more months of relatively little rainfall, as in the southeast, soil leaching and erosion are considerably reduced, and there are sizable grassy areas, interspersed with clumps of trees, which provide pasture for livestock. Above 2,000 to 3,000 feet there are commercially significant stands of pine trees that are used for the manufacture of paper. But man's presence in these islands for long periods of time has resulted in large tracts of *alang-alang,* grasses that overtake the abandoned plots of shifting agriculture.

Cultural Diversity

Indonesia's people are highly diversified in religion, culture, and language. This has been a continuing problem and challenge for the republic, so much so that its motto is "Unity from Diversity"—more a hope for the future than a fact of the present.

Although 85 per cent of the people are Muslims, the influences of Hinduism, Buddhism, and earlier animistic beliefs have tended to modify Islamic practice. More than 8 per cent are Christians, concentrated mainly in northern Sumatra, central and northern Celebes, and various eastern areas, including West Irian. Most of the people of Bali and neighboring Lombok Island have retained a form of the ancient Hindu religion, while a considerable proportion of the 3.5 million people of Chinese origin hold Confucian or other ancestor-oriented beliefs. Animist peoples are found in the more isolated interior rainforest or upland areas, usually on the larger islands.

Since independence from Dutch rule was achieved in 1949, the national language has been "Bahasa Indonesia," an outgrowth of the Malay language spoken widely in eastern Sumatra and in coastal areas generally throughout the archipelago. Its use is a unifying factor of considerable importance. It is used in schools beginning in the fourth grade; the local language, if different, may be used in earlier grades.

Most Indonesians are of Malay ethnic stock, either the pre-Christian-era immigrants of the Deutero-Malay type, such as the Javanese, or the even more ancient Proto-Malay type exemplified by the Batak peoples of northern upland Sumatra. Scattered groups of forest peoples represent several other early groups, including Negrito and South Indian Veddoid stocks. Another non-Malay group is the distinctive Papuan peoples of West Irian; they represent a transitional group between Asian peoples and the dark-skinned Melanesians of the western Pacific islands.

The three largest cultural groups occupy the politically and geographically central region of Java-Madura. The Islamic Sundanese live in the western highlands; the Madurese in Madura and in east Java. The Javanese, by far the largest cultural group, have spread to most parts of the island but predominate in the center and east.

Cultural variety is greatest in the outlying regions. In Sumatra, independent Muslim Atjehnese, probably the first to become converts in Indonesia, occupy the northernmost plains; Gajo peoples live in adjacent interior uplands. Various Batak peoples reside around Danau Toba, the largest body of fresh water in Indonesia. Most Bataks are Christians, but one of the major groups, the Mandailing, are Muslims. The Minangkabau in west-central Sumatra, who are strongly Islamic, have contributed many of Indonesia's notable political leaders. The Malays along Sumatra's eastern coast and nearby islands are probably the most numerous Sumatran group; their seagoing interests carried their language so widely that it became the coastal vernacular throughout Indonesia and the basis for the national language. Lampung people live in the south in a province established in 1964, but today they are outnumbered by immigrant settlers, mainly from Java, Madura, and Bali. Aside from some 1.5 million immigrant laborers and settlers, most from Java, the 700,000 Chinese are the largest nonindigenous group in Sumatra. In addition, there are some 35,000 Indians and Pakistanis, a few thousand Arabs, and several hundred Westerners in plantation, mining, and urban areas.

In Borneo the coastal zones are occupied by Malay peoples; those in the southeast are called Bandjarese. Most practice shifting cultivation, but in the more densely occupied southeast, the *sawah* (wet-rice terraced field) is typical. Extensive interior stretches of Borneo are lightly populated; animist people, most of them Dyaks, have settled along the rivers, where they practice shifting cultivation, fishing, collecting, and hunting.

The Dyaks live in settlements of communal longhouses. Approximately 400,000 people of Chinese origin and increasing numbers of settlers from Java are the principal nonindigenuous groups.

In Celebes the seafaring Muslim Makasarese-Bugis occupy the island's southwestern arm. The Toradja of central Celebes and the Minahassan on the northeastern arm are other sizable groups. The latter are highly Christianized, and they have long been active throughout the country in the civil and military services.

In eastern Indonesia, the 2 million syncretic Hindu-Buddhist Balinese in Bali and Lombok Island are the single largest cultural group. The variety of peoples, languages, religions, and cultures increases eastward. Many of these peoples, such as the Papuans of West Irian, are not yet completely integrated into the national political system, in part because of poor transportation and communications.

Population Distribution

The most striking feature of Indonesia's population distribution is its extreme unevenness. Nearly 80 million people, almost two thirds of the Indonesian total, live in the Java-Madura region, which comprises only 7 per cent of the national area. The other island complexes, often referred to as the outer islands, have 93 per cent of the nation's land but only slightly more than one third of its people.

Administratively, Indonesia is subdivided into twenty-six provinces, including Djakarta Raya (the capital city area) and two special autonomous areas, Jogjakarta in south-central Java and Banda Atjeh (Kutaradja) in northern Sumatra. The capital of each province is also its principal regional center, in both size and diversity of functions and services.

Most urban centers are classified as one of two types. Approximately fifty cities, including most of the provincial capitals, are *kotapradja*, autonomous municipalities having their own city governments. They range in size from Djakarta, whose estimated population is more than 5 million, to Sawahlunto, a coal-mining center in the west Sumatran highlands, which had just over 12,000 people in the latest census count (1961). The second category of places designated as urban communities includes capitals of *kabupaten* (subdivisions of provinces); however, in the 1961 census several leaders of *kabupaten* capitals gave no population figure to officials on the grounds that their communities were not urban.

Altogether, only 18 per cent of the population lives in officially designated urban places. (A revised and broader definition of "urban" probably would show another 2 or 3 per cent of the people to be urban dwellers.) This is slightly higher than in other nations in Southeast Asia, such as Burma (15.8), Cambodia (12.8), and Thailand (13), and many less developed nations elsewhere, but low compared with highly industrialized nations like the Netherlands (80) and the United States (70).

Agriculture: Methods and Problems

Farming is the predominant economic activity: It provides income and employment for about 66 per cent of the population. Agricultural products bring in more than half the national income and earn 70 per cent of the nonpetroleum export revenue. Nevertheless, agriculture poses problems for further economic development. Over-all production is rising, but in the densely populated Java-Madura region not enough food is raised to support the population (food, mainly rice, is brought in from the outer islands and from Burma, Thailand, and the United States). The average Indonesian farmer is only beginning to have the means to buy the new higher yielding varieties of rice evolved by the International Rice Research Institute in the Philippines and the fertilizer needed to grow them.

The majority of farmers use simple hand tools and draft animals such as the water buffalo; many farms are too small to permit efficient use of plows or power tools. Even on the larger units (estates), mechanization is limited because of the availability of cheap labor, and it is not encouraged because of the lack of alternate employment opportunities either on the land or in the cities.

The paucity of land surveys and opposition from large landowners have delayed implementation of the land-reform laws passed in 1960. Some sharecroppers are still paying 60 to 70 per cent of their harvest as rent and must buy seeds and fertilizer out of their share.

There are two distinct types of farming in Indonesia, as in many other former colonial territories: large estates, geared to commercial production of export crops, and small holdings, which produce most of the food and some commercial crops. According to recent estimates, about half the small-holder farms of Java-Madura are less than 1.2 acres, and half of those in the outer islands are between one and five acres. On these small holdings, intensive subsistence *sawah* cultivation is characteristic in most of the densely populated areas: most of Java-Madura and Bali; several sections of Sumatra, Borneo, and Celebes; and a few eastern islands. In Java

Intricately terraced rice fields, a common sight in densely populated Java (Indonesia), reflect the skillful and intensive use of land in a hilly environment. Almost 70 per cent of Java is cultivated yearly—one of the highest proportions of cropland in any large area in the world.

and Madura the intensive farming system also includes *tegalan*, dry fields where maize (corn) and other unirrigated crops are grown, and *pekarangan*, household gardens for fresh fruit and vegetables.

Near major transportation corridors or centers of population, small-holder semicommercial farming is also practiced. Small-holder crops, grown largely for export, include natural rubber in Sumatra and Borneo, pepper in Sumatra and its southeastern islands, coffee in the hills of Sumatra and Java, and copra in Celebes and the eastern islands. Near major cities most small-holder commercial farming is market gardening and fruit production.

Shifting, or slash-and-burn, cultivation, known as *ladang* in Indonesia, is practiced over broad areas. It is most common in rainforest zones, where soils are relatively thin and erode or leach rapidly once the protective forest cover is cleared. In such areas unirrigated rice, cassava, maize, and a variety of vegetables and fruit supply year-round subsistence for generally sparse populations.

Animal husbandry, particularly dairying, is very limited. Cattle and water buffalo are used as draft animals in agricultural areas, and horses supply transportation in urban areas. Only Madura, Bali, and Sumbawa and Sumba in Nusa Tenggara have surplus livestock to supply other parts of Indonesia. In a few non-Muslim areas swine are raised. Chickens, ducks, geese, and goats are the most ubiquitous animals, the former providing eggs and meat, the latter, meat and milk.

Plantation agriculture developed rapidly in the late nineteenth century with Western capital and management and local and imported labor. Java had major plantations producing natural rubber, tea, sugar, leaf tobacco, and cinchona bark for quinine. Northeastern Sumatra was the other major estate area, and today it is easily the leading one. Cigar-wrapper leaf tobacco, natural rubber, palm oil and kernels, tea, and hard fibers are produced. However, estate production has declined since independence as a result of several factors: population pressure and take-over of some land by squatters; reform laws; formation of labor unions; and inadequate capital, machinery, and spare parts, and research. As a result, small-holder production, particularly of natural rubber, has surpassed estate output in recent years.

The country's most crucial agricultural problem is to raise food production fast enough to keep pace with the rapidly expanding population. The national rate of growth is about 2.4 per cent per year, compared with a world average of 1.9 per cent. Some additional land is available for farming, but most of the production increase will have to come from higher yields on already intensively cultivated plots. This problem is further discussed on pp. 196–200.

Fishing, Forestry, and Mining

The fish catch in most years passes the 1-million-ton mark, but it is low in relation to the number of fishermen and the need for fish—most Indonesians' chief source of nonvegetable protein. Much fishing is carried on as an adjunct to agriculture; two fifths of the catch comes from inland fresh waters, flooded rice fields, or coastal salt-water lagoons. Improvements in vessels (including motorization), fishing methods, and facilities for preserving fish could greatly increase the catch.

Half of Indonesia's wood production comes from Java, although its forest cover since World War II has been considered insufficient for minimal levels of river-basin flood and erosion control. Sumatra, Borneo, and

West Irian have about three fourths of the nation's forests, but they are exploited primarily for firewood, construction, and other local needs. Both domestic and foreign enterprises are beginning to expand production in these areas.

The chief minerals exploited are petroleum, tin, bauxite, and nickel. The annual output of nearly 40 million tons of petroleum represents only 1.7 per cent of the world total but is more than half the oil produced in all of South, Southeast, and East Asia, outside the People's Republic of China. The principal sources are the eastern Sumatran plains and eastern Borneo. There are smaller fields in northern Java, the surrounding seas, and western West Irian. The greatest recent expansion in oil production has been in east-central Sumatra, particularly the Minas and Duri fields. A pipeline constructed in the 1950's moves the oil north from here to Dumai, now the country's largest port in tonnage handled. Natural gas, associated with the petroleum fields, is used in the manufacture of much-needed urea fertilizer and in the production of carbon black. Various on-shore and offshore areas have been assigned to Japanese, Australian, and U.S. companies for exploration and development. Foreign firms provide the initial capital, which they recover from 40 per cent of production, the remaining 60 per cent being divided between the firm and the Indonesian Government.

Almost 10 per cent of the world's tin comes from the southeastern Sumatran islands of Bangka, Belitung (Billiton), and Singkep and their offshore margins. New large dredges are helping to increase tin output to well over the 1968 figure of 17 million tons, and various expansion projects, using Brazilian, U.S., Australian, and Dutch capital, are being considered. Bintan Island, immediately south of Singapore, produces all of Indonesia's bauxite, more than 912,000 tons a year; almost all of it is exported to Japan. Further exploration, sponsored by Japan, is under way, and if reserves prove to be adequate a refinery will be built on the island. The mining of nickel ore, in southeastern and south-central Celebes, has expanded rapidly in recent years; production of nickel metal content reached 7,900 tons in 1968. A consortium of U.S., Dutch, and Canadian mining companies has signed an agreement that gives them rights to mine nickel in West Irian. A provisional contract has also been signed by a Japanese group for exploration of deposits on Halmahera Island.

Other minerals of some significance are manganese ore, gold, silver, diamonds, copper, and iron. Although known resources of iron ore are limited, capital provided by the Soviet Union is being invested in an iron and steel mill in northwestern Java.

Manufacturing, Transport, and Communications

Coal- and oil-powered generators provide more than half the electric power for industrial and urban needs. Many manufacturing concerns operate their own power systems to obtain dependable energy supplies. The Djatiluhur Hydroelectric and Irrigation Project southeast of Djakarta (western Java) was completed in the early 1960's and was the country's first large multipurpose hydroelectric project. Most of western Indonesia's hydroelectric potential, however, remains undeveloped. The Asahan Falls Project in northeastern Sumatra near Medan, the country's largest water-power site, has not yet been completed.

Much of the manufacturing is still of the household or handicraft variety, with a few people working in small shops using little mechanical power or technical equipment. Typical of such industries are rice milling; wood-, leather-, and silver-working; and making and printing traditional *batik* cotton cloth.

The great majority of the middle-sized and large factories are concentrated in the larger cities of Java and in the major regional centers of the outlying islands. Notable centers of industry are Djakarta, Surabaja, Bandung, and Semarang in Java; Medan and Palembang in Sumatra; and Makasar in Celebes. Representative industries in these centers include the production of food, beverages, textiles, paper, matches, glass, and tires and other rubber goods; assembly of imported parts; and manufacture of agricultural equipment, small engines, cement, construction machinery, and chemicals. Much of the petroleum refined in Indonesia's plants is exported.

Political, economic, social, and technological problems have plagued manufacturing since independence; in recent years, many industries have been operating at only 25–30 per cent of capacity. Among the problems have been shortages of imported raw materials, spare parts, and equipment; scarcity of foreign exchange and managerial and technical experience; and inadequate interisland shipping facilities.

Sea routes are the major links with the outlying islands, yet the managerial skills and funds needed to keep ports and channels properly dredged and docking, loading, and storage facilities in good repair have been lacking. Nor is there an efficient ship-to-shore communications system. Facilities for building, maintaining, and repairing ships are inadequate, and schedules are frequently ignored.

There are some forty airports large enough to handle two-engine medium-sized or large aircraft. Another twenty airstrips—many in isolated areas of West Irian and Borneo—are used by smaller aircraft. International air traffic focuses on Djakarta and to some extent on Medan. Tourism and the need for refueling on the Australian route are stimulating the use and development of larger airports such as those at Denpasar on Bali and Surabaja in eastern Java.

Only Java-Madura has a fairly extensive railway network; most of the rest of the trackage is in several widely separated systems on Sumatra. Highway mileage also is highly concentrated on Java. Riverways and oil pipelines provide additional transportation linkages. With the possible exception of pipelines, all transport facilities and equipment are sorely in need of rehabilitation. This is one of the nation's most pressing economic problems, and much emphasis is put on it in the Five-Year Plan instituted in 1969.

Radio Republik Indonesia reaches all parts of the country, and in communities where few radios are owned individually, loudspeakers broadcast major programs in Bahasia Indonesia or in the local language. To date, only Djakarta and nearby parts of west Java have television service. Educational facilities also have been highly concentrated in the Java-Madura area. Although more schools and colleges are being built in the outer islands, the flow of able young people into Java-Madura in search of education, jobs, and the amenities of urban living is likely to continue for some time. The marked contrasts in economic, cultural, and political opportunities between the densely populated Java-Madura area and the outer islands remains a crucial problem for the Indonesian nation.

focus *on the Population Crisis and Economic Development*

Within the Republic of Indonesia the major crisis area is Java-Madura. The basic problem is that too many people are trying to make a living on too little land. Clifford Geertz has referred to this situation and its associated processes as "agricultural involution"—that is, people working ever more intensively on ever smaller plots of land. To understand this crisis in Java and to assess possible ways to mitigate or solve the problems involved, one should consider several interrelated factors, such as Java's location, its agricultural assets, its growth of population, the migration to the cities, and employment opportunities.

Java's central location within the Indonesian island world has always been one of its chief assets. The ports that developed along its broadest northern plain during the past millennium became the focus of trade, both from fertile interior valleys and volcanic slopes to the south, and from other islands and lands. The pre-eminence gained through trade was later reinforced by political power centered in Java.

Its principal agricultural assets include a mild climate, adequate rainfall fairly evenly distributed throughout the year, and volcanic soils and their alluvial, downstream derivative materials, which are highly fertile and can be intensively cultivated. As Geertz puts it,

> The output of most [wet rice] terraces can be almost indefinitely increased by more careful, fine-comb cultivation techniques; it seems almost always possible somehow to squeeze just a little more out of even a mediocre *sawah* by working it just a little bit harder. Seeds can be sown in nurseries and then transplanted instead of broadcast; they can even be pregerminated in the house. . . . Timing is also important: [Wet rice] should be planted in a well-soaked field with little standing water and then the depth of the water increased gradually up to six to twelve inches as the plant grows and flowers, after which it should be gradually drawn off until at harvest the field is dry. Further, the water should not be allowed to stagnate but . . . kept gently flowing. . . . Yield can be increased by planting shoots in exactly spaced rows, more frequent and complete weeding, periodic draining of the terrace during the growing season for purposes of aeration, more thorough ploughing, raking, and leveling of the muddy soil before planting, placing selected organic debris on the plot, and so on; harvesting techniques can be similarly perfected both to reap the fullest percentage of the yield and leave the greatest amount of the harvested crop on the field to refertilize it, such as the technique of using the razor-like hand blade found over most of inner Indonesia; double cropping and, in some favorable areas, perhaps triple cropping, can be instituted. The capacity of most terraces to respond to loving care is amazing.*

Java's location, its political power, and the high potential productivity of its *sawah* areas, in contrast to the low potential productivity of the slash-and-burn areas in the outer islands, have been important factors in bringing about the uneven distribution of population in Indonesia and the present crisis.

* Clifford Geertz. *Agricultural Involution: The Process of Ecological Change in Indonesia.* Berkeley: University of California Press, 1963, pp. 31, 35.

Sir Thomas Stamford Raffles, as British Governor of the East Indies in the Napoleonic period, estimated Java's population at 4.5 million. If this figure is approximately correct, the present estimated population of nearly 80 million represents an eighteen-fold increase in just over 150 years. Population growth was most rapid during the colonial period. By 1906, Java had 30 million people, almost 75 per cent of Indonesia's total. Although the rate of growth in Java-Madura is now slowing in relation to other parts of Indonesia, it continues nonetheless to be very high, close to the national average of 2.4 per cent per year. Unless this rate can be reduced, about 1.5 million people will be added annually to this already overcrowded area. Some recent estimates suggest that the annual rate of population increase both in Java-Madura and in the nation as a whole is actually in excess of 3 per cent per year. If these are true, the population crisis in Java is even more acute.

Moreover, Java-Madura is a land of intricate landscapes. There are great local variations in soil fertility, terrain, rainfall amount, and seasonality. As is true everywhere, people tend to congregate in the most favored places. Densities per square mile reach the staggering figure of 16,300 in Djakarta Raya and nearly 2,250 in Jogjakarta, 1,680 in central Java, 1,400 in east Java, and 1,200 in west Java. The island of Madura has an average density, based on 1961 data, of 1,000 persons per square mile; this has probably now risen to about 1,200. The average in the United States is about 57.5 people per square mile.

The rapid rate of population growth and high rural densities have brought a decrease in the amount of agricultural land per person and agricultural involution. This plus political upheavals, roving bands of guerrillas, and the impact of radio broadcasts and newspapers has stimulated a steeply rising migration to the cities. More often than not, those who hoped to find employment there do not have the skills needed for urban jobs, join the ranks of unemployed or underemployed, and find themselves living in the crowded, dilapidated, unsanitary shantytowns that characterize so many of the less developed nations. Industry has not expanded enough to absorb the massive number of unskilled laborers arriving in the cities each year. Before 1965 Java-Madura received a large proportion of Indonesia's funds allocated for economic development, and new factories were built, but much of the investment went into projects of marginal economic value.

In seeking solutions to the population crisis in Java-Madura, five principal, and to some extent overlapping, options can be considered: (1) outmigration, in which considerable numbers of people from Java-Madura are relocated in Sumatra or other outlying areas; (2) industrialization, to increase the production of goods needed locally, earn income through the export of surpluses, and provide greater employment opportunities to formerly rural people in the factory and service sectors of the economy; (3) increased agricultural productivity, whether by new methods, better seed stock, use of more fertilizer, or more rational pricing policies; (4) population control by various means, officially recognized and encouraged; (5) and outside support, utilizing the surplus production of outlying areas of Indonesia and international aid to provide the extra foodstuffs and goods needed in Java.

The basic question is how to raise money to implement any or all of these measures. Under Sukarno several economic-development projects were carried out, such as the Djatiluhur hydroelectric scheme and those in the Djakarta area—the Asian Games Sports Complex, major public buildings, the Hotel Indonesia, several large monuments, and the Djakarta bypass highway. But no broadly integrated plan was evolved.

The attempted coup and the assumption of the Presidency by General Suharto led to a reassessment of economic-development priorities. Because agriculture remains the principal source of national income, the principal employer, and a major earner of foreign exchange, the first priority of REPELITA, the Five-Year Plan initiated in 1969, is to improve this sector. The target is to make the nation independent of rice imports, which have averaged at least $100 million a year since 1953, by increasing production from the 1968 level of 10 million tons to 15.4 million tons. To effect this, the area planted in rice will be increased from 19 to 23 million acres. In addition, irrigation works are to be improved or extended on 3.5 million acres, high-yielding rice strains will be introduced on 10 million acres, and fertilizer production and use will be raised from 100,000 to 1.4 million tons. Yields from inland fisheries, using lagoons, freshwater ponds, lakes, and flooded rice fields, are also to be increased.

The second priority is transportation, emphasizing the importance of road and rail systems for moving goods to local markets as well as connections to seaports for the import and export of goods. The plan calls for rehabilitation and improvement of highway and railway systems to provide improved links between agricultural areas and markets.

In manufacturing, the emphasis is on industries related to agriculture or those that will produce goods currently imported. In the second category, factories are needed to turn out more paper, textiles, clothing, tires for bicycles and motor vehicles, various construction materials, and many other goods.

Priority is also being given to a family-planning program. Even a healthy economy might find it difficult to keep pace with a 2.4 per cent annual increase in population. In 1969 a committee was formed to launch a program designed to provide knowledge and facilities to people who want to determine for themselves the size of their families.

Much of the capital needed for the Five-Year Plan is slated to come from increased exports of basic mineral, forest, and agricultural products. Increased foreign investment in such fields as mineral and forestry exploitation is expected to provide new exportable items and to raise the exports of others.

The new approach to planning is as important as the operational details of REPELITA. Past development plans in Indonesia have tended to be grandiose in intentions but limited in results. REPELITA's goals are more modest, and sounder economic and financial studies preceded its implementation; thus it is more likely to reach announced goals within the time period allotted. However, as in many other less developed nations, external factors may add to the republic's already difficult problems, especially the worldwide decreasing value of raw-material exports and the rising cost of manufactured goods to be imported. Furthermore, in 1970 Indonesia still had a foreign debt of $2.2 billion, scheduled for repayment in thirty years, and that year received an additional $600 million in foreign aid. Nevertheless, the Indonesians appear to be hopeful that they can move ahead on economic, political, and social evolution, which in the long run will enable them to meet their domestic and international obligations.

Suggested Readings

American University. *Area Handbook for Indonesia.* Washington, D.C.: U.S. Government Printing Office, 1970. A comprehensive analysis of social, political, and economic aspects of the area and its national security.

Business International Corporation. *Doing Business in the New Indonesia.* New York, 1968. Discusses the economy, foreign trade, and labor, taxation, investment, and marketing policies.

GEERTZ, CLIFFORD. *Agricultural Involution: The Process of Ecological Change in Indonesia.* Berkeley and Los Angeles: University of California Press, 1963. An analysis of factors contributing to the evolution of Indonesia's agrarian economy from the era of classical kingdoms to the early 1960's.

GRANT, BRUCE. *Indonesia.* New York: Cambridge University Press, 1964. A good summary of history, cultural characteristics, and political events of the early 1960's.

LEGGE, J. D. *Indonesia.* Englewood Cliffs, N.J.: Prentice-Hall, 1964. A commentary on the history of Indonesia, emphasizing its contribution to the making of the modern republic.

MACKIE, J. A. C. "Civil-Military Relations and the 1971 Elections in Indonesia." *Australian Outlook,* XXIV, no. 3 (Dec., 1970), pp. 250–61.

SHAPLEN, ROBERT, "A Reporter at Large: Indonesia." *New Yorker,* XLIV (Nov. 23, 1968), pp. 172*ff.*; XLV (May 24, 1969), pp. 42–46*ff.*; XLV (May 31, 1969), pp. 39–44*ff.* Surveys recent trends and events in Indonesia.

THOMAS, R. MURRAY. "Effects of Indonesian Population Growth on Educational Development, 1940–1968." *Asian Survey,* IX (July, 1969), pp. 498–514. Discusses recent trends and possible solutions to some major problems.

See also Suggested Readings for Part I, pp. 57–59.

13 THE PHILIPPINES

Alden Cutshall

The Physical Setting • *The Cultural Scene* • *An Agricultural Economy* • *Fishing and Forestry* • *Minerals and Mining* • *Expanding Industry* • focus *on the Revolution in Rice*

During the quarter-century since it achieved independence, the Republic of the Philippines has been attempting to transform a traditional, agricultural, colonial, family-oriented economy into an industrial, national, market-oriented system. As in most other less developed nations, this transition has brought recurring problems of economic instability. Domestic savings and foreign-exchange resources have fallen short of investment requirements. With an import-dependent economy, inflation resulting from excess credit expansion and other factors has created balance-of-payment difficulties. However, production is now carried on to an increasing extent by an emerging Filipino entrepreneurship with local capital and a labor force growing in skills, and with increasingly complex methods and more sophisticated technology. In some fields significant progress has been made; in others, changes have barely begun.

Augmenting the economic problems is a tremendous upsurge in population, the result of a decreasing mortality rate due to improved health conditions, and a high birth rate. The population has more than doubled since independence to an estimated 38.3 million and has been increasing at about 3 per cent per year. Projections suggest a 3.4 rate for the 1970's.

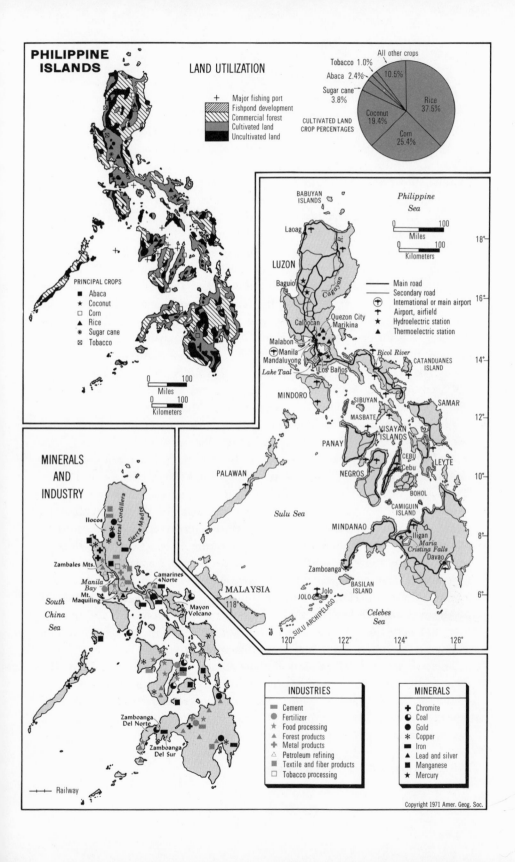

PHILIPPINE ISLANDS

LAND UTILIZATION

+ Major fishing port
Fishpond development
Commercial forest
Cultivated land
Uncultivated land

CULTIVATED LAND CROP PERCENTAGES

- Tobacco 1.0%
- Abaca 2.4%
- Sugar cane 3.8%
- Coconut 19.4%
- Corn 25.4%
- Rice 37.5%
- All other crops 10.5%

PRINCIPAL CROPS

- ■ Abaca
- ★ Coconut
- □ Corn
- ▲ Rice
- ⊙ Sugar cane
- ⊠ Tobacco

0 — 100 Miles
0 — 100 Kilometers

BABUYAN ISLANDS

Philippine Sea

Laoag

LUZON

Baguio

Cagayan R.

Caloocan

Quezon City
Marikina

Malabon

Manila
Mandaluyong

Lake Taal

Los Baños

Bicol River

CATANDUANES ISLAND

0 — 100 Miles
0 — 100 Kilometers

— Main road
— Secondary road
⊕ International or main airport
✛ Airport, airfield
★ Hydroelectric station
▲ Thermoelectric station

MINDORO

SIBUYAN

MASBATE

VISAYAN ISLANDS

PANAY

CEBU
Cebu

LEYTE

NEGROS

BOHOL

SAMAR

CAMIGUIN ISLAND

PALAWAN

Sulu Sea

MINDANAO

Iligan
Maria Cristina Falls
Davao

Zamboanga

18°
16°
14°
12°
10°
8°
6°

MINERALS AND INDUSTRY

Ilocos

Central Cordillera

Sierra Madre

Zambales Mts.

Manila Bay

Mt. Maquiling

Camarines Norte

South China Sea

Mayon Volcano

MALAYSIA

118°

JOLO
Jolo

BASILAN ISLAND

SULU ARCHIPELAGO

Celebes Sea

120°   122°   124°   126°

Zamboanga Del Norte

Zamboanga Del Sur

＋—＋ Railway

INDUSTRIES

- ■ Cement
- ● Fertilizer
- ★ Food processing
- ▲ Forest products
- ✚ Metal products
- △ Petroleum refining
- ■ Textile and fiber products
- □ Tobacco processing

MINERALS

- ✚ Chromite
- ◖ Coal
- ● Gold
- ✳ Copper
- ■ Iron
- ▲ Lead and silver
- ■ Manganese
- ★ Mercury

Copyright 1971 Amer. Geog. Soc.

The Physical Setting

The more than 7,000 Philippine islands and islets (740 of them large enough to be inhabited) have a combined land area of 115,600 square miles, about the size of Italy or the state of Arizona. Unlike Italy or Arizona, however, the Philippines is not compact but extends over almost 16 degrees of latitude. The distance from one extremity to the other is about 1,150 miles, roughly comparable to the distance from New York City to Miami or from Stockholm to Rome.

The Philippines is an insular arc of extremely varied topography with volcanic masses forming the cores of most of the larger islands. Indeed, 65 per cent consist of mountains or uplands, and the more rugged interior of many islands is marked by folding, faulting, and in some cases by recent volcanic activity as well. Of the several active volcanoes, Mount Mayon in southeastern Luzon, best known for its beautiful symmetrical shape, is perhaps the most active. Taal Volcano, twelve miles in diameter, in a crater lake of the same name, is some forty miles south of Manila and has been active intermittently since 1965, as has Mount Catarman on the island of Camiguin off the northern coast of Mindanao.

The country can be divided into three regions or sections: Luzon and attendant islands; the Visayas, including Palawan and Mindoro (the central Philippines); and Mindanao, including the Sulus, often called the southern Philippines. About 37 per cent of the land area is in Luzon. 29 per cent in the Visayas, and 34 per cent in Mindanao.

The tropical position and archipelagic character of the country ensure warm, uniform temperatures and generally adequate rainfall throughout the year. The annual range of temperature is less than four degrees at Jolo in the extreme south and seven degrees at Laoag on the northwest tip of Luzon. Temperatures above 100° F. are rare and have occurred only at interior, lowland stations, such as the Cagayan Valley of northeast Luzon. Likewise, sea-level temperatures below 70° are uncommon and below 60° are unknown; but temperatures in the 60's do occur at Baguio (elevation, 4,860 feet) and other upland stations.

The average annual rainfall for the nation as a whole is about 100 inches, but, for a number of reasons, it varies greatly in both amount and seasonality from place to place. Most of the country receives adequate moisture during the months of the southwest (summer) monsoon. The eastern coastal areas and most of the southern islands receive heavy rain during the period of the northeast (winter) monsoon as well. In either case, there are local areas that lie in the rain shadow of some of the higher mountains. Generally, April is the month of least precipitation over most of the country, and November is the wettest month except in those western areas that receive the full effect of the southwest monsoon, which gives maximal moisture in July and August.

Soils vary markedly, but, for a moist tropical environment, they are relatively fertile. The most valuable soils are in the relatively level alluvial areas, as exemplified by the central plain of Luzon, the Cagayan Valley, and western Negros. Residual soils of greatest fertility reflect a basaltic volcanic parent material, as in the area south of Manila, or limestone bedrock, of which there are several small areas.

The Cultural Scene

An ancient Philippine legend says that once there was only water and sky and a bird. Exhausted from its flight and eager to find a place to rest, the bird provoked a quarrel between ocean and sky. As the ocean lashed at the sky with crashing waves, the sky, growing angry, threw huge rocks to subdue the ocean. Those rocks were the world's first land, the Philippines, where the bird finally alighted. However delightful, this legendary theory is refuted by scientists and archaeologists, who have found evidence of fossil remains and stone tools discovered in several provinces dating more than a quarter of a million years ago from a people who are thought to have wandered in from the south and west over then existing land bridges.

The first known civilization on the islands started some 25,000 years ago with the ancestors of today's Negritos, a pygmy-like people with Negroid traits who today live in the remote uplands of Luzon and some of the other larger islands. The first seafarers descended upon the Philippines about 4,000 years ago from east China and Formosa, with another influx in 2000 B.C. They had more advanced knowledge of agriculture with refined stone tools for cultivating grains.

The largest and most significant migrations took place between 300 B.C. and 200 B.C., with the Malays (Indonesians), who brought with them their iron-age tools and crafts of pottery and weaving. These early Filipinos formed many separate communities, known as *barangays* after the crude boats in which they arrived. The communities were usually situated by waterborne trade routes in harbors offering protection from both the elements and other *barangays*. The early settlements attained a certain sophistication and traded extensively with Indian, Chinese, and Arab merchants.

Finally, in the fourteenth and fifteenth centuries, Muslim traders came into the Malay area reaching as far as Luzon. But the Muslim influence was relatively limited, partly because the central government never espoused the principles of this faith. In the sixteenth century, ardent Roman Catholic Spanish missionaries began to arrive after the Spanish gained control of the area.

Economically the Filipinos remained subsistence farmers and fishermen. However, with the more advanced techniques and irrigation methods brought in by the Spaniards came commercial crops—sugar cane, coconut, and tobacco. The Spanish also brought the concept of private property in lieu of the communal ownership characteristic of the *barangay*. The Philippines became the western terminal of the galleon trade developed by Spanish and Mexican entrepreneurs and merchants. Spain monopolized this Philippine trade until 1837, when Manila became an open port.

With the end of the Spanish-American War in 1898, the Philippines was transferred to the United States, which maintained it as a colony, with the stated intent of protection and development of a democratic form of government. After a ten-year commonwealth period, the Philippines became an independent republic shortly after the end of World War II, at a time when the economy was at its lowest ebb: Cities and port facilities had not yet been reconstructed, and commercial agriculture was far below 1939–40 production. This precarious economic situation was made worse by a communist-led postwar rebellion of ex-guerrillas, landless farmers, and others (originally the Peoples Army Against the Japanese, called Huks, for short). This uprising was not controlled until the mid-1950's, under the leadership of Ramón Magsaysay and with U.S. military assistance and funds. At the same time, economic and social reforms were instituted to raise the level of living and the morale of the Filipinos. Since then the Philippine Government has continued to pursue economic and social reforms.

Today the Philippines is a kind of Asian melting pot. As a result of intermixing over many centuries, 99 per cent of the Filipinos are a brown-skinned blend of basic Malayan stock. But there are some marked exceptions, primarily among the highland people. Along with the diminishing numbers of Negritos are the skilled Ifugao mountaineers of northern Luzon, who live amid world-famous rice terraces first built by their an-

The jeepney is a Philippine institution. Born out of necessity at the end of World War II, it is an elaborately decorated, locally constructed body on a jeep chassis. Originally surplus army jeeps were used; now new jeep chassis are imported to meet the demand. The jeepney is faster than the bus and less expensive than the private taxi. In most cities jeepneys are required to follow a fixed route, but in some they are available for charter.

cestors and extended in more recent years; the Bukidnons of interior Mindanao; and many other small groups who differ from the majority of the inhabitants and from each other. Most of these minority groups live in relatively inaccessible areas and generally have remained outside Filipino society.

In addition, there are Chinese and European minorities and mixtures. Numerically the Chinese are a tiny minority (less than 1 per cent of the population), but they have been, and continue to be, active in wholesale and retail trade, banking, transport, and other aspects of the economy. Many have intermarried with Filipinos, and their children have become integrated into Filipino society. Both Spaniards and Americans have contributed an ethnic and cultural imprint. Pure, or nearly pure, Spanish strains remain in only a few areas, but there are thousands of Spanish *mestizos* (people of mixed blood). There have also been many American-Filipino marriages, first dating from the American occupation seventy years ago, but probably occurring in greatest numbers in the immediate postindependence years.

This European and quasi-European segment generally has had a high economic status, in striking contrast with the multitudes of poor both in the cities and in rural areas. High-ranking governmental officials and wealthy Filipino landowners, too, may live in spacious splendor in sharp contrast to the poor fisherman and his urban or agricultural counterpart. Despite recent land-reform programs, many small peasant farmers still pay far too large a share of their crop to the landlord and are burdened with debts incurred for seeds, tools, and fertilizers. The government program includes the purchase and subdivision of a few large estates and the opening of new government-owned lands for resale on easy installment plans to tenants, plus the granting of loans to newly established owners; but few people have benefited from this program. In many places land reform is still a dream. Although social and land reforms are given high priority on the list of government projects in the next decade, as in many other parts of the world the rich and powerful tend to be interested primarily in remaining rich and retaining social prestige and political power, and very little is done to ease the hardships of the poor on the farms and in the cities. As Dennis Bloodworth noted in *An Eye for the Dragon,* "the distance between the poor and rich strains the eyes."

Equally fundamental, perhaps, are religious and linguistic differences. The largest cultural minority is the Moros or Muslim Filipinos (5 per cent), concentrated in parts of Mindanao and the Sulus. About 84 per cent of the people are Roman Catholic (this includes two indigenous Christian cults, Aglipayan and Eglesia ni Cristo); some 5 per cent are members of the Independent Church of the Philippines, 3 per cent are Protestant, and almost 3 per cent follow other religions, mostly pagan.

English is the *lingua franca,* and approximately 40 per cent of the people understand it. In an attempt to develop a common language other than English, the government has supported the creation of a national language (Pilipino) based on Tagalog, and has made this language compulsory in the schools. Probably half the population is now fluent in Pilipino. Spanish is the third official language, but probably no more than a half million people, largely the social elite, speak or understand it as a second language. Despite the multiplicity of tongues (there are some seventy-five languages and local dialects), the Philippines has achieved one of the highest literacy levels in monsoon Asia, about 75 per cent.

An Agricultural Economy

Agriculture is the source of livelihood of about 57 per cent of the total labor force, and goods of agricultural origin bring in three fourths of the export revenue. In volume, production more than doubled from 1949 to 1960, then continued to increase at a slower rate during the 1960's. Nonetheless, improvement in agriculture has been slow and has lagged behind industrial evolution.

Philippine farms are neither so labor intensive as those of most other Southeast Asian nations nor so capital intensive as those of Western nations. There are three types of farming: plantation, small holdings, and shifting (slash-and-burn) cultivation. Locally called *kaingin*, this last process makes use of simple tools and relatively simple cropping technology. It is a primitive, subsistence type of economy and is practiced in the rugged interiors of the larger islands and in some lowland frontier areas.

Plantation cultivation, called *hacienda* agriculture in Luzon and the Visayas, dates from the Spanish period, although some farms of this type were established at a later date, using American, European, or Filipino capital. Some plantations have large acreages of rice or corn, but most are geared to the export market (sugar, coconuts, abaca, and tobacco, for instance).

The great majority of farms are small. The average size is 8.5 acres, but more than half the total are under five acres and in crowded sections they are becoming smaller. Subsistence-type tillage is widespread, especially in the older, densely settled areas (Ilocos coast, Cebu, and parts of the central plain of Luzon, for example). Rice or corn is generally the dominant crop, though both may be replaced by sweet potatoes (*camotes*) in areas of rugged terrain or by cassava (*manioc*) in some communities in the south. Bananas and other tropical fruits, coconuts, and peanuts and some vegetables are also grown in most places for home use.

The small holding may be a commercial rather than a so-called subsistence farm. Most of the coconuts, abaca, and tobacco and much of the sugar cane are grown by farmers who cultivate only a small acreage. Tropical fruits and vegetables for village and city markets also are normally the product of small operators. Only rubber and pineapples (for two major cannery operations) are exclusively plantation crops.

Rice, referred to as *palay* in the Philippines, is the principal crop on about half the farms; it is grown on more farms than any other crop and occupies 40 per cent of the cultivated land. It is the traditional staple food for some three fourths of the population. Primary rice-producing areas are the central plain of Luzon, the Panay Plain, the Bicol region, and parts of the Cagayan Valley. Culture methods are comparable to those in other Southeast Asian lands, but, for preparing the paddy field, the *carabao* (water buffalo) gradually is giving way to a small walking tractor made in Britain or Japan. When adequate water is available, either from rainfall or from irrigation storage facilities, double-cropping of rice is practiced. (This is the case over most of the Bicol Plain.) Upland (dry-land) rice culture is widespread but accounts for only 30 per cent of the annual production.

Although the Philippines has been on the verge of rice self-sufficiency for many years, it continued to be an importer until a surplus was achieved beginning with the 1968–69 crop as a result of the use of improved seed, such as the new varieties developed at the International Rice Research Institute (see pp. 215–19). The country is not yet a significant rice exporter, however, because improper milling conditions result in a high percentage of broken grains; hence Philippine rice is not yet competitive on the world market.

Corn, known in the Philippines as *mais,* was introduced into the Visayan Islands more than 500 years ago and has since spread to all parts of the archipelago. It is the second most important food crop and occupies some 15 per cent of the cultivated area. It is usually ground into granules or grits about the size of rice grains and cooked in a similar manner. In fact, it is sometimes called "corn-rice." This corn-rice provides a more nutritious and cheaper diet than polished rice. Corn is the primary staple in areas where rainfall is erratic or soils are too porous or slopes too steep for economical rice culture. The principal corn-producing areas are Cebu, eastern Negros, much of Mindanao, and the sandy alluvial soils of the middle Cagayan Valley of Luzon.

Sugar has occupied a dominant position in the economic structure of the Philippines for more than a half century. It is a high-value crop, and more than a million tons have been processed each year since 1920, except during the war and immediate postwar period from 1942 through 1950. Current annual production is almost 2 million tons a year. Less than a half dozen countries produce more sugar from cane than the Philippines. Sixty-five per cent of the total comes from the island of Negros. The sugar districts of western Negros, central Luzon, and elsewhere reflect the combination of level land and moisture in sufficient quantity to permit an

extensive acreage of cane and thereby support commercial sugar processing. But political rather than environmental factors have helped to promote the sugar industry; for several decades it has had access to a favored
American market. The future of the industry will also be dependent in
part on political factors, for the present U.S. sugar act expires in 1971
and the Laurel-Langley trade agreement in 1974. Probably both will be
renegotiated in some form, for the Philippine sugar industry affects all
strata of Filipino society.

The coconut industry provides about 40 per cent of the annual foreign
exchange earnings, and in most years the Philippines supplies 60 per cent
of the world's copra exports, 23 per cent of the world's export of vegetable
oil, and more than half the commercial shredded coconut. Of these exports, 28 per cent go to the United States and 60 per cent to Europe. The
total area planted in coconuts is about 4.5 million acres. The industry
consists primarily of small enterprises; most coconut groves are plots of
less than 12.5 acres. The principal areas of commercial production are
central and southeastern Luzon and Mindanao.

The output of abaca, known commercially as Manila hemp, has declined in recent years because of plant disease, competition from synthetic
fibers, and a variety of other factors. Nevertheless, the Philippines has retained a virtual monopoly on abaca and supplies more than 90 per cent
of the world's diminishing demand. Requiring moisture throughout the
year, production is principally along the eastern margins of the country
and in interior Mindanao.

Tobacco is grown, at least in small amounts, in almost all provinces,
but two districts are responsible for most of the commercial production.
The middle Cagayan Valley in northeast Luzon is the leading area for
cigar filler and the basis of the Manila cigar industry. It is a dry-season
crop, planted on porous alluvial soils that carry corn during the wet
season. The Ilocos coast of northwestern Luzon and northern portions
of the central plain have become the principal area for "Virginia-type"
cigarette tobacco, a crop that had its beginnings in 1950. Production of
cigarette tobacco has been encouraged by rigid import controls on foreign
commodities that might be produced domestically and by abnormally high
price supports. In this part of Luzon rice is the wet-season crop and
tobacco the second or dry-season crop, but tobacco has become the first
crop in terms of income produced per acre. In contrast to the other major
commercial crops, tobacco is produced almost totally for the domestic
market.

Fishing and Forestry

A wide variety of fish is available in Philippine waters, and the fishing industry employs about 688,000 persons. Inshore fishing predominates, and traditional methods are used. The most important catch is scad, followed by slipmouth, herring, anchovy, tuna, mackerel, and many others. Most of the large fishing boats are based at Manila. Of the total catch of about 770,000 tons a year, about one third comes from commercial operations, more than half from subsistence fishing, and about 13 per cent from fishponds. Although the volume of production has tripled since 1947, the fishing industry is unable to supply the nation with sufficient seafood to meet the growing demand.

Fishpond culture is one of the most intensive uses of land for food production, and few places in the world can match the intensive development of the deltaic swampland around Manila Bay. Similar, though less intensive, development occurs in several of the Visayan Islands (especially Panay) and to a modest extent in Mindanao. Some 350,000 acres are in fishponds. Bodies of primarily brackish water are divided into a series of diked ponds for controlled production of selected species of fish and jumbo shrimp, which are raised from fry to marketable size. The *bañgos* or milk fish is the most widely used species in the fish-culture industry.

Tropical evergreen hardwoods cover about half the country, commercial forests more than one third. Lumber, logs, and plywood make up the bulk of the forest products, which collectively rank second in value among Philippine exports (after coconut products). The top buyer of logs is Japan; most of the lumber is shipped to the United States. Bamboo and rattan are the principal secondary forest products, primarily for the domestic market.

Minerals and Mining

Philippine minerals are varied and widely dispersed over the islands, but most of them are markedly limited in quality, quantity, or both. However, among the Southeast Asian nations, only Indonesia and Malaysia have greater mineral wealth (primarily petroleum and tin, respectively). The most valuable metallic minerals mined in the Philippines are copper, gold, iron ore, and chromite. Other metals produced include mercury, manganese, lead, silver, zinc, and molybdenum. Some low-quality coal (central Cebu and southwestern Mindanao) has been mined for many years. Other nonmetallic minerals are limestone, marble, sand and gravel, rock asphalt, sulphur, asbestos, and gypsum. Salt is obtained by evaporation of seawater during the dry season. Crude petroleum and natural gas have never been found in quantities of commercial significance. At present the total mineral-resource base is not known, as most of the country has not been systematically and scientifically surveyed.

The copper deposits are small compared to those of Chile, the Soviet Union, and the United States, but they provide nearly 85 per cent of the income from minerals. Most of the copper comes from central Cebu, southwestern Negros, central Samar, southeastern Mindanao, the Zambales Mountains of Luzon, and Rapu Rapu Island (southeast Luzon). Production increased from slightly more than 10,000 tons (copper metal equivalent) in 1950 to more than 110,000 tons in 1968.

Postwar production of gold has been markedly less than in the 1920's and early 1930's, and in recent years the country has supplied only about 1 per cent of the world's total. Nevertheless, it is the eighth-ranking gold producer and the leading one in Asia. The principal gold area is the complex Baguio mineral district, but almost 20 per cent of the total is a by-product of the expanding copper industry.

Iron deposits of different types occur in several places, the main producing ones being in Camarines Norte, Zamboanga del Sur, and Davao. Largest reserves are the nickeliferous lateritic ores of Surigao, Davao, and Samar; they are largely unused because of the high cost of removing the nickel.

In terms of the value of production, chromite ore has ranked third or fourth in recent years. The major deposits of chrome are in the Zambales area of western Luzon. Chromite ore is shipped primarily to the United States; smaller amounts are sold to Japan, Canada, Western Europe, and Australia.

Expanding Industry

Although some elementary processing has been traditional for decades, if not centuries, modern industrial activities are relatively new in the Philippines. It is only since the nation became independent, and especially since 1950, that industrialization has been strongly encouraged by the government. Much of the listed manufacturing is simply assemblage or packaging of some kind, but the average annual growth rate has nevertheless been phenomenal; manufacturing has become a major sector of the national economy (19 per cent of the Gross National Product), and it includes a reasonable variety of products destined increasingly for domestic consumption. Establishments tend to be small, and most of them employ fewer than twenty workers, although there are marked exceptions; about eighty concerns employ 500 or more workers each.

Strong government protection has been helpful, through foreign import and exchange controls, through the decontrol of the Philippine peso, and through partial tax exemption for the so-called pioneer (new and necessary) industries. More than 25 per cent of the value of Philippine manufacturing is food processing, followed in order by chemicals and chemical products, metal products, textiles, beverages, tobacco products, and wood products. Textiles and cement have probably expanded the most rapidly in recent years, and shoe manufacture has become a semimodern industry, rather than a cottage industry.

Textiles, clothing, and shoes have benefited greatly from government protection. Textile manufacturing, chiefly from imported cotton, absorbs some 13 per cent of the metropolitan Manila labor force and includes several large new integrated plants mostly in its suburbs (Quezon City, Malabon, Mandaluyong, and Marikina). Clothing manufacture too is concentrated in Manila, much of it within the city.

A modest development of heavy industry has taken place. There are several small rolling mills, one integrated steel plant, and a variety of fabricated-metal plants manufacturing such things as bodies for trucks, buses, and jeepneys, steel office furniture, castings, hardware and hand tools, small mechanical rice threshers, steel pipe, and structural forms. Four small petroleum refineries, with a combined capacity of 49.8 million tons per year, began operation between 1954 and 1962. There are now four fertilizer plants and several modern cement plants.

Much of this expanding industry is in Manila (population 4.3 million) and a few other cities such as Cebu and Davao; and Iligan, on the northern coast of Mindanao, is the center of a rapidly growing industrial complex, a result of the availability of cheap electric power from the Maria Christina Falls. Iligan industries include the integrated steel mill, two fertilizer plants, a flour mill, and a cement plant.

In summary, the Philippines is the only nation in Southeast Asia where the population is predominantly Christian, English is the language of instruction at all levels, and the "national dress" is basically patterned after European models. The years of American rule left a considerable imprint on the viewpoints of Filipinos on government, education, health, and sanitation. The pattern of culture is not East Asian, nor is it representative of Southeast Asia, nor is it a blend of East and West. It is best characterized as having some elements of Western culture within an Asian matrix.

focus *on the Revolution in Rice*

Rice is the principal food of more than 60 per cent of mankind. The people of Asia produce and eat more than 90 per cent of all rice grown, yet rice yields in the tropical parts of this region have been among the world's lowest.

Although poor preparation of wet-rice fields, limited weed and insect control, inadequate fertilization, and other factors collectively have contributed to the low yields, traditional varieties of tropical rice possess peculiarities that have made it difficult to increase yields. Most species of tropical rice naturally grow to a height of five or six feet, and heavy fertilization results in a taller stock or bigger leaves. This contributes to a greater amount of "lodging" (the plant leans, falls over, and lies in a tangled mass), which, in turn, contributes to greater damage by weather, insects, and rodents.

In 1960, recognizing the need to improve rice production in Asia to meet the rapidly rising population, the Ford and Rockefeller foundations jointly, in cooperation with the government of the Philippines, established the International Rice Research Institute (IRRI) as a world center for the improvement of rice. The Institute came about, at least in part, because agricultural scientists had concluded that the only solution was to "re-engineer" the structure of the tropical rice plant to develop short-stemmed varieties that would not fall over when subjected to torrential rains, high winds, or heavy fertilization. There was encouragement, too, from the fact that high-yielding varieties of wheat, corn, sorghum, and millet had been developed in recent years, the best known of which were the Mexican wheats developed by the Rockefeller Foundation. These varieties had quadrupled Mexican wheat yields to forty bushels per acre and were setting new records in West Pakistan, parts of India, and elsewhere.

The Institute is situated adjacent to the College of Agriculture and Forestry of the University of the Philippines at Los Baños, Laguna, forty miles southeast of Manila. The area has an annual precipitation of about eighty inches, which falls during a rainy season normally extending from mid-May until November or early December. But the site is near the foot of Mount Maquiling, and so irrigation water is available during the dry season. Hence, three crops of rice per year are possible on the experimental fields, thereby shortening the over-all time span for producing and testing new varieties.

The professional staff of the Institute has included top rice scientists from all major rice-producing countries; total employment approaches 700, 90 per cent of whom are Filipinos. They have conducted research in plant-breeding, genetics, agronomy, soil chemistry, soil microbiology, plant pathology, plant physiology, entomology, agricultural economics, communication, and statistics. The Institute also trains extension workers from other Southeast Asian nations. Philippine extension personnel are trained at the nearby University of the Philippines Agricultural and Forestry campus. In cooperation with the U.S. Agency for International Development, the Institute carried out a project in agricultural engineering to develop small, light-weight mechanical rice-threshers. One or more of these machines, inexpensive and easy to maintain, is now produced

Courtesy The Rockefeller Foundation
The International Rice Research Institute in the Philippines has developed a lightweight, mechanical rice-thresher, and a small walking tractor made in Britain or Japan is becoming available; yet traditional methods of preparing the land with a carabao remain widespread. Even these methods can produce high yields with the new varieties of rice evolved by the Institute.

commercially. The Institute also tackled the problem of rats, a serious one in the tropics. They eat the grain in the field and also feed on young rice plants soon after transplanting. IRRI has developed an electric fence which kills rats. But the major efforts of the Institute have been devoted to the development of new strains of rice.

New Varieties of Rice

Some 10,000 varieties of rice were collected from 73 countries in the search for seeds that might be crossed to develop the heartiest, most adaptable, most nutritious strain for the humid tropics. Probably 8,000 of them were tested or studied, at least in a preliminary manner. The first real evidence of success (1963) appeared with the crossing of Dee-geo-woo-gen, a short-stemmed Taiwan rice, with Peta, a tall Indonesian variety that has also been grown widely in the Philippines. This resulted in the first strains of the famous IR-8, released in early 1968.

IR-8 is outstanding in many ways. Having a short (36–42 inches), stiff stalk, it remains erect during heavy tropical rainstorms, high winds, and heavy applications of fertilizer. It produces many tillers (stems from the single transplanted seedling). It gives excellent yields with heavy fertilization and without fertilization yields as much as other varieties—facts confirmed in tests outside the Philippines as well as at various sites within the Philippines. It matures rapidly (120–130 days) and is tolerant of a wide variety of soil and climatic conditions, is moderately resistant to virus diseases, and is less susceptible to other diseases than many varieties produced at the Institute. Unfortunately, IR-8 has a poor grain quality because of chalkiness. It is a "soft" rice whose grains are easily broken during the milling process, which reduces its marketability, and its taste is unacceptable to most rice eaters in Asia. Science was able to change the architecture of the plant; changing taste preferences is another matter.

The second variety, IR-5, was released in 1969. Taller than IR-8 (51–58 inches), it is susceptible to lodging, insects, and fungus and is very light-sensitive. The one redeeming feature is the extremely high yield that can be obtained (more than 5,000 pounds per acre) if the negative factors can be controlled. It, too, is a "soft" rice, and the great quantities of fertilizer necessary to obtain the high yield imparts a taste that is not appreciated by most rice users, especially Indonesians.

In early 1970, two other varieties were released, IR-20 and IR-22. The former does not break so easily as IR-8, but it hardens when cool, and taste quality remains generally unacceptable. Nonetheless, it is being grown in several countries. IR-22 appears to be the best variety yet released, primarily because it tastes better and has better milling qualities than previously released varieties. Fortunately, too, it has a flag leaf—a single leaf that rises higher and extends partly over the head of the stalk —which makes the grain less accessible to birds.

In summary, the Institute has been successful in developing new and important varieties of rice—and they are new varieties; technically they are not hybrids, hence not comparable to the hybrid corn of the American corn belt and elsewhere. It is not profitable to use any of them without careful water control, heavy fertilization, periodic application of insecticides, and chemicals for control of fungus diseases. However, if the farmer can and will follow the rules, yields can be doubled, even tripled in some instances. The IR varieties have produced record yields in every tropical country where they have been tried—in Asia, in Africa, and in the Americas.

IR-8 has now been planted in many countries throughout South and Southeast Asia and in Peru, Brazil, and West Africa. Both West Pakistan and the Philippines have now become rice-surplus areas, and South Vietnam expects to become an exporter by 1972. The new rice is unpopular in Indonesia, probably because most farmers are not yet able to purchase the necessary fertilizer. It is not widely used in Burma, perhaps as a result of economic and political instability, and has only limited acceptance in Thailand, where there are popular Thai varieties that supply current domestic needs and the export market. Although it is not yet widely used in Cambodia and Malaysia, excellent results have been reported there. The only tropical areas where environmental factors have limited the planting of IR-8 is East Pakistan. Apparently IR-8 is too light-sensitive for the prolonged cloudy skies during the growing season on the Ganges (Ganga) Delta. It is reliably reported that IR rice is being grown in the People's Republic of China and North Vietnam, although neither country received seed stock through the normal channels distributing seed rice.

The Impact of IRRI Rice on the Philippines

The new developments have had a major effect on farming operations. Probably more than half the Philippine rice acreage is now IR rice. This means a higher income for the farmer and implies a better living for him and his family. It has no doubt contributed to the rapid introduction of mechanization in the form of a light-weight walking tractor and the mechanical thresher. High yields and associated higher incomes have encouraged the expansion of pump irrigation to make a second crop possible.

Industry also is reflecting the impact of the rice revolution. Fertilizer manufacture has expanded greatly in the past few years. One new factory, a $30 million plant, now employs almost 400 persons. A chemical concern has developed and markets an effective insecticide against rice stem-borers. New opportunities have arisen for the small businessman. There is now a network of fertilizer dealers. Engineering firms that specialize in the construction of costly irrigation and drainage systems (water control) are more prevalent. One small entrepreneur has developed his own mail-order business in growing the new varieties and selling certified seed. The provincial governments have been forced to construct more farm-to-market roads in rural areas; hence, there are greater employment opportunities in roadbuilding. More storage facilities are needed; hence, the construction industry and cement manufacture should expand.

What has taken place in the Philippines over the past few years may well be duplicated in other less developed nations. The construction of a new fertilizer plant in India and of new grain-storage facilities in West Pakistan are related, in part, to the introduction of new varieties of rice in those nations. As yet, the use of IRRI rice has not greatly affected total world production, but it may profoundly alter the economics of the rice industry. Malaysia and Ceylon, for instance, which have traditionally emphasized export crops and imported great quantities of rice, have launched plans to attempt to attain sufficiency in rice by using the new varieties. Thailand has publicly expressed concern about the probable loss of its established export markets. In recent years, the United States has exported rice to 110 different countries; no doubt this number will be reduced as many buyers become self-sufficient in rice or even rice-exporters.

Suggested Readings

American University. *Area Handbook of the Philippines.* Washington, D.C.: U.S. Government Printing Office, 1969. A comprehensive analysis of social, economic, and political aspects of the area and its national security.

Asian Social Institute. *Pattern for Rural Reform.* Manila: Solidaridad, 1969. Discusses socio-economic problems and social and psychological factors in rural development.

CUTSHALL, ALDEN. *The Philippines: Nation of Islands.* Princeton, N.J.: Van Nostrand, 1964. A compact volume emphasizing physical-cultural-political relationships.

KRINKS, P. A. "Peasant Colonization in Mindanao." *Journal of Tropical Geography,* XXX (June, 1970), pp. 38–47. Discusses unassisted migration and settlement in marginal lands and the resulting damage to forests and soils.

Philippine Population in the Seventies. Proceedings of the Second Conference on Population, November 27–29, 1967. Manila: Community Publishers, 1969. Discusses population and the food situation, employment and education, population growth and economic development, and problems and targets for the future.

RAVENHOLT, ALBERT. *The Philippines: A Young Republic on the Move.* Princeton, N.J.: Van Nostrand, 1962. A discussion of the historical development, economy, society, and problems of the country as viewed by a longtime resident.

SIBLEY, WILLIS E. "Social Organization, Economy, and Directed Cultural Change in Two Philippine Barrios." *Human Organization,* XXVIII, no. 2 (Summer, 1969), pp. 148–54. Explores the reasons for the successes and failures of two development projects and suggests alternatives for improving the probability of success in future work.

VAN DER KROEF, JUSTUS M. "Patterns of Cultural Conflict in Philippine Life." *Pacific Affairs,* XXXIX, nos. 3 and 4 (Fall and Winter, 1966–67), pp. 326–38. Analyzes the divisive role of group loyalties in the search for national unity.

WERNSTEDT, FREDERICK L., and J. E. SPENCER. *The Philippine Island World.* Berkeley and Los Angeles: University of California Press, 1967. An authoritative study of the archipelago that provides a physical, cultural, and economic survey of the country, then discusses its various regional sectors.

See also Suggested Readings for Part I, pp. 57–59.

INDEX

Abaca, 211

Agency for International Development (AID), 144, 216

Agriculture: in Burma, 68–71, 74–81; in Cambodia, 106–9; development of, 51, 55–56; in Indonesia, 188, 189, 191–93, 197, 199; in Laos, 123–25; in Lower Mekong Basin, 13, 19–20, 26–29; in Malaysia, 158–60, 164; in North Vietnam, 135–38; in Philippines, 206, 209–11; in South Vietnam, 135, 139–42; in Thailand, 87, 88, 90, 93, 95 (*see also* Rice production)

Andaman Sea, 67

Angkor Thom, 104

Angkor Wat, 104

Animal husbandry: in Burma, 70–71; in Cambodia, 107, 108; in Indonesia, 191, 193; in Malaysia, 160

Animism: in Cambodia, 114; in Indonesia, 188–89; in Thailand, 87

Annam, 131, 135, 137

Arakan Coast, 67, 71, 80

Asahan Falls Project, 195

Asian Development Bank, 6, 7: and Mekong Project, 21, 29

Association for Southeast Asia (ASA), 6, 12

Association for Southeast Asian Nations (ASEAN), 6, 12

Australia, 6

Bahrin, Tunku S., 164

Bajau, 156

Bali, 188–91, 193, 196

Banda Atjeh, 190

Bandung, 195

Bangka, 194

Bangkok (*see* Krung Thep)

Bassac River, 103–4, 107

Batavia (*see* Djakarta)

Battambang, 110, 115, 116

Bawdin Mines, 72

Belitung, 194

Bengal, Bay of, 68

Bhamo, 67

Bhumibol Dam, 89

Bicol Plain, 210

Bien Hoa, 134

Bintan Island, 194

Birth control (*see* Family planning)

Black, Eugene R., 14

Bloodworth, Dennis, 208

Bogor, 21

Bolovens Plateau, 122, 125

Borneo, 5, 152, 154, 188–89, 191–94, 196

Brahmaputra Valley, 83

Broek, Jan, 5

Brunei, 5, 154

Buddhism: in Burma, 65, 70, 104; in Cambodia, 105–6, 113, 116; in Indonesia, 188; in Laos, 129; in Thailand, 87; in Vietnam, 132

Bukidnons, 207

Bukit Timah, 168

Burma, 3–5, 7–9, 63–81: agriculture in, 68–71, 74–81; and China, 11, 67; climate and landscape of, 66–69; fishing and forestry in, 71–72; government of, 63–65, 73–74; history of, 63–64; industrialization in, 66, 73; and Mekong Project, 13, 16, 22; mineral resources of, 72–73; population of, 63, 65–66; rice production in, 74–81; and Thailand, 83–85

Burma Road, 67

Cagayan Valley, 205, 210, 211

Cai Bau, 138

Cambodia, 5, 7, 9, 100–117: agriculture in, 106–9, 112; climate and landscape of, 102–3; economy of, 106–10; exports and imports of, 107–8, 109–10; government of, 111–12; history of, 100, 104–5; and Mekong Project, 13–16, 21, 23, 26; population of, 103–4, 112–17; social change in, 105–6; and Vietnam war, 100, 112

Camiguin, 204

Catarman, Mount, 204

Catholicism: in Cambodia, 113; in Philippines, 206, 208 (see also Christianity)

Cebu, 209, 210, 213, 214

Celebes, 188, 190–92, 194–95

Ceylon, 5, 219

Chaîne Annamitique, 134, 135, 137

Chakri Dynasty, 85

Chams, 117

Chang Hai Ding, 184

Chao Phraya River, 83, 88

Chao Phraya Valley, 87, 88

Chauk, 72

Cheng Heng, 100

Chhlong, 109

Chiang Mai, 87

Chin Hills, 65

China, People's Republic of, 9, 10–12, 14: and Burma, 11, 67; and Cambodia, 116; and Laos, 121; and North Vietnam, 133, 139; and Thailand, 11–12, 86; and Vietnam, 131

Chindwin River, 67, 70–71

Chinese: in Burma, 63, 65; in Cambodia, 104, 113, 115; in Indonesia, 11, 188–90; in Laos, 128–29; in Malaysia, 155–56, 158, 160, 162–64; in Philippines, 11, 207; in South Vietnam, 134; in Southeast Asia, 10, 11, 38; in Thailand, 36, 86, 87

Cholon, 37–38, 142

Christianity: in Indonesia, 188–90; in Philippines, 208, 214 (see also Catholicism)

Chulalongkorn, 85

Cities, 31–56: growth of, 35–37, 43–47, 49–53; morphology of, 38–40, 48; problems of, 31–42, 47–49, 53; trends in, 49–56 (see also Urbanization)

Climate: in Burma, 66–68; in Cambodia, 102–3; in Indonesia, 185–88, 197–98; in Laos, 122; in Malaysia, 154–55; in Philippines, 204–5; in Singapore, 169; in Thailand, 88–89; in Vietnam, 134–35

Coal (see Mineral resources)

Cochin China, 37, 131

Coconut production: in Malaysia, 158; in Philippines, 211

Coedès, Georges, 57

Cohe, Louis A., 13–30

Colonialism: in Burma, 75–78; and cities, 35–37, 47; in Thailand, 85

Commerce, 9–10: and urbanization, 35–37, 44 (see also Trade)

Communication: and cities, 54; in Indonesia, 196

Communism: in Laos, 119; in Malaysia, 163; in North Vietnam, 134, 136–39; policies toward, 9, 11; and South Vietnam, 133, 146–47; and Thailand, 98

Corson, William, 147

Cutshall, Alden, 203–19, 220

Da Nang, 142

Danau Toba, 189

Davao, 213, 214
Davis, Kingsley, 31n., 32n.
De Young, John E., 99
Delta Development Project, 23, 26, 27
Denpasar, 196
Diem, Ngo Dinh, 145–46
Djakarta, 32–42, 47, 153, 185, 190, 195–96, 198–99
Dommen, Arthur J., 128
Donnison, F. S. V., 81
Dumai, 194
Dwyer, D. J., 43n., 57
Dyaks, 189–90

East Malaysia (see Malaysia)
Ebhihara, May, 117
Economic Commission for Asia and the Far East, 21, 22
Education: in Burma, 74; in Cambodia, 105–6; in Indonesia, 196; in Laos, 128; in Malaysia, 156, 158; in Singapore, 176–77; in South Vietnam, 143; in Thailand, 96
Eisenhower, Dwight D., 145
Electric power: in Burma, 73; in Cambodia, 109; in Indonesia, 195; in Laos, 123; in Malaysia, 161; in North Vietnam, 139; in South Vietnam, 142; in Thailand, 89, 92–93
Elephant Mountains, 108
Employment: in Burma, 73; in Cambodia, 106; in cities, 40–41, 49–51; in Indonesia, 191, 198; in Malaysia, 161–62; in Singapore, 172–74; in South Vietnam, 143
Ethnic groups (see Chinese; Indians; Minority groups)

Family planning: in Indonesia, 200; in Singapore, 170; in Thailand, 95
Farming (see Agriculture)
Fisher, C. A., 57
Fishing: in Burma, 71; in Cambodia, 108–9; in Indonesia, 193; in Laos, 125; in Malaysia, 160; in Philippines, 212; in Thailand, 90; in Vietnam, 135

Flood control: in Lower Mekong Basin, 19–20, 26; in North Vietnam, 136
Food crops (see Agriculture)
Foreign Exchange Operations Fund, 126
Foreign investment: in Cambodia, 111–12; in Indonesia, 194, 200; in Singapore, 173; in Thailand, 91, 93
Forestry: in Burma, 71–72; in Cambodia, 109; in Indonesia, 193–94; in Laos, 122, 125; in Malaysia, 155, 160; in Philippines, 212; in Thailand, 89
France: and Cambodia, 105, 117; and Indochina, 3, 9; and Laos, 119; and Mekong Project, 21–22; and Vietnam, 131, 138
Fryer, Donald W., 31–42, 57
Furnivall, John S., 76, 81

Geertz, Clifford, 196–97, 200
Germany, East, 139
Germany, West, 23, 142
Ginsburg, Norton S., 3–12, 32n., 43–56, 166n.
Golay, Frank H., 57
Goldstein, Sidney, 99
Government: of Burma, 63–65; of Cambodia, 111–12; of Indonesia, 185–90, 199–200; of Laos, 127–29; of Malaysia, 161–64; of North Vietnam, 134, 136–38; of Philippines, 206, 208, 214; of Singapore, 166, 172–73, 176; of South Vietnam, 133–34, 143–50; of Thailand, 85, 95, 97–98
Grant, Bruce, 210
Great Britain, 3, 5, 6: and Burma, 9, 65, 75–78; and Malaysia, 152–54, 162; and Singapore, 8, 37, 168
Greater East Asian Co-Prosperity Sphere, 3, 10
Gross national product: Cambodian, 110; Lao, 126; Thai, 93
Gullick, J. M., 164

Haiphong, 138, 139
Halpern, Joel M., 128

Hanoi, 35–37, 134, 138, 139
Hartshorne, Richard, 7
Hinduism, 188
Ho, Robert, 165
Homalin, 67
Hon Gai, 138
Hong Kong, 8–9
Hong River, 134, 135, 136, 138
Housing: in cities, 41, 46; in Singapore, 171, 177–83
Htin Aung, U., 81
Hué, 36, 134, 135
Hughes, Helen, 183
Huke, Robert E., 63–81
Huks, 206

Iban, 156
Ifugaos, 206
Iligan, 214
Ilocos, 209, 211
Immigration, rural-urban, 49–52
Imperialism, 3 (see also Colonialism)
Indians: in Burma, 65; in Cambodia, 117; in Indonesia, 189; in Malaysia, 155–56, 162; in Singapore, 168–70
Indicative Basin Plan, 23–30
Indochina: and China, 11; and France, 3, 131 (see also specific country)
Indochina war (see Vietnam war)
Indonesia, 3–9, 11, 185–200: agriculture in, 188, 189, 191–93, 197, 199; climate and landscape of, 185–88, 197–98; economy of, 191, 198–200; government of, 185, 190; and Malaysia, 163; population of, 185, 188–91, 196–200; transportation in, 195–96
Industrialization: in Burma, 66, 73; in Cambodia, 109; in cities, 44–45, 49–51; in Indonesia, 199; in Laos, 105–6; in Lower Mekong Basin, 19–20; in Malaysia, 161; in North Vietnam, 138; in Philippines, 203, 213–14, 219; in Singapore, 172–75; in South Vietnam, 142; in Thailand, 90–91
International Rice Research Institute (IRRI), 140, 191, 210, 215–19: rice strains, 80, 217–19

Iron ore (see Mineral resources)
Irrawaddy River, 67, 68, 70, 75, 80
Irrigation: in Burma, 71, 80; in Cambodia, 107; in South Vietnam, 141
Islam: in Indonesia, 188–89; in Malaysia, 152, 155, 163; in Philippines, 206, 208; in Thailand, 86, 87

Jacobs, Norman, 99
Japan, 3, 8, 10, 12: and Mekong Project, 22–23; occupation of Burma by, 63, 78; and Vietnam, 131
Jars, Plain of, 122
Java, 7, 36, 144, 188–99
Jogjakarta, 190, 198
Johor, 154, 159, 161, 168
Jurong, 172, 174–75

Kachin, 65–66
Kadazans, 156
Kalimantan (see Borneo)
Kampot, 109, 115
Karens, 65, 76, 87
Kawthule, 65
Kayah, 65
Kelantan, 154, 159, 161
Keppel Harbor, 175
Kha, 128
Khmer Empire, 104–5
Khmer Republic (see Cambodia)
Khmers: in Cambodia, 100, 104, 113, 114–15; in South Vietnam, 114; in Thailand, 83, 86
Khorat Plateau, 88
Kinabalu, Mount, 154
Kinta Valley, 161
Kirk, Donald, 118
Klang Valley, 161
Kompong Cham, 107, 110
Kompong Som, 104, 109, 110
Kra Isthmus, 88
Kratie, 14–16, 103
Krinks, P. A., 220
Krung Thep, 19, 21, 32–36, 40, 82, 85, 87, 91, 92, 94, 116
Kuala Lumpur, 35, 37, 161

LaBar, F. M., 130
Land ownership: in Burma, 76, 79; in Cambodia, 108
Land reform: in Indonesia, 191; in North Vietnam, 136–37; in Philippines, 208; in South Vietnam, 139–40, 143–50; in Thailand, 96
Language: Burmese, 66; Cambodian, 104, 106; Filipino, 208; Indonesian, 188–89, 190; Malaysian, 155, 156, 158; Singaporean, 176
Lao, 128: in Cambodia, 116–17
Lao Cai, 138
Lao Theung, 128
Laos, 4, 7, 9, 119–29: agriculture in, 123–25; and Cambodia, 116–17; climate and landscape of, 121–22; economy of, 123–26; government of, 127–29; industry in, 125–26; and Mekong Project, 13, 16, 21–23; population of, 127–29; and Thailand, 83
Legge, J. D., 201
Leifer, Michael, 118
Livestock (see Animal husbandry)
Lombok Island, 188, 190
Lon Nol, 100, 113–14
Los Baños, 21, 215
Lower Mekong River Basin, 13, 16–30
Luang Prabang, 119, 121, 127, 128
Luzon, 144, 204–5, 206, 209–11, 213

McGee, T. G., 57
Mackie, J. A. C., 201
Madrasi, 76
Madura, 189–93, 196, 198
Magsaysay, Ramón, 206
Magwe, 69, 80
Majapahit Empire, 152
Makasar, 195
Malacca, 152, 154, 166
Malay Peninsula, 83, 88, 152, 160, 168
Malays, 155–56, 162–64: in Indonesia, 189; in Philippines, 205–6; in Singapore, 170
Malaysia, 3–8, 11, 152–64: agriculture in, 158–60, 164, 218, 219; climate and landscape of, 154–55; economy of, 161, 164; exports and imports of, 162; government of, 161, 162–64; history of, 152–54; manufacturing and mines in, 160–62; population of, 155–56, 158; and Singapore, 168
Maluku Islands, 188
Mandalay, 66, 80
Manila, 32–34, 36–40, 42, 47, 48, 49, 53, 204, 206, 212, 214
Marcos, Ferdinand, 10, 11
Martaban, Gulf of, 68
Maung, Mya, 81
Mawchi Mines, 72
Mayon, Mount, 204
Medan, 195–96
Mekong Committee, 21–23, 27–30
Mekong Development Project, 13–30, 141
Mekong River, 14–16, 83, 87, 88, 89, 93, 102–4, 107–9, 117, 121, 123, 127
Melanau, 156
Meo, 87, 125, 128
Mindanao, 204, 207, 208, 210, 211, 212, 213
Mindoro, 204
Mineral resources: in Burma, 72–73; in Cambodia, 109; in Indonesia, 194; in Laos, 122–23; in Malaysia, 160–61; in North Vietnam, 138; in Philippines, 212–13; in South Vietnam, 142; in Thailand, 89
Minority groups: in Burma, 63, 65–66; in Cambodia, 104, 112–17; in Indonesia, 189–90; in Malaysia, 155–56, 158, 162; in Philippines, 207–8; in Singapore, 170; in Thailand, 86–87; in Vietnam, 134 (see also specific group)
Mogok, 72
Mole, Robert L., 150
Moluccas, 152
Mongkut, 85
Mons, 75, 83, 104, 117
Monsoon, 13, 16 (see also Rainfall)
Montagnards, 134
Morgan, Theodore, 57
Moros, 208,

Moulmein, 66, 68
Mountbatten, Louis, 20
Mumford, Lewis, 44
Murphy, Rhoads, 58
Murut, 156
Muscat, Robert J., 99
Muslims (see Islam)
Myingyan, 72
Myitkyina, 69, 72
Myrdal, Gunnar, 58

Nakhon Ratchasima, 87, 92
Nam Dinh, 139
Nam Phung Dam, 89
Nationalism, 7–8: in Lower Mekong Basin, 13–14
Ne Win, 63
Negri Sembilan, 154
Negritos, 189, 205, 206
Negros, 205, 210, 213
Netherlands, 3–5, 9
Neville, Warwick, 183
New Zealand, 6
Ngo Dinh Diem, 145–46
Ngum River, 121, 123
Nguyen Van Thieu, 147–49
North Vietnam, 4, 7, 9, 133–39: agriculture in, 135, 136–38; and Cambodia, 114–16; and China, 11; climate and landscape of, 134–36; government of, 134, 136–38, 145; industrialization in, 138–39; and Laos, 121; and Mekong Project, 13, 22; population of, 133–34, 136
Nusa Tenggara, 193

Oil (see Petroleum production)
Ooi Jin Bee, 165, 166n., 184
Organization of Southeast Asian Ministers of Transport and Communication, 21
Oshima, Harry T., 184

Pa Mong, 23, 27, 123
Pa Mong Dam, 89
Pahang, 154, 159, 161

Pakistan, 6
Pakistanis: in Cambodia, 117; in Indonesia, 189; in Malaysia, 155–56
Pakse, 121, 128
Palawan, 204
Palembang, 195
Panay Plain, 210, 212
Papuans, 189, 190
Pearson, H. F., 184
Pegu, 74–75
People's Action Party, 166, 176
Per capita income: in Burma, 73; in Laos, 126; in Lower Mekong Basin, 19; in Malaysia, 164; in North Vietnam, 137; in Singapore, 166
Perak, 154, 161
Perlis Kedah, 154
Petroleum production: in Burma, 72–73; in Indonesia, 194; in Laos, 123; in Malaysia, 161; in South Vietnam, 142; in Thailand, 89, 91
Philippines, 3–8, 10, 11, 203–19: agriculture in, 206, 209–11; climate and landscape of, 204–5; economy of, 203, 214; exports and imports of, 211, 212; government of, 206, 214; history of, 205–6; industrialization of, 203, 213–14; mining in, 212–13; population of, 203, 205–8; and Spain, 7, 206, 207
Phitsanulok, 92
Phnom Penh, 16, 20, 103, 104, 105, 106–10, 112, 115, 117
Phumiphon Adunyadet, 85
Pinang, 4, 21, 154, 168
Plain of Jars, 122
Poipet, 109–10
Poole, Peter A., 112–17, 118
Population growth: in Burma, 79; in Cambodia, 103, 112; in Indonesia, 193, 196–200; in Laos, 128; in Lower Mekong Basin, 19; in Malaysia, 155; in Philippines, 203; in Singapore, 170; in South Vietnam, 143; in Thailand, 87, 95–96; and urbanization, 34–35, 49–52
Port Swettenham, 161
Prosterman, Roy L., 143–50

Quang Yen, 138

Raffles, Thomas Stamford, 154, 166–68, 170, 198
Rainfall: in Burma, 68, 70, 81; in Cambodia, 102–3; in Indonesia, 187–88; in Laos, 122; in Malaysia, 154–55; in Philippines, 204–5, 215; in Singapore, 169; in Thailand, 88; in Vietnam, 134–35
Ramkamhaeng, 83, 86
Rangoon, 35, 37–38, 47, 66, 67
Ravenholt, Albert, 220
Regional associations, 4–7
Regionalism, 3–12, 20–21
Religion (*see specific religion*)
Rent control in Singapore, 178
Rice production: in Burma, 68–70, 74–81, 218; in Cambodia, 107; in Indonesia, 191, 197, 199, 218; in Laos, 122, 123–24; in Malaysia, 159–60; in North Vietnam, 135, 136, 137; in Philippines, 209–10, 215–19; in South Vietnam, 135, 137–41, 218; in Thailand, 88, 90, 96, 218
Rubber production: in Cambodia, 107–8; in Indonesia, 193; in Laos, 125; in Malaysia, 158, 164; in South Vietnam, 141–42; in Thailand, 90
Rural-urban relations, 31, 44, 45, 47, 55: in Indonesia, 190, 198; in South Vietnam, 143; in Thailand, 96–97 (*see also* Immigration, rural-urban)

Sa Dikin, 42
Sabah, 6, 152, 154, 156, 160, 161, 168
Sagaing, 80
Saigon, 19, 21, 32–34, 37–40, 134, 140, 142
Salween River, 67–68
Samar, 213
Sambor, 23
Sansom, Robert, 146, 150
Sarawak, 152, 154, 155, 156, 159, 161, 168
Savannakhet, 121, 127, 128
Schaaf, C. Hart, 14

SEATO, 6, 9, 12
Selangor, 154
Semarang, 195
Sewell, W. R. D., 58
Shan, 65, 67, 83
Shand, R. T., 58
Shaplen, Robert, 58, 201
Shifting cultivation (*see* Slash-and-burn cultivation)
Shipping: in Indonesia, 195; in Singapore, 175–76
Si Ayutthaya, 36, 83–85
Siam (*see* Thailand)
Sibley, Willis E., 220
Siem Reap, 110, 116
Sihanouk, Prince, 100, 113, 114, 116
Singapore, 5, 6, 12, 21, 38, 40, 47, 49, 166–83: climate and landscape of, 168–69; economy of, 171–75; government of, 166, 172–73, 176; history of, 36–37, 154, 166–68; housing in, 177–83; and Malaysia, 168; population of, 32–35, 169–70; trade by, 8–10, 41, 168, 174–75; urban growth in, 41–42, 170–71, 179–83
Singkep, 194
Sirik Matak, 113
Sittang River, 67, 68, 70, 75
Sittwe, 68
Sjoberg, Gideon, 45
Slash-and-burn cultivation, 71, 101, 109, 125, 192, 209
Social change: in Cambodia, 105–6; in cities, 43–45 (*see also* Land reform)
Soil: in Burma, 71; in Indonesia, 192; in Laos, 122; in Malaysia, 158; in Philippines, 205; in Thailand, 89
South China Sea, 9, 154, 160, 168
South Vietnam, 4, 7, 9, 133–35, 139–50: agriculture in, 135, 139–42; and Cambodia, 114; and China, 11; climate and landscape of, 134–35; economy of, 142–43; government of, 133–34, 143–50; and reform in, 139–40, 143–50; and Mekong Project, 13, 16, 22–23, 26; population of, 133–34, 143
Southeast Asia Treaty, 85

Southeast Asia Treaty Organization (SEATO), 6, 9, 12
Southeast Asian Ministers of Education Organization, 21
Spain and Philippines, 7, 206, 207
Spencer, J. E., 220
Spoelstra, Nyle, 57
Srivijaya Empire, 83, 152, 166
Stanford Research Institute, 144, 151
Steinberg, David J., 58, 118
Sternstein, L., 99
Stouffer, Samuel, 51
Straits Settlements, 168
Stung Treng, 27, 110
Suburbanization, 46, 48
Suddard, Adrienne, 130
Sugar production in Philippines, 210–11
Suharto, 185, 199
Sukarno, 5, 6, 42, 185, 199
Sukhothai, 83, 87
Sulus, 204, 208
Sumatra, 7, 8, 83, 152, 155, 185, 188–96, 199
Sumba, 193
Sumbawa, 193
Surabaja, 47, 195–96
Syriam, 72, 75

Taal Volcano, 204
Tahan Mountain, 154
Takhmau, 109
Tay Bac, 134
Tenant farming (see Land reform)
Tenasserim Coast, 66, 67, 71, 80
Tet, 147, 148
Thai Nguyen, 138
Thailand, 3–7, 36, 82–98: agriculture in, 87, 88, 90, 93, 95; and Burma, 83–85; Cambodians in, 116; and China, 11–12, 86; climate and landscape of, 88–89; economy of, 90–94; government of, 85, 95, 97–98; history of, 83–85; and Mekong Project, 13, 16, 21–23; population of, 86–87, 95
Thailand, Gulf of, 88, 89, 100, 102–3, 107, 108, 110

Thais, 86: in Cambodia, 116; in Laos, 128
Thakhek, 121, 122, 127
Thalun, 75
Thieu, Nguyen Van, 147–49
Thomas, R. Murray, 201
Thompson, Kenneth, 152–64
Thon Buri, 36, 87
Tin production: in Burma, 72; in Indonesia, 194; in Laos, 122–23; in Malaysia, 160–61, 164; in Thailand, 89, 91, 93
Tinker, Hugh, 81
Tobacco production: in Laos, 125; in Philippines, 211
Tonkin, 131, 136, 137
Tonle Sap, 23, 26
Tonle Sap Lake, 102, 104–5, 107–9
Tonle Sap River, 102–4
Tourism: in Singapore, 174; in Thailand, 93
Trade in Singapore, 8–10, 41, 168, 174–75 (see also Commerce; Shipping)
Transportation: in Cambodia, 109–10, 112; and cities, 37, 40, 41, 45, 52–55; in Indonesia, 195–96, 199; intra-urban, in Laos, 127; in Malaysia, 162; in Singapore, 171; in Thailand, 92
Trengganu, 154, 161

Unemployment (see Employment)
Unger, Leonard, 82–98, 119–29
Union of Soviet Socialist Republics, 133, 139
United Kingdom (see Great Britain)
United Nations: and Mekong Project, 22; and Singapore, 171
United States: and Cambodia, 109; and Laos, 126; and Mekong Project, 22–23; and Philippines, 7, 206, 208, 211, 215–16; and South Vietnam, 133, 145–47, 149–50; and Southeast Asia, 3, 6, 9, 10, 12; and Thailand, 82, 85–86
Urban growth in Singapore, 170–72, 179, 181–83

Urbanization, 31–37, 47: in Cambodia, 112; in Indonesia, 198 (*see also* Cities; Rural-urban relations)

Van der Kroef, Justus M., 220
Van Niel, Robert, 58
Van Roy, Edward, 99
Vegetation (*see* Agriculture; Forestry)
Vientiane, 119, 121, 122, 127, 128–29
Viet Bac, 134
Viet Cong, 146–47, 150
Vietminh, 131, 145, 146
Vietnam, 131–50 (*see also* North Vietnam; South Vietnam)
Vietnam war, 133, 140–41, 143–50: and Cambodia, 100, 112; and Laos, 121, 128; and Thailand, 82–83, 86, 93, 98
Vietnamese: in Cambodia, 104, 113–15; in Laos, 128–29; in Thailand, 87
Visayas, 204, 209, 210, 212
Volcanoes, 204

Wang, Gungwu, 165
Water management (*see* Flood control; Irrigation; Mekong Development Project)
Water supply (*see* Rainfall)
Wernstedt, Frederick L., 220
West Irian, 5, 185, 188–90, 194, 196
West Malaysia (*see* Malaysia)
Wheeler, Raymond A., 14, 23
White, Gilbert F., 23, 58
Wikkrametelike, R., 184
Willmott, William E., 118
Withington, William A., 100–112, 185–200
World Bank, 22, 29

Yagyaw, 80
Yao, 87, 125, 128
Yenangyaung, 72
Yeung, Yue-man, 166–83
You Poh-Seng, 183, 184
Yunnan Province, 67, 83

THE CONTRIBUTORS

Louis A. Cohen is Acting Director of Engineering Services Division, Committee for Coordination of Investigations of the Lower Mekong Basin.

Alden Cutshall is Professor of Geography, University of Illinois at Chicago Circle.

Donald W. Fryer is Professor of Geography, University of Hawaii.

Norton S. Ginsburg is Professor of Geography, University of Chicago.

Robert E. Huke is Chairman and Professor of the Geography Department, Dartmouth College.

Peter A. Poole is Assistant Professor of International Relations, Howard University.

Roy L. Prosterman is a Professor in the School of Law, University of Washington.

Kenneth Thompson is Professor of Geography, University of California, Davis.

Leonard Unger is United States Ambassador to Thailand and former Ambassador to Laos.

William A. Withington is Associate Professor of Geography, University of Kentucky.

Yue-man Yeung is Lecturer in Geography, University of Singapore, and Ph.D. candidate, University of Chicago.

DATE DUE

NOV 2 '75			
DEC 2 '75			
NOV 10 '81			
OCT 2 6 1981			
SEP 3 0 '88			
GAYLORD			PRINTED IN U.S.A.